MW01122273

Humber College Library
3199 Lakeshore Blvd. West
Toronto, ON    M8V 1K8

# Performing Architectures

**Methuen Drama Engage** offers original reflections about key practitioners, movements and genres in the fields of modern theatre and performance. Each volume in the series seeks to challenge mainstream critical thought through original and interdisciplinary perspectives on the body of work under examination. By questioning existing critical paradigms, it is hoped that each volume will open up fresh approaches and suggest avenues for further exploration.

## Series Editors

Mark Taylor-Batty
University of Leeds, UK

Enoch Brater
University of Michigan, USA

## Titles

*Adaptation in Contemporary Theatre*
by Frances Babbage
ISBN 978–1–4725–3142–1

*Authenticity in Contemporary Theatre and Performance*
by Daniel Schulze
ISBN 978–1–3500–0096–4

*Beat Drama: Playwrights and Performances of the 'Howl' Generation*
edited by Deborah R. Geis
ISBN 978–1–472–56787–1

*Drama and Digital Arts Cultures*
by David Cameron, Michael Anderson and Rebecca Wotzko
ISBN 978–1–472–59219–4

*Social and Political Theatre in 21st-Century Britain: Staging Crisis*
by Vicky Angelaki
ISBN 978–1–474–21316–5

*Theatre in the Dark: Shadow, Gloom and Blackout in Contemporary Theatre*
edited by Adam Alston and Martin Welton
ISBN 978–1–4742–5118–1

*Watching War On The Twenty-First-Century Stage: Spectacles of Conflict*
by Clare Finburgh
ISBN 978–1–472–59866–0

# Performing Architectures

## Projects, Practices, Pedagogies

Edited by
Andrew Filmer and Juliet Rufford

*Series Editors*
Enoch Brater and Mark Taylor-Batty

HUMBER LIBRARIES LAKESHORE CAMPUS
3199 Lakeshore Blvd West
TORONTO, ON.   M8V 1K8

*methuen* | drama
LONDON · NEW YORK · OXFORD · NEW DELHI · SYDNEY

METHUEN DRAMA
Bloomsbury Publishing Plc
50 Bedford Square, London, WC1B 3DP, UK

BLOOMSBURY, METHUEN DRAMA and the Methuen Drama logo are trademarks of
Bloomsbury Publishing Plc

First published in Great Britain 2018

Copyright © Andrew Filmer, Juliet Rufford and contributors, 2018

Andrew Filmer, Juliet Rufford and contributors have asserted their right under the
Copyright, Designs and Patents Act, 1988, to be identified as authors of this work.

For legal purposes the Acknowledgements on p. xiv constitute an extension
of this copyright page.

Series design by Louise Dugdale
Cover image © Double Cyclops

All rights reserved. No part of this publication may be reproduced or
transmitted in any form or by any means, electronic or mechanical, including
photocopying, recording, or any information storage or retrieval system,
without prior permission in writing from the publishers.

Bloomsbury Publishing Plc does not have any control over, or responsibility for,
any third-party websites referred to or in this book. All internet addresses given in this
book were correct at the time of going to press. The author and publisher regret any
inconvenience caused if addresses have changed or sites have ceased to exist, but can
accept no responsibility for any such changes.

A catalogue record for this book is available from the British Library.

A catalog record for this book is available from the Library of Congress.

ISBN:  HB:     978-1-4742-4798-6
        ePDF:   978-1-4742-4800-6
        eBook:  978-1-4742-4799-3

Series: Methuen Drama Engage

Typeset by Integra Software Services Pvt. Ltd.

To find out more about our authors and books visit www.bloomsbury.com and sign up for
our newsletters.

# Contents

# Figures

# Contributors

**Klaus van den Berg** (PhD Indiana University) is a theatre historian who has taught at Kennesaw State University and the University of Tennessee, Knoxville and worked as a professional dramaturg in US and European theatres. His research centres on visual culture and the dramaturgy of space with particular focus on scenography in performance, the role of spectacle in contemporary society, the interlacing of urban landscapes and performance venues, and the image as a central issue of critical theory. He is currently working on a book that will provide the first in-depth account of Walter Benjamin's concept of *Bildraum* (image-space) as a foundational concept for the theory and practice of twentieth-century performance. His most recent publications related to the Benjamin project are essays on Marlene Dietrich's transformation of her live performances into a cinematic image-space in *European Drama and Performance Studies* (2015) and designer Karl-Ernst Herrmann's scenographic approach to Shakespeare performances in *Designers' Shakespeare* (2016).

**Himanshu Burte** is an architect and urbanist based in Mumbai where he teaches at the Tata Institute of Social Sciences. He is the author of *Space for Engagement: The Indian Artplace and a Habitational Approach to Architecture* (2009). His research and teaching interests include the politics of urban space and its transformation, sustainable architecture, theatre space and contemporary Indian architecture.

**Andrew Filmer** is Senior Lecturer in Drama, Theatre and Performance at Aberystwyth University. His research focuses on space, place and location in contemporary theatre and performance, sites of encounter between architecture and performance, and the performance of running. He has published in *Performance Research*, *New Theatre Quarterly* and *Theatre Research International* and, with Juliet Rufford, co-convenes the International Federation for Theatre Research's Theatre Architecture Working Group.

**Dorita Hannah** is Research Professor of Interdisciplinary Architecture, Art and Design at the University of Tasmania, Australia, and Adjunct Professor of Stage and Space at Aalto University, Finland. Space and performance form the principal threads that weave through her creative work, teaching and research. Specializing in theatre architecture and performance design, Hannah also publishes on practices that negotiate between architecture, art and design, including her own transdisciplinary work in Australia, New Zealand, Europe and the United States. Her practice-led research focuses on live events, installations and exhibitions as well as a specialization in theatre architecture. She co-chairs the Performance + Design Working Group for Performance Studies International (PSi), sits on several editorial boards and has created exhibitions and events for the Prague Quadrennial of Performance Design and Space as design director, architectural commissioner and theory curator. Focusing on spatial performativity, Hannah's book *Event-Space: Theatre Architecture and the Historical Avant-Garde* will be published in 2018.

**Breg Horemans** graduated as Master in Architecture from LUCA, Ghent, in 2008. He worked at Wiel Arets Architects on urban and architectural competitions and building projects (2009–2013). In 2012 he met visual artist Eleni Kamma, for whom he designed installations such as *P like Parrot* (Museum Alex Mylona, Athens) and *From Bank to Bank on a Gradual Slope* (Villa Romana, Florence). In the same year the theatre production company Huis van Bourgondië asked Horemans and theatre maker Gert-Jan Stam to develop the DIT-theatre pavilion *KHOR I* for the World Horticultural Expo in Venlo (Netherlands). The interdisciplinary approach of this project triggered Horemans and Stam to found their collective TAAT: Theatre as Architecture Architecture as Theatre.

**Evelyn Furquim Werneck Lima** holds a BA, MA and PhD (UFRJ/EHESS). She is Full Professor at the Universidade Federal do Estado do Rio de Janeiro/Post-Graduate Programme in Performing Arts and a researcher for the National Council of Technological and Scientific Development. She is the leader of the Research Group for Theatrical Spaces Studies and the author of *Architectures and Set Designs: Lina Bo Bardi and the Theatre* (2012, with Monteiro), *Architecture and Theatre: From Palladio to Portzamparc* (2010, with Cardoso), *From the AvantGardes to Tradition* (2006), *Architecture for Performing Arts* (2000/Brazilian Institute of Architects Award) and *President Vargas Avenue: A Drastic Surgery* (1990/Architect Olga Verjovski Award). She has edited *Architecture, Theatre and Culture: Revisiting Spaces, Cities and Playwrights of the Seventeenth Century* (2012), *Space and Theatre* (2008) and *Space and City* (2007), among others. She has coordinated the Laboratory of Theatrical Spaces and Urban Memory Studies since 1994.

**Mike Pearson** is a former Professor of Performance Studies at Aberystwyth University. He creates theatre as a solo artist; with artist/designer Mike Brookes in Pearson/Brookes; for National Theatre Wales; and with senior performers' group Good News From The Future. He is the co-author with Michael Shanks of *Theatre/Archaeology* (2001) and the author of *In Comes I: Performance, Memory and Landscape* (2006), *Site-Specific Performance* (2010), *Mickery Theater: An Imperfect Archaeology* (2011) and *Marking Time: Performance, Archaeology and the City* (2013). As a director, his productions for National Theatre Wales include *The Persians* (2010), *Coriolan/us* (2012) and *Iliad* (2015).

**Natalie Rewa** is Professor of Drama in the Dan School of Drama and Music at Queen's University in Kingston, Ontario, Canada, and author of *Scenography in Canada: Selected Designers* (2004). She was the co-curator of the Canadian delegation to PQ07 and the co-editor of *Imprints of Process*, the catalogue for the exhibit, the editor of *Design and Scenography* (2009) and the guest editor of the special issue 'Costumes and Costuming' of *Canadian Theatre Review* 152 (2013). Her research has appeared in *Canadian Theatre Review, Theatre Research in Canada, Australasian Drama Studies* and *Scene*.

**David Roberts** is Architectural Design and History & Theory Teaching Fellow at the Bartlett School of Architecture. Alongside his work at University College London, he is part of collaborative art practice Fugitive Images and of architecture collective Involve. He uses poetry and performance to explore the relation between people and place. His collaborative research, art and cultural activist practice engages community groups whose homes and livelihoods are under threat from urban policy. He has exhibited, lectured and published work related to public housing, architecture, critical methodologies and site-specific practice. His PhD thesis in architectural design, 'Make Public: Performing Public Housing in Regenerating East London', was supervised by Professor Jane Rendell and Dr Ben Campkin and won a RIBA President's Award for Research in 2016.

**Juliet Rufford** is an artist, curator, educator and researcher-writer whose work spans theatre and performance studies, architecture, scenography and the politics of space. She has held academic posts at London's Victoria & Albert Museum and Queen Mary University of London, and has also taught drama, theatre and performance at a number of other higher education institutions within and outside the University of London (including Birkbeck and Goldsmiths colleges and Sussex University). An artist contributor to the 2011 Prague Quadrennial of Performance Design and Space's Architecture Section and to the 2012 Venice Architecture Biennale (as part of Haworth Tompkins's creative team), she has also acted as an education consultant to the Bartlett School of Architecture (MArch Design for Performance and Interaction) and as a guest lecturer at Chelsea College of Art (BA Interior and Spatial Design). Together with Andrew Filmer, she co-convenes the International Federation for Theatre Research's Theatre Architecture Working Group. Her articles have appeared in journals including *Contemporary Theatre Review*, *Journal of Architectural Education* and *New Theatre Quarterly*. Her small book *Theatre & Architecture* was published in 2015.

**Alex Schweder** coined the term 'Performance Architecture' to encapsulate the notion that architecture both gives cues for how we are to behave and offers itself as a prop for inhabitants to form and perform their identities. His works along these lines have been exhibited and collected internationally by the Museum of Modern Art, Tate Britain, Performa 17, the Tel Aviv Museum of Art, the San Francisco Museum of Modern Art and the 2014 Venice Architecture Biennale. He is a fellow of the American Academy in Rome and currently lives and works in New York City.

**Gert-Jan Stam** started writing for theatre in 2007 after a career in the visual arts. His debut one-act play *Shame* got him on the Forum of Young European Playwrights in 2008, where he worked under the guidance of acclaimed British playwright Mark Ravenhill. His collaboration with the Irish actress Jody O'Neill resulted in *I love guns*, which premiered at the Absolute Fringe in Dublin in 2010. A radioplay version was broadcasted on Croatian radio that same year. His first Do-It-Together theatre play was *OK OK*, a collaboration with British theatre maker Ant Hampton. *OK OK* was translated into German, Czech, Arabic, Chinese and Japanese, among other languages. In 2012 he founded TAAT together with the Belgian architect Breg Horemans.

**Cathy Turner** is Associate Professor in Theatre and Performance at the University of Exeter. Her research concerns performance as spatial practice (particularly artists' walking) and dramaturgy as an analytical lens. Her book *Dramaturgy and Architecture* (2015) discusses European exchanges between theatre and architecture since the late nineteenth century. She is the joint author, with Synne Behrndt, of *Dramaturgy and Performance* (2nd edition 2016), which was one of the first to consider dramaturgy beyond a concern with dramatic texts. She is a core member of Wrights & Sites, a group of artists whose work is concerned with the pedestrian's relationship with space and place, often through artist books, or 'Mis-Guides'. The company's recent work *The Architect-Walker: A Mis-Guide* was published in 2017. She is currently researching performance in relation to gardens and horticulture.

**Beth Weinstein** is Associate Professor of Architecture at the University of Arizona and PhD candidate at the University of Tasmania. Her research and practice explore architecture in relation to performance, through writing, drawing, event-making and intervening in urban and landscape spaces. She curated *the Collaborative Legacy of Merce Cunningham* exhibition (2011) and has contributed chapters to *Architecture as a Performing Art* (2011), *Disappearing Stage: Reflections on the 2011 Prague Quadrennial* (2011) and *The Routledge Companion to Scenography* (2017). She co-chairs PSi's Performance+Design Working Group and has served on the editorial boards of the *Journal of Architectural Education* and *Theatre and Performance Design Journal*.

# Acknowledgements

The editors would like to express their thanks to all past and present members of the Theatre Architecture Working Group of the International Federation for Theatre Research.

We would also like to express our gratitude to the following colleagues who generously reviewed manuscripts during the preparation of this book: Synne Behrndt, Carol Brown, Matthew Butcher, Minty Donald, Ella Finer, Karoline Gritzner, Andrew Houston, Gay McAuley, Michael McKinnie, James O'Leary, Roger Owen, Amitabh Rai, Alan Read, Heike Roms, Ashis Sengupta, Kim Solga, Jeremy Till, Joanne Tompkins, Sebastian Truskolaski, Maurya Wickstrom, Fiona Wilkie, Piotr Woycicki and Keren Zaointz.

We would also like to thank Bruce Barton, Bernadette Cochrane, and Miranda Heckenberg for their advice and assistance.

The editors and publisher gratefully acknowledge the permission granted to reproduce the copyright material in this book. Every effort has been made to trace copyright holders and to obtain their permission for the use of copyright material. The publisher apologizes for any errors or omissions and would be grateful if notified of any corrections that should be incorporated in future reprints or editions of this book.

# Introduction: Performing Architectures

Andrew Filmer and Juliet Rufford

*Performing Architectures* examines the relationship between theatre, performance and architecture in an 'expanded field' of spatial and artistic practice. The book's title evokes our sense of the dynamism and plurality of this field. It posits performance and architecture as bound up in action together – rather than categorizing performance as a dynamic/temporal agent and architecture as a static/permanent object – and also frames architecture as not only that which houses performance but also that which might be performed, and that which might perform.[1] If the title suggests the plurality of what we mean by the term 'architecture' – encompassing a range of different buildings, different design and construction strategies and different orders of space and experience – it also suggests that 'performing' may take place in spatial as well as theatrical and cultural contexts. By combining a critical discussion of theatre architecture with a broader consideration of the relationship between performance and architecture, this book explores the creative intersection of performance and architecture as distinct but related disciplines.

The book has emerged from the work of the Theatre Architecture Working Group of the International Federation for Theatre Research (IFTR), and it reflects the shared interests of that community of scholars. Since its establishment by Frank Hildy in 2006, the Working Group has expanded its interdisciplinary scope to not only explore all that theatre architecture has been historically, is at present and might be in the future but also consider the relationship *between* theatre and architecture. We have done this because we have witnessed a renewed encounter between performance and architecture that is generating vibrant critical and creative work among architects, urban planners, artists, and theatre and performance makers. A number of recent publications have engaged with this work but most have done so from an architectural perspective, reflecting that discipline's current interest in performance and performativity.[2] By contrast, *Performing Architectures* views architecture from the perspectives of theatre and performance studies and addresses the architectural in theatre and performance. The ten chapters of this book – set in dialogue with three shorter contributions by artists – use the event of theatre and a range of metaphorical and real stages to articulate the multiple points of exchange between performance and architecture.

The aim of *Performing Architectures* is to further an interdisciplinary conversation between theatre, performance and architecture. The book does this by offering an introduction to the current points of interdisciplinary exchange between these fields. This includes exploring the spatiality of theatre and performance along lines that are distinctly different from existing texts, which draw on cultural and economic geography and interdisciplinary spatial theory, and investigating how performance might contribute to the development of socially engaged architectural practice and more embodied approaches to architectural pedagogy. In what follows, we discuss the key contexts for the chapters in this book. First, we look at theatre architecture and theatre's renewed concerns with staging and spacing. Next, we further examine architecture's engagement with concepts of performativity and event. We then provide an orientation towards issues of interdisciplinarity, before finishing with a guide to the shape of the book and its individual chapters.

## Theatre: Stages and spaces

Consideration of the specific role of architecture, and of architectural thinking and practice in theatre and performance studies has, for the most part, focused on theatre architecture. There are good reasons for this focus. Besides the oft-remarked duality of the term 'theatre' (from the ancient Greek *theatron*) as both the physical form and the activity of performance, the fact that accepted theatrical taxonomies such as proscenium arch theatre, black box theatre and theatre-in-the-round link performance genre and style directly to theatre architecture signals an awareness that theatrical performance is defined by the specifics of architectural space and form. Of all architectural typologies, the theatre building is 'one of the most persistent architectural objects in the history of Western culture' (Carlson 1989: 6). As such, theatres have generated an extensive literature of treatises, studies and historical surveys (see, for instance, Leacroft and Leacroft 1984) and, more recently, technical and planning manuals (see, for instance, Appleton 1996, the three volumes of Brett 2004, and Strong 2010). Whereas the theatrical event is fleeting, the theatre building endures; it provides historians with valuable clues about theatre-as-activity and furnishes theatre makers with starting points for future productions. Theatre architecture, particularly that of backstage and rehearsal spaces, has a significant bearing on theatrical possibility since differently shaped, sized and technically equipped spaces will enable or restrict what it is possible to achieve in production. Then again, a theatre's front-of-house spaces affect social and emotional experiences of being at the theatre even as its auditorium sets up particular performer–spectator and spectator–spectator relations, and frames acts of perception and cognition.

The spatial turn of the late twentieth century – catalyzed by the work of French theorists Michel Foucault (1986), Henri Lefebvre (1991) and Michel de Certeau (1984) – has generated a range of critical studies that have investigated the function of space in theatrical processes of production and reception and extended analysis beyond the physical location of the theatre. These studies have proved especially productive in three broad areas: in their consideration of theatre architecture as an index to broader social and cultural issues, including social class and identity (see Boyer 1996; Kershaw 1999; Knowles 2004); in their investigation of the semiotic, phenomenological and heterotopic dimensions of performance space (Carlson 2003; McAuley 2000; Tompkins 2014); and in their examination of the theatre building as an urban institution, closely connected to the economic and political management of the city (Bennett 1990; Carlson 1989; Harvie 2009, 2013; McKinnie 2007, 2013). From these works we have learnt why the theatre's stages and social spaces have taken the forms they have, how the theatre building signifies within its urban setting, how theatre space offers opportunities for contesting and reimagining wider social spaces, and how theatre architecture acts as an aestheticizing environment, conditioning acts of performance and spectatorship.

The emergence of performance, as a critical concept and a field that extends and contests theatre, has also contributed to a rethinking of the role and function of traditional models of theatre architecture. In the 1930s, Antonin Artaud insisted on the physical reality of the stage and the need for it to be given 'its own concrete language to speak' (Artaud 1958: 37). Artaud's desire was for a theatre no longer subjugated to the dramatic text but rather defined through the performance of space, light, objects and the proximity of living, pulsating bodies. His vision was a spatial one: with an emphasis on immediacy and sensuality he rejected the division of stage and auditorium and sought to replace them with 'a single site' (96). Artaud's legacy in performance studies is discernible in the attention practitioners have given to the body and in their thorough exploration of the fluid and interactive potential of performance space in purpose-built theatres and in 'found' spaces (see Schechner 1968, 1988). The performative turn – prompted by J. L. Austin's (1962) philosophy of language and Judith Butler's (1990) development and application of Austin's work to the study of gender – has shifted our understanding of the performativity of space: space is produced through action and movement and is itself active and affective. These expanded understandings of performance space and spatial performativity have spurred the development and proliferation of site-specific theatre and spatially inventive performance practices, which, in turn, are critically reassessing – and in many cases rejecting – theatre architecture (see, for instance, Pearson 2010; Tompkins and Birch 2012).

This brief survey suggests that the key critical issues in the design of theatre architecture and performance space are now entangled in broader questions about the relationship *between* performance and architecture. At a time when practitioners are intertwining reality and performance, and engaging more directly with social processes (see Lavender 2016), the question of what a theatre building might *be* is deceptively difficult, requiring an architecture that is performative, porous and unfixed. Dorita Hannah, curator of the Architecture Section of the 2007 Prague Quadrennial of Performance Design and Space, has made clear her sense that we are in the midst of a generational shift away from older ways of producing, receiving and designing theatre and are having to rethink our sense of theatre's relationship to social life and established social codes. Hannah writes:

> When I run studio projects on theatre architecture, or am called upon to critique student work that focuses on performing arts spaces, I am often struck by the apparent redundancy of this typology. Few students frequent the theatre and many wish to break its confines, extend its limits, and challenge the social behaviour it accommodates. The playhouse seems an irrelevant architectural genre in this age of liquescence, where nothing is stable, where fiction constantly folds into reality, and where sedentary structures can no longer house the mediatized spectacle of daily life (2008: 42)

And yet many of the authors in this book (including Hannah) agree that there remains a vital artistic, social and critical role for theatre architecture even as rapidly evolving technologies irrevocably alter perception and subjectivity. The chapters that address theatre architecture in this book explore the ideological nature of the organization of theatre spaces, question how modes of performing, spectating and participating are encouraged or discouraged, and examine the changing relationship of theatre buildings to theatre practice and to urban space.

If the combined effects of the spatial and performative turns have transformed the way we understand, and design, theatre architecture and performance space, they have also radically altered approaches to dramaturgy and scenography. Both dramaturgical and scenographic practice now possess an expanded and inclusive critical remit that extends well beyond the stage, and both now operate as valued mediators between theatre and architecture. The importance of dramaturgy and scenography has come to the fore through the emergence, on the one hand, of a postdramatic theatrical aesthetics that emphasizes theatre as an event characterized by shared space, and, on the other, of a growing desire by artists and institutions to intervene directly in the production and performance of public space. While certain playwrights – chiefly Sarah Kane, but also Henrik Ibsen and Martin Crimp – have been identified as 'architects of drama' (Cohn 2001; see also Rufford 2007: 132–158; Turner 2015: 24–51), we now see a marked emphasis on the architectural in the varied forms of experimental and 'unhoused' theatre that form the spectrum of contemporary performance practice. Dramaturgy, which historically has been confined to the analysis and editorial 'sharpening' of the dramatic text, encompasses an increasingly diverse set of concerns. It not only structures 'the totality of the performance-making process' (Trencsňyi and Cochrane 2014: xi) but also helps organize and articulate spectatorial processes of perception and reception. Understanding dramaturgy as the dynamic and contextual practice of 'crafting' or 'building' a theatrical event, Cathy Turner has examined how it operates 'as a form of involvement in architecture' (2015: 19) and allows us 'to think in terms of interacting, unfolding and to some degree unpredictable space-time compositions, rather than thinking of performance largely in terms of its action, and architecture in terms of its immutable spaces' (2010: 161). Similarly, scenography has shaken off historic associations with scenic decoration and pictorial illustration to reassert the multi-sensory, social and visuospatial nature of theatre and has acted as the driving force behind recent forays into performative environments and constructed situations. Indeed, as Christopher Baugh's work on the history of scenography in the twentieth century reveals, scenographic experimentation has played a major role in the gradual de-framing and destabilization of theatre architecture and, in its challenge to the inherited typology of the playhouse, has posited new spaces and forms of theatre and performance (Baugh 2005). So great has been the expansion of scenography beyond the traditional stage and into areas of architectural, performance and urban practice that Thea Brejzek argues for a new understanding of scenography as 'the practice of constructing social space in a constant making and re-making of time-space according to an intended and/or evolving narrative' (2012: 23). Awareness of scenography's expanded field, and of dramaturgy as both an architectural and a theatrical practice, is reflected across all three parts of this book and is felt especially keenly in those chapters concerning practices which take place at the meeting points of architecture and performance.

## Architecture: Performativity and event

For architects, the concepts of performance and performativity have influenced theory and practice, prompting renewed attention to the body and lived experience, and to notions of event, agency, contingency and temporality. They have also supplemented the long-standing metaphor of the *theatrum mundi* – what Gray Read calls the 'deep tradition of thought that casts architecture as both set and player in the ongoing theatre of social life' (in Feuerstein and Read 2013: 1). Theatrical performance and the space of the stage have long served as sites of experimentation for architecture. As Chris Salter writes, 'Architecture seems to have historically needed the theatre to assist in pushing conceptual and structural boundaries – to practice scenography on the stage in order to carry it over into the urban wild' (2010: 84). This braiding together of theatre and architecture can be witnessed in, for instance, Renaissance architect Inigo Jones's use of perspectival staging techniques in his design for the Covent Garden district of London through to more recent collaborations between architects and theatre makers, like that between Diller Scofidio + Renfro and The Builders Association for *JET LAG* (1998).

Architect Bernard Tschumi's work is seminal in contemporary engagements between performance and architecture because of his exploration of the disjunction between the *conceptualization* of space in architecture and the *lived experience* of space and his insistence on the centrality of movement, action and event to architecture. Since the mid-1970s Tschumi has championed pleasure, disorder and indeterminacy in his theoretical and built projects, introducing the notion of 'event' and 'event-space' to architectural discourse (Hays 2000: 216). Breaking from debates over the relationship between form and function in architecture, Tschumi instead asserted:

There is no longer a causal relationship between buildings and their context, their use, and, of course, their very improbable meaning. Space and its usage are two opposed notions that exclude one another, generating an endless array of uncertainties. (1996: 21)

In response, he has explored the programmatic and political possibilities of this 'array of uncertainties' through developing techniques of crossprogramming, transprogramming and disprogramming space, all of which deliberately collide different spatial types and activities in ways that echo, and improvise upon, the cultural practice of crossdressing. In his first realized project – Parc de La Villette, Paris – Tschumi developed a conceptual scheme for this large city park that involved the superimposition of three distinct spatial systems – a grid of points, marked by twenty-six small buildings he called *folies*, a system of lines and a system of unprogrammed surfaces. This superimposition generated a montage of spatial sequences and juxtapositions for users of the park, operating against any sense of stable composition (Tschumi 1987).

Through the course of his career, Tschumi has placed an emphasis on radical indeterminacy and anti-fixity as the chief goal of an architecture of event-space as well as exploring the psychological processes awoken by provocative spatial attitudes and the active political force of architecture. His abiding sense, on the one hand, of the *disjunction* between abstract and lived space, and, on the other, of the *conjunction* of time and space, action and situation, invites us to celebrate the fictional element in all architecture – the fact that, of necessity, architecture imagines social relations and projects hypothetical situations. More generally, by (re)viewing architecture from a perspective afforded to us by Tschumi, we might say that architecture is analogous to theatre and performance in that it is conscious of the world 'as is', curious about the world 'as if' and oriented towards a world in which the crucial question is 'what if?'

The force of performance, and broader fascination with the performative, is apparent in emerging architectural discourse. But the dominant understanding of performance in architecture remains a technical one, most commonly referring to the operation and responsiveness of a building's materials, components or systems (for instance, temperature regulation). Iain Borden's work on skateboarding offers one notable exception to this. His engagement with performativity privileges the actions of moving, sensing bodies as a means of critiquing the object-driven focus of architectural history. For Borden, the contribution of a radically embodied practice like skateboarding to architecture lies 'in the performative, representational aspects of skateboarding – its spaces of representation – wherein skateboarders re-image architectural space and thereby recreate both it and themselves into super-architectural space' (2001: 89). David Leatherbarrow's chapter in Branko Kolarevic and Ali Malkawi's *Performative Architecture: Beyond Instrumentality* (2005) crucially argues for the uncertainty of the event-character of architecture to be brought into dialogue with its rational, technical and aesthetic dimensions. Much of *Performative Architecture* is engaged with the broad questions of architecture's technical and environmental performance, foregrounding the responsive nature of the so-called 'performative architecture' in which interactive systems enable responsiveness, efficiency and indeterminacy. Leatherbarrow, however, sets out a clear argument for the value of a performative understanding of architecture – entailing 'a shift of orientation from what the building *is* to what it *does*' (2005: 7) – that encompasses 'instrumental reason and the rationality on which it depends, plus situated understanding that discovers in the particulars of a place, people and purpose the unfounded conditions that actually prompt, animate and conclude a building's performances' (18). The thrust of Leatherbarrow's argument is that architecture needs to broaden its definition of performance.

A concern with ethical architectural practice motivates the interest in cultural and aesthetic performance in Marcia Feuerstein and Gray Read's edited collection *Architecture as a Performing Art* (2013). In the introduction, Read reconceives the figure of the architect as a director of action, a figure who (like a stage director) designs buildings not as objects but rather as actions that might play a meaningful role in social life (2013: 2). This idea is further developed by Alberto Pérez-Gómez, who offers a recovery of the figure of the architect that appears in the plays of Euripides and Aristophanes. This is the architect not so much as 'master craftsman' but 'as a hero and legislator who opens a clearing for political and social order, a public space (both physical and political) as a site for collective orientation, which is not invented or created, but drawn from the pre-existing orders of culture and the cosmos' (Pérez-Gómez in Feuerstein and Read 2013: 17). Though drawn from ancient drama, this vision of the architect as a civic figure, a thinker and director of action, is remarkably contemporary and is one where theatre, performance and architecture are intimately entwined.

## Interdisciplinarity

*Performing Architectures* is written with a due sense of the tensions and ruptures between performance and architecture, as well as their shared concerns. The chapters of this book do not seek to dissolve or merge disciplines, and neither do they advocate an anti-disciplinary approach. The arguments and case studies making up this collection seek to demonstrate that a rigorous interdisciplinarity can strengthen disciplinary expertise even as it broadens critical and creative awareness of issues, methods and values that lie beyond conventional disciplinary boundaries.

The work of architectural theorist Jane Rendell is a source of inspiration in thinking about the space between theatre, performance and architecture as an expanded – or even *exploded* – field of interdisciplinary possibility. In *Art and Architecture: A Space Between* (2006), Rendell introduces the term 'critical spatial practice' to describe work that exists in a place between disciplines and that raises questions about the conditions of social and political life (6). In coining this term, Rendell identifies how art offers architecture a means of developing as a critical practice, and she interrogates examples of interdisciplinary spatial practice which exemplify this criticality by embodying the sort of reflective, transformative potential that she finds in critical theory. What interests Rendell about the works of art/architecture she discusses (which include urban interventions by the architectural practices of Cornford & Cross, FAT and muf art/architecture as well as works by sculptor Rachel Whiteread and artist Krzysztof Wodiczko) is that they suggest new ways in which the disciplines of art and architecture can exert a critical and transformative pressure on one another even while addressing wider social and political issues (2006: 10–12). Referencing Rosalind Krauss's influential 1979 description of an 'expanded field' of architecture, landscape and sculpture, Rendell argues that today's field of critical spatial practice has in fact *exploded*, with the result that categories are no longer held in tension, and artworks and artists now operate across disciplinary boundaries (2006: 43). In response, Rendell proposes that 'we need to understand artworks as products of specific processes, of production and reception, that operate within a further expanded and interdisciplinary field, where terms are not only defined through one discipline but by many simultaneously' (2006: 43). The chapters in *Performing Architectures* offer insights into works drawn from this vibrant field of artistic and curatorial experimentation operating in the space between art, architecture and performance. Here, the definition of whether a given work *is* performance or architecture is much less interesting than observing what the work *does* through the way in which it brings these different fields into contact.

Pedagogical concerns, including curriculum design and delivery, significantly condition the disciplines of theatre, performance and architecture. Architecture is already recognizing the value of performance in the education of architects:

it enables students to test and develop concepts and designs through embodied knowledges, processes of prototyping and acts of inhabitation, and to form more nuanced understandings of architecture–user relations. Performance as a pedagogical method, therefore, serves the development of 'other ways of doing architecture' (see Awan, Schneider and Till 2011) by breaking down architecture's presumed autonomy as a discipline and offering critical perspectives on its dominant working methods and modes of visual representation, and their attendant assumptions. The specific use of architectural theories or practices in performance pedagogy is rarer, although there are notable examples. Jacques Copeau famously included architecture in his training course at the Théâtre du Vieux-Colombier in the early twentieth century (see Rufford 2015: 1–2) while, more recently, architecture has been invoked as a framework for movement training as part of the Laboratoire d'Etude du Mouvement (LEM) run by Jacques Lecoq and Krikor Belekien (Barbieri 2007). The use of spatial grids and references to the physical environment formed by architecture is a key component of Anne Bogart's Viewpoints methodology (Bogart and Landau 2014).

## Performing architectures

This book locates its enquiry into the interdisciplinary terrain between theatre, performance and architecture in three areas. First, it focuses on theatre *projects*, examining the architecture of contemporary theatre and performance spaces, assessing prevalent ideologies that have shaped theatre design and exploring the changing situation of theatre architecture in urban space. Second, it addresses performance *practices* that closely engage with or critically re-examine architecture, and architectural practices which employ performance frames or techniques to transform or question how we experience and understand the built environment. Third, it focuses on interdisciplinary *pedagogies*, examining what might be gained for students of one discipline in the encounter between that discipline and the other.

Each of the chapters in *Performing Architectures* glances between the author's main subject and its disciplinary 'other' and the individual chapters are designed as stand-alone investigations and as invitations for further debate in theatre and performance and/or architecture. The three parts of the book are intended to act as explorations of specific areas of interest within and between disciplines. However, the decision to group these three major areas of concern together is aimed at stimulating holistic approaches to the study and practice of each. Rather than separating discussions of theatre architecture from discussions of theatre and performance that engage with architecture, we think these discussions should inform one another. How one conceives and makes performance cannot be separated from questions of the spaces in which performance is framed and articulated, and the powerful influence of theatre architecture over patterns of performance and spectatorship can be gauged from the fact that so many non-theatrically housed performances consciously or unconsciously reproduce the spatiality of the theatre auditorium. Practices of all kinds are also significantly informed by the ways in which they are taught, and pedagogy, practice and research form a continual feedback loop. The emphasis on interdisciplinary pedagogy at the end of this book emerges from a desire to address particular disciplinary issues or problems. But, beyond that, interdisciplinary pedagogy can also assist in developing a metacognition of one's own discipline, by providing an epistemological 'outside' from which to critically and creatively review central tenets.

The chapters in the first section – 'Projects' – identify some of the most important concerns in the design of architecture for theatre and performance today, placing these concerns in specific historical, cultural and political contexts. Dorita Hannah's chapter provides the critical frame for this section through her discussion of Friedrich Nietzsche's spatial thinking. Starting with Nietzsche's profound disappointment with Richard Wagner's Bayreuth Festspielhaus (Festival Theatre), Hannah articulates how Nietzsche's project of Dionysian thinking and its critical relation to emerging Modernist thought serves as a challenge to conventional theatre architecture, much of which continues to emulate the disciplining spatiality of the Festspielhaus. Hannah sets out a vision of an architecture in a state of restless *becoming* rather than *being* and her exposition of Nietzsche's thinking demonstrates its enduring importance in debates on theatre spectatorship, space and participation.

Evelyn Lima examines two theatres by Italian-Brazilian architect Lina Bo Bardi: the iconic Teatro Oficina and the SESC Pompeia Theatre, both located in São Paulo, Brazil. The Teatro Oficina is exemplary of the sort of theatre architecture envisaged by Nietzsche – a dynamic choric space where the boundary between spectator and performer is always in question. The two theatres analyzed in this chapter, though hugely significant, are still not widely known and discussed. Lima paints a picture of the culturally radical nature of Bo Bardi's architectural practice which, conducted in collaboration with artists and artisans, enabled the development of such provocative spaces of assembly. Through the chapter Lima demonstrates the influence of Antonio Gramsci's Marxist thought on Bo

Bardi's architectural practice, and describes her negotiation of European and indigenous Brazilian ideas and practices.

Klaus van den Berg examines the place of the theatre building in the global city, asking how, in an age of unparalleled and rampant urban development, the theatre might respond to regional particularities and urban sprawl. Drawing on the notion of urban site dramaturgy and Walter Benjamin's concepts of *Bildraum*, *Spielraum* and *Ausstellungsraum*, Van den Berg discusses the critical potential of theatre architecture that intervenes in the fragmented spatiality of the post-urban city. The chapter interrogates four significant theatres of the past thirty years by Peter Latz, Cesar Pelli, Rem Koolhaas and Jean Nouvel, respectively, and outlines how, by arresting and mediating historical forces, these theatres articulate the global city as a performance space.

Leaving the city, Himanshu Burte examines The Company Theatre's (TCT) five-acre residency in the hills outside Mumbai, India. Burte's chapter is focused on spaces of theatre making rather than performance. Noting the struggle of non-traditional Indian theatre makers to secure spaces for rehearsal and preparation in India's cities, Burte argues that the significance of the architecture of TCT's residency lies in its interaction with, and participation in, the company's ongoing practices of living and making. Burte's discussion of TCT's 'Big House' echoes Hannah's discussion of the value of an architecture of *becoming* through his focus on the iterative nature of the residency's architecture.

The concluding contribution in this section is from the Dutch-Belgian collective TAAT (Theatre as Architecture Architecture as Theatre), and it documents key aspects of their project *KHOR II*, a life-sized building kit. Since 2012, TAAT's work has explored how theatre architecture serves as a place of assembly and acts as a catalyst for the formation and interrogation of community. The *KHOR II* theatre installation is constructed by volunteer participants in a single day and is then used for the performance of a 'Do-It-Yourself' theatre play and, additionally, for workshops that reflect on the possibilities for community building. TAAT's contribution to the book takes the form of excerpts from the manual used by participants as well as transcripts of past participants' responses to the project. Many of the issues of contemporary theatre architecture raised in the other four chapters in this section can be seen in TAAT's work, including the use of provisional, flexible structures, a consideration of the theatre as a site of reflexivity where surrounding social and spatial contexts are interrogated and played with, and an emphasis on embodied co-presence and participation.

The chapters in the second section – 'Practices' – explore case studies where performance and architecture operate in combination or in counterpoint. The first chapter in this section, co-authored by Cathy Turner and Mike Pearson, examines the troubled work *Prydain: The Impossibility of Britishness*, produced by Welsh theatre company Brith Gof in 1996. This was the last of Brith Gof's large site-specific performances before Pearson left the company in 1997, and the chapter reflects on the tensions between the different approaches to performance taken by Pearson and co-artistic director Clifford McLucas as they prepared for this production. While Pearson focused on the body and the face-to-face encounter of performer and audience, McLucas, influenced by Bernard Tschumi, developed an architectural approach to dramaturgy. This chapter questions the limits of reciprocity between performance and architecture in site-specific theatre, articulating the particular dangers of a systematizing architectural approach to theatre while acknowledging architecture's usefulness in revealing and performing political structures.

Andrew Filmer's chapter reflects on the possibilities for architectural experience in theatre and performance by examining how spectators might occupy the scene in reflexive theatre events. Through thick descriptions and dramaturgical analysis of two recent productions by National Theatre Wales – including *Iliad*, co-directed by Mike Pearson with Mike Brookes – Filmer notes the different opportunities provided for spectators to occupy and inhabit these works. This chapter addresses the inhabitational possibilities of architectural dramaturgies and the way in which theatre might operate as a site of habitation, not promising immediacy or unreflective involvement, but instead offering opportunities for perceptual and cognitive exploration.

David Roberts's chapter exemplifies the vital role that performance can play in developing collaborative socially engaged architectural practices. The project Roberts describes challenges the narratives of failure that have developed around post-war social housing schemes in the UK by encouraging residents of London's Balfron Tower to speak of their lived experiences. Roberts demonstrates how performance can be used not only as a method of engagement – his chapter discusses the use of enactment as part of an oral history project – but also as a mode of analysis and a means of activism. Roberts's chapter describes how architects and architectural historians can use playful and unusual ways of interacting with users of architecture and displays a thoughtful and ethical engagement with the lives and circumstances of others.

Natalie Rewa analyses the staging of architectural models as scenographic elements in performance, revealing how the presence of an architectural model can alter the perception of the stage by inviting critical reflection and introducing an interplay of associations. Rewa examines how models are introduced, interacted with and handled in three very different theatre productions: Robert Lepage's *887* (2015), Michael Levine's design for the 2006 staging of *Der Ring des Nibelungen* for the Canadian Opera Company and *Me on the Map*, a participatory urban planning event created by Adrienne Wong and Jan Derbyshire (2013–2015). Rewa's discussion reveals the vitality of the architectural model as a means of exploring spatial aspirations and debating spatial production.

This section concludes with a reflection by artist Alex Schweder on his durational inhabited work *In Orbit*, performed in 2014 with long-term collaborator Ward Shelley. Schweder's works of 'performance architecture' are well known for their interrogation of the intimate relations between subjects and spaces. In his contribution to this book, Schweder frames the process of making and performing *In Orbit* through the lens of autobiography. Providing an account of the methodology of inhabitation that he and Shelley have developed, Schweder's brief critical-creative text weaves between intention and experience, the personal and the professional, to reveal the productive tensions between architecture and autobiography.

The final section in the book – 'Pedagogies' – is devoted to the possibilities and potentials of interdisciplinary pedagogy. Juliet Rufford explores how architectural theory and practice can inform the teaching and learning of devised postdramatic performance. Noting how students of theatre and performance frequently struggle with shaping and structuring a piece of performance and how they tend to fall back on restrictive spatial codes and conventions, Rufford outlines how architecture can offer guiding principles and tools for performance composition and for making critically informed dramaturgical decisions about the relationship between content, form, matter and space. The disciplines of performance and architecture are fundamentally interested in 'world building', imagining and structuring shared spaces of event and action, and Rufford's chapter makes a persuasive case for how an integrative interdisciplinary engagement with architecture can benefit performance pedagogy.

Beth Weinstein argues for a more nuanced understanding of performance in architectural pedagogy – one that draws much more directly than architecture has done to date on performance studies. Noting the absence of tools to directly explore human spatial performance in architecture, she identifies how performance can operate as a critical tool during three phases in the architectural life cycle: pre-design programme analysis, design and building processes, and inhabitation. Through a series of paired case studies, including one that discusses Alex Schweder's teaching at the Pratt Institute, Weinstein demonstrates how multimodal performance-oriented pedagogy can help extend architecture students' abilities to work with time, space and event.

We finish the book with an interview with artist and theatre maker Robert Wilson, in which Wilson describes The Watermill Center, the artistic laboratory on Long Island, New York, which he founded in 1992. Likened to the Bauhaus in its fostering of interdisciplinary creative endeavour, Watermill operates as a site for artistic experimentation and formation through its annual education and residency programmes. The interview provides an insight into how Wilson's careful arrangement of architecture, landscape and objects at Watermill embodies his pedagogical vision and aesthetic sensibility, resulting in an environment that inspires and constrains those who make work there.

As this brief overview of chapters suggests, *Performing Architectures* seeks to speak across disciplines and conventions rather than stay within familiar discourses and appeal to like-minded readers. The three sections of the book articulate key sites of engagement between theatre, performance and architecture, and address developments in theory and practice that intersect both fields. For all that, there have been inevitable limitations to what we can include, and some topics, which otherwise deserve greater attention, remain undeveloped. For instance, while the book includes chapters from scholars in Brazil and India, these only go a small way to addressing sizeable gaps in our knowledge of non-Western theatre architecture and performance space, particularly the ways in which indigenous or local cultural concerns adapt, appropriate and contest European theatre typologies. The chapters in this book also focus largely on the analogue and physical realities of space rather than on the interface between the digital and the physical. Discourses of performance are increasingly used in architecture to describe the use of interactive systems, surfaces and interfaces, and the ways in which digital design tools and virtual reality technologies have extended the formal possibilities of architectural design. Models from theatre and performance are also being drawn on to explain the interactions between pervasive computing technologies, publics and urban space (see, for instance, Geiger 2015), and architecture is used as a metaphor and a structuring principle in artistic explorations of aurality (see Blesser and Salter 2007; Petralia 2010). Discussions of these developments lie beyond the scope of this book.

*Performing Architectures* demonstrates how the aims, concerns and practices of theatre, performance and architecture overlap through shared interests in space, action, perception, event and the imagination of possible worlds. Through bringing together discussions of contemporary theatre architecture, cross-currents in artistic practice and a consideration of the uses of interdisciplinarity in architecture and performance pedagogy, we hope that this book contributes to pushing these disciplines closer together and serves to encourage further explorations of the rich and productive spaces between them.

# Notes

1  This sense of the tripartite nature of engagements between performance and architecture draws heavily on Dorita Hannah's editorial in a special issue of the Czech design magazine *ERA21* in 2011, where she described architecture as 'a performative medium' and identified 'the broad and dynamic role performance can play in the built environment; from sites as active public events (performative architecture); to spaces specifically designed to house the event (performance architecture); to aesthetic events that integrate art and architecture (performing architecture)' (2011: 5).

2  See, for instance, Branko Kolarevic and Ali Malkawi's edited collection *Performative Architecture: Beyond Instrumentality* (2005); the May 2008 special issue of the *Journal of Architectural Education* on 'Performance/Architecture' edited by Dorita Hannah and Omar Kahn; Marcia Feuerstein and Gray Read's *Architecture as a Performing Art* (2013); Michael Hensel's *Performance-oriented Architecture* (2013); Jordan Geiger's edited volume *Entr'acte: Performing Publics, Pervasive Media, and Architecture* (2015); and the 2015 special issue of *Performing Arts Journal* (no. 109) on 'Performance and Architecture' edited by Cathryn Dwyre and Chris Perry. A notable exception to this is Alan Read's *Architecturally Speaking: Practices of Art, Architecture and the Everyday* (2000), which operates dialogically between art, architecture and urban studies.

# Part One

# Projects

2

# What Might Be a Nietzschean Architecture?

Dorita Hannah

*Being an event rather than an object, performance is radically unstable in the meanings it generates and in the activities it engages.*

McAuley 2000: 16

*The tendency of twentieth-century art is to revolve around the act rather than the work, because the act, as the intense power of beginning, can only be thought in the present.*

Badiou 2007: 136

## Event-space

In *Architectures of Time: Toward a Theory of the Event in Modernist Culture* (2001), Sanford Kwinter articulates the temporal turn in twentieth-century Modernism, insisting that 'any proper understanding of architecture must also confront *its* character as an *illocutionary event*, or at the very least as an element inseparable from and in constant interface with the world of force, will, action and history' (14). It was this notion of the *evental* – as active and disruptive of the old – that signalled a break with architectural history in which past epochs had expressed their 'will to form' (13). Through the twentieth century's spatio-temporal revolutions in science, arts and communication, architecture could now be understood as an intimate system of forces giving shape and rhythm to everyday life – shifting from the static spatialization of time (object) to a more dynamic temporalization of space (action), emphasizing movement, relativity and duration. This realignment of architecture from passive *being* to active *becoming* foregrounds spatial performativity, which is most dynamic in theatre itself, where fictive and real spatio-temporalities variably intersect and alternate.

'Theatre' conventionally refers to both *dramatic practice* (event) and the *building* (space) housing that practice. As an *art form*, it incorporates the theatrical artifice of fleeting events that utilize the ephemeral elements of gesture, light and sound alongside the disposable materials of costume, prop and setting, while, as *built form*, it provides a seemingly stable environment conceived to persist beyond the transitory performances it houses. As *event-space* – a term attributed to contemporary architect Bernard Tschumi, in which architecture could not be dissociated from the events that 'happened' in it (1996: 139) – theatre harnesses 'spacing' as architectural performativity, described by Jacques Derrida as a means of 'taking place' through 'the event': an architectural 'acting out' that puts something 'into form' (1997a: 324–336). Navigating between the space of architecture and architectural space, spacing is an architectural act for both the designer formulating architecture and the inhabitant experiencing it. As 'the provocation of an event' (335), it constitutes an act always in the making, whereby inhabitants are constantly reconstructing their perception of, and engagement with, the built environment through embodied occupation. Despite innovative rethinking of theatre architecture over the last century – finally overthrowing the 300-year-old baroque archetype with multiple experimental and hybrid forms in new and adapted buildings – the persistent form of a rationally planned auditorium, in which parallel rows of seats face a framed and separated stage house, tends to dominate a globalized imaginary, alongside the ubiquitous black box studio that replicates the stage itself as a spatial void within which theatrical images are technologically manufactured. This cookie-cutter archetype found in performing arts centres worldwide enacts a disciplinary spacing and is the direct legacy of Richard Wagner's Bayreuth Festspielhaus, a coherent anti-Italianate model that opened in 1876 and was eventually embraced by architecture's Modern Movement as rational and democratic.[1] Yet, as David Wiles suggests, 'Theatre architecture turned out to be one of modernism's greatest failures, flexible, versatile theatres stripped of social messages proving a conceptual impossibility. The *machine à jouer* proved as chimeric as Le Corbusier's *machines á vivre*' (2003: 22).

This contribution to *Performing Architectures* revolves around the influential part played by late nineteenth-century German philosopher Friedrich Nietzsche in rethinking the potential of theatre architecture as action rather than object. Generally recognized as *the* philosopher of the avant-garde and the original postmodern thinker, he fiercely opposed the abiding model of the highly decorated, multi-layered, baroque auditorium with its framed technological stage, which the nineteenth-century European bourgeoisie had appropriated for performing their new-found post-revolutionary status. He was initially influenced by Wagner, to whom he dedicated his first book, *The Birth of Tragedy* (1872), having spent time with the composer during the conception and planning of the Bayreuth Festspielhaus while exiled in Switzerland. In fact, *The Birth of Tragedy* was published the same year construction began on the building for which Nietzsche held so much hope as a new kind of performance space as both art and architecture. However, by the time the building opened, the young philosopher had lost faith in his mentor. Nietzsche was bitterly disappointed with the Festspielhaus, which negated the visceral public engagement that was so critical to his participatory formulation. As a disciplinary mechanism, the architecture of the Festspielhaus reinforced rather than effaced the framed distance. Despite Wagner's initially radical intention to subvert architectural monumentality by establishing a temporary structure,[2] the rigid form of the Festspielhaus failed to fulfil his acolyte's demand for an undermining of enduring structures in favour of a new performative spatiality which recognizes unstable terrain, advocates the real over the representational and integrates performers and audience in a choric ground designed to unite them.

Although little has been written on the architectural thinking of Nietzsche – who was not always explicit in his references to the built environment – this chapter probes his writing in order to reveal just how radical his spatial thinking was, especially in relation to performance space and spatial performativity. Beginning with his bitter disappointment in Wagner's Festspielhaus, it goes on to unpack a series of Nietzsche's enduring discursive ideas: first, in relation to de-monumentalizing theatre architecture in favour of choric space that eliminates the boundary between performers and spectators; second, in his recognition of a new post-revolutionary anti-scenic paradigm emerging from the death of God; and third, in his understanding that, while the artist resisted the status quo, the architect reinforced society's power structures. Nietzsche's interrogation of how performance space itself performs in and as the event is haunted by his erstwhile mentor, whose enduring architectural project was variously a source of inspiration, disenchantment and frustration in relation to the philosopher's commitment to building thought.

## Building thought

*If we desired and dared an architecture corresponding to the nature of our soul*
*(we are too cowardly for it!) – our model would have to be the labyrinth!*

Nietzsche 1997a: 104

In his essay 'Why Peter Eisenman Writes Such Good Books', Jacques Derrida
asks, 'What might be a Wagnerian architecture?' (1997b: 337). Referencing
Nietzsche's own 'Why I Write Such Good Books' from *Ecco Homo*, Derrida
exposes the central query, and that of this particular chapter, to be: what might
be a Nietzschean architecture for the artwork – as both event and space – which
the philosopher had hoped Wagner would fulfil? This of course is a challenging
task as Nietzsche rarely wrote directly about architecture, and his philosophies
have been appropriated and interpreted to shape both conservative and radical
agendas in all aspects of art and politics. However, the role of spatialization
in his thinking serves to undermine the proper place of both architect and
architecture, just as his writings on tragedy aim to destabilize theatre as
bourgeois entertainment. As Nadir Lahiji points out in the *Missed Encounter
of Radical Philosophy with Architecture* (2014), Nietzsche inspired a new form
of architectural thinking through the notion of building thought, but the
philosopher's simultaneous ungrounding of thought influenced the ensuing
theatrical avant-garde that went on to test alternative sites for housing the event
as event (6). According to Lahiji:

> Nietzsche, the artist-philosopher, regarded himself as 'a kind of architect of
> imagination' and wanted to see the edifice of his own thought as 'the mind
> that builds'. He wanted this 'art of thinking' to be synonymous with an 'art of
> building' in which the verbal noun *building* would be a fundamental human
> activity in creating form. (6)

In 1994, the Getty Institute broached the question of Nietzschean
architecture in a conference held in Weimar with a subsequent publication five
years later entitled *Nietzsche and 'An Architecture of Our Minds'* (Kostka and
Wohlfarth 1999), referring to his suggestion that the 'labyrinth' provides a
fitting architectural prototype to match the Modernist soul (Nietzsche 1997a:
140). However, as Gary Shapiro notes in a review of the anthology, none of the
contributors addressed Nietzsche's writing on the Greek theatre in *The Birth of
Tragedy*, 'which is probably his most extended treatment of an architectural work'
(2002: 102). Such an undertaking discloses the philosopher's spatial speech as

one that reconciled distanced Apollonian aesthetics with immersive Dionysian frenzy. While the boundaries between the real and imagined architecture of Nietzsche's philosophies create an evasive territory, nowhere is this slippery spatiality more relevant than in the theatre, which is predicated on the co-presence of real and imagined spaces. Nietzsche's writings also reveal a distance between radical propositions for possible architectures and the architectural profession's complicity in the powers that prevent their realization.

## Architecture *against* Wagner

*Had we even been supplied with nobler material than our estimates allowed of, we should have shrunk in terror from the task of erecting a monumental pile, and been obliged to look around for assistance such as we could scarcely anywhere have found just now. For here presented itself the newest, the most individual problem, and, since it could never yet have been attempted, the most difficult for the architect of the present (or the future?) day.*

Wagner 1896b: 337

*For an event to possess greatness two things must come together: greatness of spirit in those who accomplish it and greatness of spirit in those who experience it. No event possesses greatness in itself, though it involves the disappearance of whole constellations, the destruction of entire peoples, the foundation of vast states or the prosecution of wars involving tremendous forces and tremendous losses: the breath of history has blown away many things of that kind as though they were flakes of snow.*

Nietzsche 1997b: 195

Nietzsche eagerly attended the foundation-laying ceremony for the Festspielhaus in 1872, which inspired him to write his meditation on 'Richard Wagner in Bayreuth', recognizing the building as an encapsulation of the composer's artwork where performance (event) and place (space) came together in a new form with a new audience, constituting a significant turning point that combined creative accomplishment and enhanced public experience. His desire for a more participatory and performative theatre architecture can be formulated as *event-space*, in which the built environment housing the event is itself an event and an integral driver of experience.[3] The building opened in 1876, a year after Charles Garnier's Palais Garnier (Paris Opera House) – a Beaux-Arts masterpiece that represented the conclusion of an epoch in which the audience as spectacle melded with a dramatically ornate, multi-leveled architecture. Seeking to remove such distraction and focus on the emphatically framed stage event, Wagner abandoned architect Gottfried Semper, who had already created plans for both a temporary and permanent theatre in Munich, instead working with architect Otto Brückwald and technician Karl Brandt, who were willing to fulfil the impresario's desire to eliminate architectural detail and monumentality in order to subdue spatial and public expression. While the Palais Garnier dedicated an extraordinary amount of floor space to lobbies, promenades and the grand staircase with its multi-leveled 'cage' of loges and balconies, Wagner all but eradicated the front of house in an effort to foreclose on audience sociality and emphasize his *Gesamtkunstwerk* ('total work of art') in which architecture played a critical role through spectatorial control. This was most evident in the auditorium itself, where an austere interior with a steeply raked fan-shaped format focused viewers on the stage, requiring them to sit in darkness and awed silence for hours at a time, although it is worth noting that Wagner did not originally intend to plunge the audience into complete darkness, claiming he was thwarted by problems with gas lighting at the opening (Wagner 1896a: 104). The uprights of an emphatic proscenium frame were repeated into the auditorium, enclosing the audience within the perspective setting of both architecture and scenery that converged on a mutually sited vanishing point towards the back of the stage. The buried orchestra pit reinforced this spatial unification of the real with the ideal by eliminating the customary visual and spatial interruption of musicians and conductor. Yet, while the devices of double proscenium, invisible orchestra and darkness worked to immerse the audience in the fictional world presented on the stage, they withheld any active participatory engagement with and between the audience, which Nietzsche advocated.[4]

Nietzsche's experience of the new theatre during the inaugural Bayreuth Festival in 1876 left him disenchanted: 'My mistake was to come to Bayreuth with an ideal. I was forced to experience the bitterest disappointment. The excess of ugliness, distortion, and overexcitement repulsed me vehemently'[5] (Nietzsche in Fischer-Dieskau 1976: 139). In his letter outlining the 'Case of Wagner' (1888), the philosopher contends that the composer had created an art that 'offers us a magnifying glass' where 'everything looks big, *even Wagner*' (Nietzsche 2000: 616). This magnification effect equates with Wagner's double proscenium, which played with scale to make the performers on the forestage appear as gods. The visionary apparatus of his festival and its venue focused and concentrated effects with what Nietzsche called 'the pressure of a hundred atmospheres' (628).

In removing the surrounding balconies and multiple viewpoints, and by tilting all audience members directly towards the stage – doubly framed by proscenium and doubly distanced by pit – Wagner had eradicated the last vestiges of audience as social performers. His emphasis on the illusory distance of the constructed scene and the immobility of the audience destroyed the choric realm advocated by Nietzsche in *The Birth of Tragedy* while exemplifying the pure Apollonian vision, which the philosopher spurned.

## (Re)birth of the will-to-destruction

Event-space emerged as a contemporary paradigm from traumatic events and perceptual shifts occurring in the early twentieth century that undermined both the theatrical *conventions* and the material *walls* of the melodramatic realistic theatre. The well-constructed playhouse seemed as meaningless as the well-made bourgeois play. Even as architecture's Modern Movement sought to industrialize, control and harmonize space, theatre's avant-garde wished to radically undermine it, celebrating the sacrificial body dancing amidst the debris. This theatrical will-to-destruction – standing in opposition to an architectural will-to-creation – was prefigured by Nietzsche in *The Birth of Tragedy* as Modernism's first dramatic manifesto, which called for a return to the feverish excesses of Dionysian rites in ancient Greek performance enacted before a more refined Apollonian approach was adopted that distanced the spectator (no longer embodied partaker) from the art form. The Dionysian performer, as 'pure primordial pain and its primordial re-echoing', is absorbed in the image, returning the precedence of the *choros* (dancing place) as a participatory space in which the image was unable to be apprehended as a whole (2000: 50). This return to an emphasis on the choric realm was intended to challenge the primacy of vision and efface the gap between the distanced view from the *theatron* (auditorium) and the exclusive performance realm of the *skene* (stage).

Nietzsche desired to undermine the monumental form of bourgeois theatre by introducing what Una Chaudhuri calls a 'rule of disorder' (1995: 21). His primary intention was to articulate and incorporate the opposing forces of Apollo (god of healing and the arts) and Dionysus (god of fertility, ritual madness and wine) – indicating representational form and nonrepresentational excess – dynamically at play within the Attic tragedies of the Dionysian festivals, as a model for generating art (see Weiss 1989, 2002). The Apollonian principle of dreams, appearance and representation (embodied in the distanced contemplation from the *theatron*) collided with the Dionysian principles of experience, intoxication and the will, found in the participatory ritual within the *choros*. As fundamentally conflicting principles, their antecedents lay in Arthur Schopenhauer's contrast between the world as 'Will' and the world as 'Representation'. However, as Adrian Poole notes, Nietzsche's notion of Will was no longer the root of all evil, pain and suffering, but an inevitable consequence of the Life-Force: 'For Schopenhauer pain means death throes, for Nietzsche pain means birth-pangs' (2005: 63). This complicated relationship between dying and birthing has spatial ramifications for the stage as *choros*, which Nietzsche referred to as the 'womb' that gave birth to drama, a 'primal ground' melding dream into communal being by presenting 'itself to our eyes in continual rebirths' (2000: 65–66).

Nietzsche wished for creative and destructive forces to operate in dynamic tension. Working with binary oppositions as essential to the tragic form, he encourages us to accept and embrace contradictions rather than dialectically subvert them, thereby revealing the essential nature of violence, pain and conflict, and the need to acknowledge and incorporate them into the artwork. Tragedy was an admonition and critique against the rigid Apollonian form, which the Dionysian act comes to shatter, revealing the inherent fragility of human structures, as individual identities, social institutions and constructed assemblages. Dionysus, as creator and destroyer, is a force driving through all forms, challenging their Apollonian individuation, differentiation and rigidity, making and remaking them. This radical critique of the human products, structures and artefacts in which we put so much faith, impacted as much on architecture as other art forms, particularly on the auditorium.

Nietzsche deliberately critiqued the Apollonian 'architectonics' of Doric art that denied the natural instincts and savage excesses of the Dionysian festival, which he referred to as 'that horrible mixture of sensuality and cruelty' (2000: 39). Through the performance of the Dionysian dithyramb, the visceral and ecstatic dancing body undermined architectonic control, causing astonishment in the Apollonian Greek 'mingled with the shuddering suspicion that all this was not so very alien to him after all, in fact, that it was only his Apollonian consciousness which, like a veil, hid his Dionysian world from his vision' (41). The communal shudder that trespasses on consciousness is a visceral experience, underscoring how the Dionysian exceeds vision, just as the dance exceeds place. The ecstatic sensorium of the performing body displaces the more static ocularcentrism of architecture, undermining its stability with Zarathustra's 'dancing-mad feet' (Nietzsche 1969: 241). As Mark Wigley contends of Nietzsche's dance, '[It] disrupts the spatial regime by locating something aspatial within it' (1995:

159). Containing a phantasmatic promise of theatre's virtuality, it troubles architecture's secure spatiality.

The inherent excesses of performance – exposed by Nietzsche in laughter and play as well as in the dance – mobilized 'things' as multiple and evental, and weakened the basis upon which thought itself had previously been constructed.[6] In *The Architecture of Deconstruction* (1995), Wigley names this philosophical instability the 'edifice complex' where metaphysics, as a sound structure erected on secure foundations and stable ground, is threatened because the ground is no longer considered stable. Nietzsche created a new philosophical space seen by Heidegger as ungrounding ground, opening up and revealing the metaphysical void (Wigley 1995: 6–13, 62). In aligning philosophy with architecture, we can see that Nietzsche's thought destabilized built form by weakening its structures and questioning its abiding qualities of strength and durability.

A reconciliation of Dionysian and Apollonian forces, therefore, constituted a revolutionary spatial event that was also aspatial. It required more than tearing down the physical and metaphorical veil-as-curtain that separated the distanced viewing place of the *theatron* from the participatory space of the *choros*. The Apollonian culture was an artistic structure that must be levelled 'stone by stone' to make visible the foundations upon which it rests (Nietzsche 2000: 41), a gesture designed to fundamentally weaken rather than annihilate architecture. Dismantling this cultural edifice also reveals the ever-present pit beyond the visible: 'the terror and horror of existence' (42, 45) covered over by Apollonian illusion as a totalizing worldview, which he likens to a 'permanent military encampment' (47). He wished to undermine architecture's supposed rationality, stability and disciplinary imperative, revealing its cracks and crevices and, eventually, that ever-present abyss, over and within which theatre could constructively play.

For Nietzsche, the true tragedy of modernity was a refusal to communally embrace a primordial unity in the face of the loss of God and Christianity's homogeneous unity, acknowledging 'life-giving' chaos as the basis of the universe. As an Apollonian force, the increasingly utopian project of modern architecture denied this tragic Dionysian vision while it attempted to build a rational, unified world over the void, rather than 'looking boldly right into the terrible destructiveness of so-called world history as well as the cruelty of nature' (59). An anarchic prophet of Modernism, Nietzsche's spatial speech continues to undermine conventional theatre architecture, revealing the Modernist tragedy as doubt in the divine, loss of a centre, confrontation of the abyss and acknowledgement of the inherent cruelty of human nature. His declaration of God's death signalled the end of representation and impacted on how both theatre and architecture are conceived, presented and experienced.

## An event still on its way

*Have you not heard of the madman who lit a lantern in the bright morning hours, ran to the market place, and cried incessantly, 'I seek God! I seek God!' As many of those who do not believe in God were standing around just then, he provoked much laughter. [...]*

*'Wither is God' he cried. 'I shall tell you. We have killed him – you and I. All of us are his murderers. [...] Who gave us the sponge to wipe away the entire horizon? [...] Is there any up or down left? Are we not straying through an infinite nothing? Do we not feel the breath of empty space? [...] God is dead. God remains dead. And we have killed him.'*

Nietzsche 1974: 181

Although Nietzsche claimed not to believe in the idea of a resounding 'great event' but in shifts that created new values (Nietzsche 1966: 131), the nineteenth century was brought to a close with the echoes of his proclamation that 'God is dead' (Nietzsche 1974: 95). One hundred years later, the philosopher Gilles Deleuze acknowledges this statement, first outlined by Nietzsche in *Gay Science* (1882), as '*the* dramatic proposition *par excellence*' in its denial of an identifiable unity from which all the differences of the world emanate and to which they return (2006: 152). Reflecting a general disbelief in the eternal, in order to place more faith in the present, God's death could also be considered *the* decisive Modern event calling into doubt the physical space of worship and therefore architectural typology: 'What are these churches now if they are not the tombs and sepulchres of God?' (Nietzsche 1974: 95). More radically, it emphasized the disappearance of any absolute reference to a closed system of spatio-temporal coordinates previously defined by Cartesian perspectivalism (also referred to as the *ancien scopic régime*), whereby space and its subjects and objects are constructed and perceived through Euclidean geometry. This signalled the end of mimetic representation that, since the sixteenth century, had bound art, architecture and theatre through scenography (*scenografia*), defining our ways of seeing and experiencing both architectural and theatrical space.[7] The framed perspectival construction within the nineteenth-century proscenium arch simultaneously distances and centralizes the spectator in the event, previously organized around the monarch's ideal view, integrating the monumental architecture of the house with the pictorial architectonics of scenery. The plane of the proscenium forms both window and mirror, beyond which a perspectival world is artificially constructed through spatial collapse and distortion. The spectator's gaze apprehends a spatial continuum via geometric projection that is dependent on a horizon line and vanishing point where 'infinity, aesthetics, mathematics and theology meet on a unified plane whose grandeur and perfection symbolizes God himself' (Weiss 1995: 59). However, Europe's revolutions had unseated the all-seeing 'I' of the monarch that had stood in for the all-seeing eye of God. As Nietzsche's madman claimed, the horizon had been wiped away and the vanishing point had opened up to reveal a gaping void, undermining hitherto rational, stable and homogenous space, which assumed the sovereignty of vision through a single immobile eye and the mathematization of psychophysiological space (Panofsky 1991: 29–30).

Nietzsche's pronouncement declared the end of the classic age as the end of illusion. It coincided with a loss of desire to represent within the field of art, discussed by Michel Foucault in *The Order of Things* (1970) as a mimetic crisis in which the world had become unrepresentable. This in turn destabilized both architecture and the stage, neither of which could now play a role in representing a closed, complete universe as a finitely constructed totality. However, just as the madman who frantically heralds God's death in the marketplace maintains 'this tremendous event is still on its way, still wandering', Nietzsche also recognized it as one in motion: 'The event itself is much too great, too distant, too far from the comprehension of the many even for the tidings of it to be thought of as having *arrived* yet, not to speak of the notion that many people might know what has really happened here, and what must collapse now that this belief has been undermined' (1974: 447). The edifice of classic representation was, therefore, in a state of slow and inexorable collapse, reconfiguring how space is constructed not only for events but also as events.

Threatening fundamental belief structures, Nietzsche also undermined the buildings that literally house such structures, thereby exposing architecture's constitutive instability: the church that housed a dead god became a mausoleum, while the new theatre could resacralize performance space as a participatory, secular and immersive rite, free from the artifice of dissimulation that weakened the theatrical power of an unmediated reality. This introduced an intricate conception of temporality to the built environment, presenting the possibility for architecture to partake in the ensuing avant-garde project through active agencies of performance – ephemerality, movement, theatricality, illocution and virtuality – in order that theatre as built space align with the art form that resisted it and become de-materialized, un-housed and de-constructed. However, as Denis Hollier contends, this necessitated loosening 'the structure that is hierarchical and at the same time creates hierarchy' (1989: 23), an action which architectural Modernism as well as contemporary practices are resistant to undertake because, as Nietzsche noted, architecture serves power.

## Nietzsche's architect(ure)

*The architect represents neither a Dionysian nor an Apollonian state: here it is the great act of will, the will that moves mountains, the frenzy of the great will which aspires to art. The most powerful human beings have always inspired architects; the architect has always been under the spell of power. His buildings are supposed to render pride visible and the victory over gravity, the will to power. Architecture is a kind of eloquence of power in forms – now persuading, even flattering, now only commanding. The highest feeling of power and sureness finds expression in a grand style. The power which no longer needs any proof, which spurns pleasing, which does not answer lightly, which feels no witness near, which lives oblivious of all opposition to it, which reposes within itself, fatalistically, a law among laws – that speaks of itself as a grand style.*

Nietzsche 1954: 520–521

In *Twilight of the Idols* (a riff on Wagner's *Twilight of the Gods*, the last of his four operas in *Der Ring des Nibelungen*), Nietzsche 'sounds out' legendary characters and iconic figures, including the architect, who occupies the same section as the artist (1954: 520). However, the artist as actor, mime, dancer, musician and poet – once one and the same figure, combining Apollonian and Dionysian tendencies – is separate from the architect, portrayed as a wilful character implicated in the construction and expression of history's powers. Henri Lefebvre later elucidates by stating that 'monumental buildings mask the will to power and the arbitrariness of power beneath signs and surfaces which claim to express collective will and collective thought', thereby managing 'to conjure away both possibility and time' (Lefebvre 1991: 143). Lahiji points out how Nietzsche's critique of a 'will to architecture' (echoed by Bataille as domineering and disciplining) was appropriated by Modernism's heroic architects who interpreted it as reinforcing the Master Builder as ideologist (2014: 8). Although Nietzsche was mindful of architecture's potential, as a form of power, to mediate between the creative and destructive forces upon which his philosophy was built, the Nietzschean architect (working for the status quo) forecloses on Nietzschean architecture (working against the status quo), once more revealing the gap between Modernism's architectural avant-garde and those in its theatrical counterpart who tested alternative sites for housing the event as event.

By mutually incorporating power systems, architecture defines, regulates and limits our daily practices (Foucault 1980: 149), and, as handmaidens to power, architects are responsible: a claim reinforced by Lefebvre's reference to the authoritarian, brutal and phallic 'logic of space' (Lefebvre 1991: 57). Such spatial hostility is acutely evident in the West since the defining spectacle of 9/11, after which freedom of movement and expression is purposefully curtailed – locally and globally – in the very name of 'freedom'. Designers of public space are more actively complicit in architecture's role to silently and subtly condition the competence and performance of the subject, especially in this age of a constructed 'war on terror' that maintains a continual state of siege. As Nietzsche wrote of the architect: 'His buildings are supposed to render pride visible, and the victory over gravity, the will to power' (1954: 521). Yet in our current age of liquescence – where nothing is stable, where fiction constantly folds into reality and where sedentary structures can no longer house the mediatized spectacle of daily life – this fatal resolve is countered by a desire to create more porous, open-ended, transparent and ephemeral environments.

Advocating a labyrinthine space, which privileges sensorial immersion rather than the spectatorial overview of reason, Nietzschean architecture challenges the Nietzschean architect. Integrating what Lefebvre calls architecture's concrete 'objectality' with its philosophical 'other' allows us to return to event-space as an aspatial spatial condition, positing an emergent, contingent and weak architecture that simultaneously houses and un-houses events.

## Event-spacing

As Modernism's philosopher of crisis, Nietzsche took centre stage in calling for a radical reworking of the space of the event. His own stage was neither centred nor framed before a baroque or even Modernist auditorium. Nietzsche's alter ego, the madman who declares God's death and therefore the end of mimetic representation, occupies what Derrida names 'the space of dis-traction' (1997a: 336). As '*the one who is spacy, or spaced out*', he cannot be housed and is obliged to wander (336). Carrying a lantern like a failed prop in the blinding light of day, this madman appears in the chaotic marketplace, a theatrical figure calling to account those who gather around him as implicated in great events. His declaration (of God's death) is also a demand that the public (as God's murderers) realize their complicity in the creation of history. Like Dionysus, Nietzsche came to shatter form. Replacing perspectival construction with the multiplicity of perspectivism, he wished to transform the 'herd' into a reflective community that is no longer dominated by a singular totalizing reality but could occupy and create multiple realities with varying interpretations of existence. Rather than distant viewers in the *theatron*, they were choric participants returning to the *agora*, those wanderers who strayed from the proper site of theatre, once held in suspicion by Plato.

Wagner's Festspielhaus provided an effective disciplinary apparatus for isolating individuals within the auditorium and successfully played into the hands of the twentieth century's Modern Movement as a model for forming well-behaved spectator-citizens. Within the darkness of this hermetically sealed and seemingly passive vessel, a homogeneous plane of well-organized viewers, each contained in their separate seat, gazes transfixed towards the light emanating from highly composed images enacted within the technological frame of the proscenium stage. Notwithstanding claims to a 'democratic' form, this prevalent model for theatre architecture reduces the potential impact of audience and architecture on the event. Enacting a violent gesture against any potential disruption, it disciplines the behaviour of the spectators, who can be likened to Plato's chained prisoners in a cave, watching shadows dancing on the walls, oblivious to the material world of light and reality outside (see Plato 1997).

For Nietzsche, the choric space – located between the raised stage and raked auditorium – is where the 'ideal spectator' is located and immersed: 'the only beholder, the beholder of the visionary world of the scene' (2000: 62). As the space of dance, it evokes the choreographic notion of 'spacing': a means of registering and apprehending changing relationships between bodies in motion and the place they occupy. Such sites of dynamic spacing can be found in a handful of venues from last century that have resisted the default model designed to ensure a globally recognizable 'theatre' by refuting darkness, immateriality, symmetry, so-called neutrality and an unequivocal delineation between performers and audience. These include Heinrich Tessenow's Hellerau Festspielhaus in Dresden (Germany, 1911), a hall of glowing white canvas walls that radically removed the raised stage with its principal designer, scenographer Adolphe Appia, creating tiered landscapes for dancers and spectators that rise from common ground; Wellington's Hannah Playhouse (New Zealand, 1973), designed by architect James Beard in consultation with scenographer Raymond Boyce as one of a handful of asymmetric performance spaces in the world, labyrinthine and resolutely architectural with its concrete towers, cranked galleries and walls of diagonally slatted timber; Manchester Royal Exchange (England, 1976), designed by Levitt Bernstein Associates in close consultation with director-designer Richard Negri as a theatre-in-the-round, configured within an open tubular steel structure of multi-level surrounding galleries; and São Paulo's Teatro Oficina (Brazil, 1984), designed by Lina Bo Bardi and Edison Elito as a theatrical slot in the city composed of glazed wall and garden, a skylight roof that slides open, vertiginous scaffolding galleries and a long central pit furrowing through the site's steeply ramping floor. These enduring iconic sites – the result of collaborations between architects and scenographers – tend to be provisional in nature, with architectures of fabric, rostra and scaffolding, or are flexible in formatting while emphatic in materiality. They also recognize the inherent uncontainability of performance, immersing audience as participants in an atmosphere that is resolutely architectural yet anti-monumental.

This chapter has sought not to relate existing projects as exemplars of Nietzsche's formulations, but rather to outline his architectural thought as a shifting, open-ended project in itself, which remains as relevant today as it has over the last century and a half. It has sought to take account of the role Wagner's own project played in Nietzsche's spatial thinking; to identify his recognition of the *event* in philosophical, political and perceptual revolutions, which brought the built environment more in line with the dynamics of performance, challenging architecture's status as a fixed and enduring object; and to acknowledge his contribution to rethinking architecture as an orchestrated set of systems, forces and complex sociopolitical and embodied relationships and experiences, in order to perceive the constructed environment more in a state of active *becoming* than passive *being*.

# Notes

1   The Italianate theatre has been linked to the baroque model that originated in the sixteenth century, which evolved into a decorated multi-layered auditorium separated from a technological stage, predicated on perspectival images, by the proscenium frame.

2  On 30 September 1850, from exile in Zurich, Richard Wagner wrote to his friend
   Theodor Uhlig of his desire for a 'rough theatre of planks and beams' in a pastoral
   setting adjacent to a city, furnished with theatrical machinery, in which an event
   could be created to which a select audience of musicians, scholars and sympathetic
   lovers of musical drama would be invited: 'When everything was in order, I should
   give three performances […] in the course of a week; after the third, the theatre
   would be pulled down and the score burned' (Wagner cited in Hartford 1980:
   19). Through this conceptually complex and radical idea, Wagner was aiming to
   emphasize performance's inherent ephemerality, while also utilizing the event as a
   money-raising strategy for his longer-term project.

3  This chapter draws together aspects of Nietzsche's spatial thinking that are outlined
   in greater length in my book *Event-Space: Theatre Architecture & the Historical
   Avant-Garde* (Hannah 2018).

4  While Jacques Rancière (2009) has argued that a distanced spectator can be actively
   engaged without embodied participation, Nietzsche was more interested in visceral
   and spatial engagement.

5  The first performance of the entire *Der Ring des Nibelung* took place at Bayreuth on
   13, 14, 16 and 17 August 1876. Also referred to as the *Ring Cycle*, it comprised four
   music dramas, loosely based on Norse sagas and the epic Middle High German
   poem 'The Song of the Nibelungs': *Das Rheingold* (The Rhine Gold), *Die Walküre*
   (The Valkyrie), *Siegfried* and *Götterdämmerung* (Twilight of the Gods).

6  Deleuze regards Nietzsche's focus on dance, laughter and play as 'affirmative powers
   of transmutation: dance transmutes heavy into light, laughter transmutes suffering
   into joy and the play of the throwing (the dice) transmutes low into high. But in
   relation to Dionysus dance, laughter and play are affirmative powers of reflection
   and development. Dance affirms becoming and the being of becoming; laughter,
   roars of laughter, affirm multiplicity and the unity of multiplicity; play affirms
   chance and the necessity of chance' (Deleuze 2006: 193–194).

7  The section and page reference for this classical work is 1449a: 18. Aristotle (1987)
   briefly referes to *skenographia* in Poetics (1449a: 18) as a 'scenic writing' linked to
   stage painting. In Book I.2 of *De Architectura* (Vitruvius 1999: 24–25), Vitruvius
   described *scaenographia* as the representational art of perspective. In 1545 the
   Renaissance architect Sebastiano Serlio utilized *scenografia* in the second book
   of his *Architettura* (1611: 45) as a means of integrating the science and craft of
   architecture, scenery and painting into a combined stage and auditorium, which
   in turn influenced the planning of buildings, cities and landscapes. Scenography is
   now generally referred to as the art of scenic design, including setting, costumes and
   lighting (Howard 2002: 125).

# 3

# Factory, Street and Theatre in Brazil: Two Theatres by Lina Bo Bardi

Evelyn Furquim Werneck Lima

This chapter discusses two innovative theatres designed by the Italian-born architect Lina Bo Bardi (1914–1992), reading them in the context of twentieth-century Brazilian culture and politics, and providing a sense of how they operate as an extant dramaturgy for the productions they house. The two theatres – the SESC Pompeia Factory Theatre, located inside a huge former industrial complex, and the Oficina Theatre, a theatrical space built as a street lined by scaffolding galleries – reveal the yearning for change in Brazil at the end of the authoritarian period of military dictatorship (1964–1985), in which artistic initiatives were metaphorically expressed to circumvent censorship, and during which Lina Bo Bardi joined artists and intellectuals to struggle against the dictatorship.[1] In her architecture, Bo Bardi championed the needs of everyday life rather than architectural formalism, and this approach – atypical in an architectural professional who had intensive contact with Milanese rationalism – was sharpened through research in the city of Salvador and the backlands of the northeastern Brazilian state of Bahia between 1958 and 1964, when she developed ideas with a group of intellectuals who valorized local culture and drew on these to strengthen new courses at the University of Bahia (Bo Bardi 1967).

Bo Bardi was acutely aware of an intellectual's responsibility to mediate between tradition and modernity. Her conception of theatre architecture was critical and atypical, imbued with a poetics drawn from local cultural forms. In a genuinely collaborative action, she consistently consulted workers and artisans, incorporating their craft skills and knowledge in her creative process. Exploring the contradictions between literate knowledge and empirical experimentation,

Bo Bardi engaged in a dialogue with industrial systems and a sense of tradition, using high-tech solutions and local materials. Valuing the working class in her theatre architecture, she practised a socialist culture reconstructed on the basis of popular participation and inspired by the ideas and practices of Antonio Gramsci, Paulo Freire and Augusto Boal. Bo Bardi's creative process sought to meet the needs of users: 'When one draws a project', she writes, 'it is necessary to make it useful to its purpose' (Bo Bardi 1992: 61). Inspired by the ethical and political function of architecture, she sought to address sociocultural deficiencies and selected materials and practices that were appropriate in the context of Brazil's national economic difficulties.

Bo Bardi's theatres arguably exemplify her Marxist approach and differ from her other well-known projects – such as the Glass House (1951) and the São Paulo Museum of Art (MASP) (1968) – through the skilful way in which they mediate different cultural influences, negotiate modern and vernacular traditions, and serve as places that encourage radical cultural production. Although much has been written about her work since her death (see, for instance, Anelli 2010; de Oliveira 2002; Lima 2009, 2013), her theatre projects have been largely neglected, with much attention instead paid to the formal aspects of her other architectural accomplishments and her achievements as an editor, theorist and exhibition designer. What is overlooked is the strong empathy Bo Bardi had for theatrical space, her working relationships with theatre and film directors, and the political, inclusive nature of her theatre architecture. Taking an anthropological approach, Bo Bardi created distinct places for performance by converting old factories into theatres, transforming streets into interior spaces and opening stages out into public spaces. She sought to integrate heterogeneous audiences and performers, and through her designs for the SESC Pompeia Theatre and the Oficina Theatre, she intervened in spectators' involvement in the spectacle, inviting them to shift, to change position and to walk on the stage. By influencing spectators' embodiment and perspective, she sought to shift their mode of participation in theatrical events.

In Brazil, despite numerous theatrical experiments in alternative spaces since the 1960s, theatre buildings remain largely designed with a clear separation between the stage and the auditorium.[2] This reflects a bourgeois ideology of theatre as an object of consumption, based on the historical importation of Brazilian cultural values from Europe, particularly Italy and France, during the nineteenth and early twentieth centuries. Since the twentieth century these values have been contested, particularly through contact with indigenous African-Brazilian culture. In the seminal 1922 São Paulo Modern Art Week, the Modernist Anthropophagics ('Cannibalists'), led by Osward de Andrade, proposed drawing on the influence of European and American artists, but freely creating their own art through 'eating', 'digesting' and 'regurgitating' the work they encountered. In theatre, Augusto Boal and José Celso Martinez Corrêa (known as Zé Celso) have been key figures in a broader resistance to colonialism that sought to develop a genuinely Brazilian culture. Although different in their purposes, Boal's Theatre of the Oppressed and Zé Celso's Oficina Group vehemently opposed the persecution and violence of the military regime and both rethought the relationship between stage and auditorium as an essential part of their resistance. From 1957 to 1971, Boal directed the Arena Theatre in São Paulo, a theatre of resistance and a 'theatre in the round'. The 1964 military coup transformed Brazil and its theatre; the dictatorship and its allies assumed the role of oppressors, while the Brazilian population assumed the position of the oppressed. After being arrested and exiled in 1971, Boal established the basis for the Theatre of the Oppressed, a methodology that considers theatre as an instrument of social resistance and inclusion. In the 1960s, Zé Celso, leader of the Oficina Theatre group and director of its collective productions, experimented with countercultural practices that formed part of the development of Tropicalism, a movement that reinvigorated Andrade's anthropophagy to develop new hybridized forms of music, theatre and poetry. Zé Celso has explained that his 1967 production of Oswald de Andrade's play *O Rei da Vela* was his most important in the struggle against colonial ideology:

> The 1967 production turned out to be the catalyst for a full-fledged movement that sprung up spontaneously around the same period: from Glauber Rocha, who was filming *Earth in a Trance* at the time, to Caetano Veloso, with his release of the *Tropicalia* album, to Hélio Oiticica, who set the stage for art to come alive, complete with earth, plants and television. So that's how the Tropicália movement came into being. (Zé Celso cited in Zancan 2012)

Before discussing the SESC Pompeia Factory Theatre and the Oficina Theatre in more detail, I first trace out some of the connections between Bo Bardi's work and that of Italian Marxist philosopher Antonio Gramsci, Brazilian pedagogue Paulo Freire and theatre theorist and director Augusto Boal. While each of these thinkers expressed themselves differently, they, like Bo Bardi, aligned themselves with the perspective of the lower classes. For Gramsci, politics 'is not a dependent sphere. It is where forces and relations, in the economy, in society, and in culture, have to be actively *worked on* to produce particular forms of power, forms of domination' (Hall 1987: 20). In his writing, Gramsci paid special attention to the concept of culture, and argued that the achievement of consciousness was the result of the efforts of the working class and its political involvement, along with its struggles to transform society (Gramsci 1975: 85). His proposed new humanism was based upon a movement of intellectual and moral reformation that would establish an organic relationship between elite and popular culture. In his prison notebooks, written in the early 1930s, Gramsci developed the concept of the 'national-popular collective will' to describe the process through which social classes might be successfully hegemonized by the Communist Party and the proletariat in order to found a new state (see Gramsci 1999: 316–330). Bo Bardi's familiarity with the work of Gramsci is attested by Brazilian philosopher Carlos Nelson Coutinho, who translated Gramsci's work into Portuguese and studied at the University of Bahia while Bo Bardi was a visiting professor between 1958 and 1963. He points out that Bo Bardi 'was the second person who talked to me about Gramsci [...]. For her Bahia [a Brazilian state in the northeast of the country] was the real expression of what Gramsci called the "national-popular"' (Coutinho 2006: 148). As most of the articles Bo Bardi wrote in magazines or newspapers were for a popular readership, Gramsci's ideas were not always directly referenced (Grinover 2010: 183). Nevertheless, her awareness of Gramsci is discernable. In one text Bo Bardi writes that she wants to preserve the genuine strength of the subaltern classes, that part of humanity which ignores literate culture but which 'has the necessary strength to develop a new and truthful culture' (Bo Bardi 1958). In another article, published two years later, she explicitly mentions Gramsci when discussing his new humanism that 'tends to fuse a technical view of the world with cultural problems' (Bo Bardi 1960: 1–2). Gramsci wrote that 'positive conditions are to be sought in the existence of urban social groups which have attained an adequate development in the field of industrial production and a certain level of historico-political culture. Any formation of a national-popular collective will is impossible, unless the great mass of peasant farmers bursts *simultaneously* into political life' (Gramsci 1999: 327). Gramsci's concept of 'national-popular' culture, and the need for intellectuals to contribute to the production of such a culture, informed Bo Bardi's designs for inclusive theatre architecture. Her designs took account of the conflicts and tensions in everyday Brazilian life and transformed pre-existing spaces into unusual places for performance. Through this she fought against injustice to establish effective conditions for social well-being.

In her architectural discourse, Bo Bardi demonstrates a familiarity with the ideas and practices of Paulo Freire, with whom she shared her Marxist convictions during the hard years of the Brazilian military dictatorship. Freire's programmes for countering adult illiteracy were officially implemented in Brazil in the 1960s. In his *Pedagogy of the Oppressed* (1968), he asserts:

> No pedagogy which is truly liberating can remain distant from the oppressed by treating them as unfortunates and by presenting for their emulation models from among the oppressors. The oppressed must be their own example in the struggle for their redemption. (Freire [1968] 1970: 54)

Bo Bardi had already expressed a similar idea when she restored and adapted the Solar do Unhão as the Museum of Popular Art of Bahia (1958–1963), exhibiting to the community art made by local artisans, and attempting to create the Popular University of Bahia in the renovated building, where skilled workers were to be the teachers and to pass on their know-how to future professionals. Bo Bardi's theatrical projects, in which an inherited bourgeois theatrical model was abandoned, reveal a similar code of values and reflect Freire's ideas about a liberating education for the lower classes. Bo Bardi's assumption was that a true and liberating pedagogy should be directed at the poor using their own models and not the models of the ruling class. In so doing, Bo Bardi echoed Freire's grounding of his pedagogy of the oppressed in the direct and indirect observation of real situations:

> Thought and study alone did not produce *Pedagogy of the Oppressed*; it is rooted in concrete situations and describes the reaction of labourers (peasant or urban) and of middle-class persons whom I have observed directly and indirectly during the course of my educative work. (Freire [1968] 1970: 37)

Like Freire, Bo Bardi was opposed to mass consumer culture, instead seeking the transformation of the capitalist state structure through the working class constructing its own culture. The *homo politicus* that Bo Bardi represented brought the relationship between individual and society to the core of her work; she searched for the authenticity of people still untainted by consumer culture, and dedicated her theatre architecture to them. It was during her stay in Bahia – one of the poorest regions of the country – from 1958 to 1964 that Bo Bardi developed a new poetics of space by exploring the use of local handicraft elements. Drawing inspiration from the imagination and materials found in popular art – and sometimes the trash found on the streets – Bo Bardi adopted ideas of *Arte Povera*. Her theatre design and theatre architecture came to reflect the unconscious practices of the popular imagination and Brazilian native culture, using this to contest inherited European theatre typologies. By using hard wooden seats (in the SESC Pompeia and Oficina Theatres), spiral staircases transformed into totems (in the Gregorio de Mattos Theatre) and circus tents (in the unbuilt Theatre of Ruins), she referenced the indigenous and vernacular Brazilian sociocultural context. In the catalogue organized for *Exhibition Bahia 1959*, Bo Bardi affirms that while a genius can create a great masterpiece or an exceptional work of art, other aesthetic expressions should be valued, such as those that 'emanate from the common man claiming his right to poetry' (Bo Bardi and Gonçalves 1959).

## The SESC Pompeia Factory Theatre: A collaborative vision

The SESC Sports and Leisure Centre of the Pompeia Factory in São Paulo, which resembles a small industrial village, was built in two phases: the renovation of the former Mauser Brothers steel drum factory between 1977 and 1982 and the construction of new towers for the sports complex between 1983 and 1986. In addition to her physical rearrangement of space, Bo Bardi assumed the management of the centre, creating a programme of pedagogy for the employees and their families, so that they could attend newly implemented courses in design, theatre, arts and handicrafts. According to Bo Bardi, architecture, like theatre, is a form of communication with the public, and in this project she built the complex and its theatre as a collective effort of multiple social actors, making the construction site her own office and listening to the ideas of employees. She created a genuine 'lived space' in the old factory, where skilled workers performed their tasks and carried out *in loco* experiments. The collective endeavour of building the whole complex, including the theatre itself, was a durational collaborative performance that reveals her Gramscian political commitment that the focus should be on providing for the elementary needs of people first, only after which quality art could emerge. Bo Bardi's decision to carry out her work on the construction site itself, sharing decisions instead of sending drawings from a remote office, transformed the construction into a collective act in which each actor/worker played his or her part.

The renovated space still resembles the former factory. The existing sheds, the exposed brick walls, the concrete structure, the cobbled paving and the ceramic tiles roof denote the idea of the old factory and highlight the tectonics of the SESC Pompeia Factory complex. The use of details such as the SESC POMPEIA sign at the entrance and metallic elements painted in red – a constant motif in Bo Bardi's buildings – grant a special character both to space and to the building, offering a contrast with its bare concrete and exposed brick. Entering the SESC Pompeia complex evokes excitement and a desire to participate in the programme proposed by the architect. In a recent article, Roger Buergel credits the success of the SESC Pompeia Factory Leisure and Sports Centre to Bo Bardi's perception of 'the site's psychic resonances' as she looked through the reinforced concrete structure of the desolate factory space, and the way she has provided 'a sense of place in a community of mostly migrant workers from the Brazilian Northeast and Europe' (Buergel 2011). Bo Bardi maintained several formal aspects of the extant factory, but her interventions feature a contemporary look and a use of materials and forms which avoid any attempt to imitate the past. The conceptual foundations of such an approach – known as 'critical restoration' – were established by Benedetto Croce in the early twentieth century and developed through contributions by Cesare Brandi (1963), among others, whose research helped to formulate the principles of the Charter of Venice (1964) and the Charter of Italian Restoration (1972). In Croce's historiographical theory, a 'past fact does not respond to a past interest, but to a present interest, in so far as it is unified with an interest of the present life' (Croce 1921: 12). Bo Bardi's theory of history is focused more acutely on the reality of labour. For her, 'history should not be understood as a "crystallization" of history, the history from the manuals or the mouths of professors, but as "history in the now" – the history of labour and toil of the people' (Bo Bardi [1958] 2001: 214). Embodying this understanding in her work at the SESC Pompeia – and the Oficina Theatre – Bo Bardi preserved 'signs of the past and of the activities of the old buildings, as well as including elements from everyday life' (Bo Bardi 1992: 61–62).

For the SESC Pompeia, Bo Bardi designed an 800-seat theatre with a rectangular platform stage set between two opposite, symmetrical and undifferentiated banks of seating, repudiating the conditions for bourgeois spectatorship and embodying a politics of visibility and participation (see Figure 3.1). If the proscenium arch theatre, with its enforced frontality, functions as a mirror of society (Aronson 2005: 40), a traverse stage with seating banks on opposite sides allows two audiences to share in and evaluate the scene more intensely. Bo Bardi provided the conditions for an intimate staging and an intense interaction between performers and spectators, as every action is visible to both sides of the banks of hard wooden chairs she designed. In this theatre, the architect also

**Figure 3.1** Stage and seating in the SESC Pompeia Theatre, São Paulo. Photo courtesy of Nelson Kon.

purposely incited strangeness and discomfort, reflecting her understanding of conditions in Greek and Roman theatres where the audience members were arranged together on stone steps: 'The wooden chairs at Teatro da Pompeia are merely an attempt to give back to the theatre its attribute of "distancing and enveloping," and not just sitting down' (Bo Bardi [1986] 1993: 226). Unlike proscenium arch theatres with multi-tiered, horseshoe-shaped auditorium and boxes, the stands do not discriminate between social classes, being suitable for a wide variety of audiences and encouraging cooperative interaction between spectators, as well as between spectators and performers. Bo Bardi believed that architecture should encourage spectators to experience theatre space, so in a move reminiscent of Bertolt Brecht, she removed everything that could enable an illusionistic staging, leaving the spectators viewing a bare stage illuminated by the light of the auditorium and providing conditions for an intense dialogue between performance and architecture. Social spaces are already layered with associations before they are used for theatrical events (see Carlson 2003), and in this case, Bo Bardi explored former workers' images of the place, re-creating the ambiance of the factory. The hard seats, arranged along the concrete steps, suggest that the audience attend the theatre not for comfort, but to stimulate thought and imagination. Bo Bardi's design of the theatre at SESC Pompeia embodies Gramscian ideas about the transforming and liberating power of the cultural actions which an intellectual should undertake, and like Freire, she sought to stimulate individuals to perceive facts for themselves.

## The Oficina Theatre: A public space for ritual and performance

Bo Bardi did not believe in the pure technical assumptions of the Modern Movement, but claimed that after rationalism, 'modern architecture resumes contact with what is most vital, primary and non-crystallized in human beings and these factors are linked to different countries' (Bo Bardi [1958] 2001: 213). It was on this basis that she explored the world of the lower classes of Brazil – their religion, performances and rituals – and drew on this in her redesign of the Oficina Theatre, recently listed by the *Guardian* newspaper as one of the ten best theatres in the world (Moore 2015). Through its history the Oficina Theatre has existed in three different internal configurations: the first (1961–1966), designed by Joaquim Guedes, had two seating areas with the stage in the middle, while the second (1967), designed by Flávio Império, had a revolving stage and concrete tiered seats. The third and current configuration, planned and built by Bo Bardi and Edson Elito in the 1980s, transformed the building into its current 'street-theatre' configuration.

Bruno Zevi, with whom Bo Bardi maintained an intense correspondence, claimed that architecture is like 'a large sculpture excavated, into which man enters and walks' (Zevi [1948] 1996: 17). Bo Bardi's early experiences with the Oficina Theatre were through her work as a set designer, transforming the interior of the second Oficina Theatre for a production of Bertolt Brecht's *The Jungle of the Cities* (1969), directed by Zé Celso. On that occasion, Bo Bardi dismantled the existing revolving stage and, in its place, set a boxing ring on a raised platform on which the scenes were presented (Lima 2008). She also participated in the collaborative performance of *Gracias Señor* (1972) with the same group, which formed a strong core of political resistance during the military dictatorship. Years later, in 1983, as Zé Celso invited her for a third time, the architect began – first in partnership with Marcelo Suzuki, and afterwards in partnership with architect Edson Elito – a new architectural project for the Oficina Theatre. Through her work with the Oficina Group, Bo Bardi developed a strong relationship with Zé Celso, which fed into her subsequent redesign of the theatre.

The Oficina Theatre is located in Bixiga, São Paulo. Originally a working-class neighbourhood with a vast Italian immigrant population, in the 1980s it became one of the main areas for leisure and culture in the city. Refitted by Bo Bardi and Elito, the Oficina is a street or alleyway in the middle of a long, narrow structure on a fifty-by-nine-metre site joining two important pedestrian areas of the city (see Figure 3.2). Bo Bardi's decision to maintain the old expressionless grey façade – which was not modified – denotes her intention to submit spectators to a 'rite of passage' as they enter the interior (Van Gennep [1908] 1960). The relationship between outdoor and interior is one of the most significant perceptions in Bo Bardi's spatial manipulation of the Oficina. In the continuous scenic area within the building, tubular scaffolding structures support long galleries and a retractable roof allows the sky to be seen from inside. In the interior of the long axial scenic space, actors, audience and technicians are in close contact.

In redesigning the Oficina Theatre, Bo Bardi challenged 'polite' architecture and the notion of theatre as a bourgeois entertainment. In this she exhibited a similar political sensibility to Augusto Boal in his development of a Theatre of the Oppressed. Both reshaped key elements of an inherited Western theatre tradition to their own ends. Boal began his experiments with participatory theatre in the 1950s and 1960s when he was the artistic director of the Arena Theatre in São Paulo, organizing performances in streets, factories, union buildings and churches, where he could reach people from the slums and the peripheral districts. He coined the word 'spect-actor' – a spectator who takes part in the action – as a way of opposing what he saw as the passivity of audience members in Aristotelian theatre (Jackson in Boal 1992: xxiv). Boal considered the term 'spectator' abject, arguing that Aristotelian theatre was authoritarian and manipulative. He pointed out that, in order to understand his poetics of the oppressed, 'one must keep in mind its main objective: to change the people – "spectators," passive beings in the theatrical phenomenon – into subjects, into actors, transformers of the dramatic action' (Boal 2000: 122). Bo Bardi's efforts to transform the Oficina Theatre into a space of dialogue between audience and performers led to her designing an open, free space for an active spectator. After workshops with the US group The Living Theater and the Argentinian group Los Lobos in 1970, Zé Celso conceptualized his theatrical experimentations as *te-ato* ('I tie you'), a ritual performance which proposes a transformation of the stage–audience relationship. In Zé Celso's *te-ato*, audience and actors converge in a sensorial encounter where nothing is left out of the scene – at any time someone from the audience can be asked to be 'devoured' – in an act of provocation. In Zé Celso's concept of *te-ato*, the body is the soul of the performance, and in her designs for the Oficina Theatre Bo Bardi provided a connection between body and space, emphasizing the deep reciprocity that human bodies share with the world around them.

Vertical lines dominate the scaffolding galleries, evoking the instability and unfinished quality of a construction site, and allowing the audience to circulate freely and participate in the performance from different vantage points. The scaffolding echoes Bo Bardi's scenography for the film *Prata Palomares* (1971), directed by Andre Farias and Zé Celso. The main scene of the film, set within a typical Brazilian Baroque church, features wooden scaffolding structures that serve either as high stages for the actors or as a support for technical equipment (Lima and Monteiro 2012: 147). Bo Bardi's design for the Oficina integrates performance and architecture, encouraging playful explorations that reveal intense relationships between people and space, and among people in place. For Bo Bardi, the project 'reflects the modern theatre, "total theatre" that comes from the 1920's, from Artaud: a naked theatre with no stage, just a place of action, a community thing, as well as a church' (Bo Bardi in Sabbag 1986: 53). This statement reveals her absolute knowledge of the historical avant-garde and understanding of the failure of the Modern Movement to house contemporary theatre. The alleyway stage of the Oficina Theatre is an allegory for public space, including the spectator in the scenic event through an informal spatial configuration that mitigates against the reproduction of existing social hierarchies. A wide glass window allows the audience to watch scenes that are linked to what is outside the building's envelope. Vegetation, light and sounds of the natural world, including a huge tree – a symbol of the African Candomblé religion – have been introduced into the interior. Along the alleyway stage, halfway between the entrance and the rear of the building, is a mechanical waterfall composed of seven tubes and a reflecting pool, referencing the Orixás of the African religion followed by many Brazilians. Bo Bardi's appropriation of everyday popular practices opens up different interpretations about elements present in life, and breaks down boundaries between reason and imagination.

Bo Bardi writes that, from an architectural point of view, 'the Oficina will search for the real meaning of theatre – its Physical and Tactile structure, its Non-Abstraction – which profoundly differentiates it from cinema and TV, at the same time permitting the total use of this media' (Bo Bardi 1999: 5). In a Brechtian manner the entire theatre apparatus is on display with technical elements forming part of the scenography of performance. Bo Bardi also allowed for the distribution of video images around the theatre, enabling simultaneous actions in different parts of the theatrical space. Brecht wanted to avoid theatrical illusion, which keeps the spectator in a state of hypnotism and passivity, by distancing them and encouraging them to evaluate facts and discern argument. On the other hand, the placing of stage lighting equipment, sound and electronic controls on one of the mezzanine levels still enables performance conditions in which a spectator might experience an almost Artaudian state

**Figure 3.2** Interior of the Teatro Oficina, São Paulo. Photo courtesy of Cassia Monteiro.

of intense identification with the spectacle. Ultimately, the Oficina Theatre encourages bodily participation and proximity coupled with a critical awareness of one's position in the theatrical event. In the current spatial configuration, the spectator participates in the production as soon as he or she enters the space. Since it opened in 1993, with the legendary production of *Ham-let*, the shows of the Oficina Group have attracted large numbers, especially because of the ritualistic character of productions such as *As Bacantes* (*The Bacchae*) (1996), and the five episodes of *Os Sertões* (*The Hinterlands*) (2001–2006), which work in close connection with the architecture.

## Conclusion

Theatre aesthetics shift and change, and contemporary spaces for theatrical action need to be in dialogue with performers and audiences as theatre makers propose more intimate relationships between them. This examination of Bo Bardi's work in the SESC Pompeia and Oficina theatres helps us to see how theatre architecture can operate dramaturgically to encourage cultural production and embody a liberational cultural project. Although both theatres were conceived in the 1980s, they remain internationally significant, serving as a provocative vision for what theatre architecture might be. The SESC Pompeia Theatre, designed as a traverse theatre in a former factory shed, still bears the memory of the place. Originally built for the working class within a trade association leisure centre, the theatre attracts people from all over the country. The symmetrically placed audiences interact with each other and are implicated in the scene/stage, and its peculiar architectural disposition allows experimental drama, musical shows and plays for young audiences to be staged at a very low cost, helping to prepare future theatregoers. In the case of the revolutionary Oficina Theatre, Bo Bardi and Elito's metaphor of the street induces the participation of all social classes as if the theatre were a public space; the spectator is invited to move through the entire theatre space, generating intense physical contact and a permanent tension between actors and audience. The 'street-theatre' extends to the entire architectural space of the building, reflecting director Zé Celso's concept of *te-ato* and providing a place for community and celebration, which involves both the profane and the sacred in ritual-like performance, and simultaneously integrates theatrical space with the city that surrounds it.

Bo Bardi believed that theatre is life and that an open and stripped-down architecture induces the spectator to participate more fully in the theatrical performance. In the former factory warehouse and in the street-shaped theatre, space functions dramaturgically to frame and shape the events that are staged within them and both venues continue to attract contemporary theatre makers and huge audiences, and inspire architects.

## Notes

1  Bo Bardi lived and worked in Brazil between 1946 and 1992 and had a strong interest in theatre, museums and art. She fought in the Italian Resistance and was a member of the Communist Party during the struggle against Fascism and the rebuilding of Italy following the Second World War (see de Oliveira 2002).
2  See, for instance, Fabio Penteado's designs for the Municipal Theatre of Piracicaba (1960) and for the Campinas Opera House and Comedy Theatre complex (awarded a Gold Medal for the first Prague Quadrennial for Theatre Design and Architecture, 1967). In 1968, the same architect created a large arena in his project for the Cultural Community Center of Campinas, introducing an alternative pattern for Brazilian theatre architecture (Giroto 2010). Despite this, it is still quite unusual for a theatre in Brazil to be designed without a proscenium arch.

4

# Imaginative Configurations: Performance Space in the Global City

Klaus van den Berg

## Urban design and global city

In a 2016 essay, urbanist Edward Soja proclaimed the 'End of the Metropolis Era' (Soja 2016: 42). Thanks to newer communication technologies, shifting labour markets, accelerated modes of travel and financial deregulation, the world's largest cities have expanded their boundaries into what Soja described as 'polycentric and complexly networked (mega)city region[s]'.[1] These new environments – from the northeastern United States (Boston/New York/Washington) to Germany's Ruhr Valley and China's Pearl River Delta – have significantly impacted the placement, visibility and functioning of cultural institutions. Proliferating hybrid geographies shrink public space; historic and perimeter centres, suburbias, edge cities and exopolises form fragmented, complex spatial relationships, challenging the very notion of a coherent urban organization with a visible reference system that enables people to experience and identify with an urban area. Drawing on Walter Benjamin's integrative approach to reading urban dramaturgy, I explore ways by which performance spaces can make critical interventions in today's ex- and post-urban spatialities. By presenting what Modernist philosopher Georg Simmel calls an *Erscheinungsreihe* (see Goodstein 2017: 233–242), a phenomenal series of performance spaces intervening in four diverse nodal points in regionalized urban space, I simultaneously explore theatre's potential to transform the globalized city and develop a new perspective on the global city itself as a performance space.

City design reflects an *urban site dramaturgy* that inscribes collective social memory and ways of thinking about political and cultural institutions in locations and spatial relations.[2] Traditionally, theatre buildings were integrated into urban configurations within architectural ensembles that expressed theatre's artistic and social importance (see Carlson 1989). Schinkel's nineteenth-century Schauspielhaus forms a centrepiece on a square flanked by churches, asserting the theatre's significance on par with religion and creating a deliberate juxtaposition between ancient square and modern boulevard; Erich Mendelssohn's early twentieth-century WOGA complex, now housing the Schaubühne Berlin, is an homage to the flow of modern street traffic and integrated into commercial development. In such configurations, street design and the placement of squares often followed principles of set design to provide structure and historical identity. The design of Palladio's Teatro Olimpico exemplifies the complex relations between the stage and baroque city design, with its invocations of facade and radiating streets that prefigure future urban design (Barnett 1986: 9). Chicago's famous, though never-executed, 1909 plan still followed this model of creating visual order and urban theatricality.

Walter Benjamin's pioneering analysis of nineteenth-century Paris excavates the very beginnings of today's global city. His large-scale montage of research notes on Paris, the *Arcades Project*, drew attention to the civic configurations that had provided structure, memory and identity, illustrating that 'the development of the boulevards represented only the first stage in the process of the essential dissolution of the urban fabric' (Vidler 2001: 77). The construction of the large-scale Palais Garnier at the confluence of boulevards – a hyper-building *avant la lettre* – conceals the dissolution of the medieval city fabric with an urban set piece. Benjamin's analyses of the physical and emotional alienation wrought by the construction of the large Parisian boulevards and shopping malls dissect experiences of dislocation familiar from everyday life in today's fragmented global city. In the twenty-first century's expanding global cities and mega-regions, sprawl and vast transportation networks create voids and hollowed-out spaces devoid of cultural reference systems.[3]

Benjamin's extensive but dispersed writings on urban space provide a theoretical framework that links social, technological, economic, psychological and aesthetic ideas to *read the city as a performance space*, an ambivalent and contested site that stages the collision of historical forces.[4] Reading this force-field of cultural memory with Benjamin clears space for a radically different urban dramaturgy, in which contemporary architecture, buildings and urban sites form a historical stage that montages past and present. His writings gather the contested, fragmented, dispersed residues and historical layers accessible in the modern metropolis into imaginative configurations using concepts that are particularly helpful for exploring contemporary performance spaces.

For Benjamin, the modern city is itself an *Ausstellungsraum*, an 'exhibition space' (Benjamin 1977b: 520). This concept, which originated in his 1939 essay on Bertolt Brecht's theatre, captures the ambivalence and contestedness of modern city-space. Benjamin devoted important sections of the *Arcades Project* to Parisian boulevards, arcades and nineteenth-century world's fairs, linking spectacle and theatricality to the cult of commodities projected in capitalist architecture. He deploys the concept of *Ausstellungsraum* to criticize the hypnotic power and dream character of an urban theatre of illusion that conceals social and economic relations even as the modern city is transformed into a site of spectacle – a process that has only accelerated and expanded in global cities.

Another key Benjaminian concept, *Bildraum* (image-space), captures the dynamic changes underway in the space of experience in the modern city. Every image-space has a 'historical index' that links the temporal experience of a building or urban site to the observer and registers the passage of time. By configuring historical seeing in image-spaces, Benjamin recaptures the past while unfolding the city as a complex visual field. His architectural writings restore or make the historical index visible and thereby show how modern city planners such as Georges-Eugène Haussmann strived to destroy that very cultural specificity.

Finally, with his notion of *Spielraum* (performing-space), Benjamin's approach facilitates thinking about expanding space creatively to develop new critical (or architectural) interventions. The concept of performing space embraces the transformative quality of the cinema – not its capacity for mimetic representation, but its strategies of editing, close-ups and telescoping reality photographically. Thus, Benjamin deploys *Spielraum* as a critical and creative form of intervention by montaging images of urban space into a historical vision of the city. The creation of a *Spielraum* is a generative practice that can create a space for artistic or architectural production as well as for critical reflection that reveals the social, cultural and economic bases of reality.

Taken together, I argue, these concepts and strategies yield a methodological road map for contemporary critics to view the global city as a new site of performance and to explore theatre buildings via Benjamin's theoretical framework. Benjamin taught us to design research dramaturgically, as a configuration of a historical situation. I extend his ideas beyond the traditional capitals of Paris and Berlin to explore four different contemporary performance spaces from diverse global city-regions: Peter Latz's Landschaftspark (Duisburg),

Cesar Pelli's Winter Garden (New York), Rem Koolhaas's Theater Center (Dallas) and Jean Nouvel's new Guthrie Theater (Minneapolis). In offering paradigmatic cases for theatre buildings intervening in the global city, my chapter explores a mega-region (Ruhr Valley), the development strategies of global developers in the traditional city (New York), a new type of global city (Dallas) and the reshaping of a cultural icon in a city that reimagines itself on the basis of its history (Minneapolis).[5] In each case, the series of concepts (*Bildraum*, *Spielraum* and *Ausstellungsraum*) enable me to trace new urban spaces through a series of mediations. I argue that performance spaces generate a new type of urban site dramaturgy: by arresting historical forces with their buildings, each makes a statement about theatre and the global city as a performance space created by the dissolution of traditional forms of urban design.

## Reclaiming industrial space for a mega-region

Since the 1980s, the Ruhr Valley region in Germany, which stretches from the Rhine cities of Cologne, Düsseldorf and Duisburg on its western edge and follows the Ruhr river to the cities of Dortmund, Essen and Bochum on its eastern border, has become a paradigmatic European version of the global city. While its individual cities are not large enough to challenge Paris, New York or even Berlin, these cities have merged into a single urban area as large as New York City, linked by a densely networked transportation system and served by a publicly funded municipal performing arts network that places its citizens within close reach of multiple cultural attractions.

A severe industrial crisis starting in the 1960s led to the closing of most coal mines and steel mills in the Ruhr Valley, a process finalized in the mid-1980s. Local mayors and the state government of North-Rhine Westphalia faced the question of what to do with the large industrial sites, unemployment and polluted environment. Instead of removing the industrial ruins, officials developed a coherent approach to the entire region within the framework of the International Architecture Exhibition (IBA). Between 1989 and 1999, the IBA Emscher Park (named after the most polluted river in the area) transformed this wasteland into 'industrial culture': a vast programme that turned the site into a progressive artistic development, sparked a revitalization of cities and attracted highly qualified workers to the region (see Hemmings and Kagel 2010). In a paradigmatic case of post-industrial urban gentrification, an elaborate high-art concept replaced the lost industries and unemployed workers. In the former heart of Germany's coal and steel industry, local and state governments collaborated with industry powerhouses to transform industrial wasteland into an urban landscape and turn abandoned machine halls into event spaces. Large performance spaces in the region such as the Duisburg Power Station and Bochum's Century Hall have turned the region into a vast *Ausstellungsraum* of industrial monuments.

IBA Emscher Park hired landscape architect Peter Latz to transform the industrial site into a central attraction for the region. Unlike Norman Foster or Rem Koolhaas, who might design a new building that inscribes the specifics of the site, the choice of Latz signalled a desire to follow Benjamin's critical strategy of *Mortifikation* (mortification): the freezing of decayed buildings into aesthetic objects, transforming them into a new vision inside an urban park (Benjamin 1977a: 353–354, 357). In his approach, the ruins remain visible resources for set design and performances, making it possible to activate their positive and negative contributions to society as former pillars of high capitalism. As Arthur Lubow has pointed out, Latz may be the 'anti-Olmsted': he shaped a recreation zone 'that is unmistakably man-made and that extends into the gritty neighboring communities. By leaving blast furnaces, gas tanks and storage bunkers intact, he implicitly debunks the fantasy of taking refuge in pristine nature' (Lubow 2004: 1). While the famous nineteenth-century American landscape architect Frederick Law Olmsted sought relief from urban reality, Latz foregrounded urban decay so that the resonances of that experience could become the foundation of an aesthetic experience which, in turn, provides the foundation for art works performed in this context.

Latz advocated placing the visitor in the position of experiencing the 'visible decay' (Lubow 2004: 6), organizing the park around its major features – the blast furnace and the power station – and creating a deliberately bifurcated space. Latz's treatment of the industrial ruins owed much to his experience with Renaissance gardens which were 'simultaneous memory structures ... or historical interpretations conveyed in myth' (Latz cited in Rohde and Schomann 2003: 63). To highlight the (post)industrial aesthetic, Latz deliberately inserted gardens as forms of transitions and contrasts to foreground the new event spaces and to create various references and different layers of time (Lubow 2004: 3; see also Wellacher 2008: 12). This approach of exhibiting the visible decay in the form of a 'leisure garden' is juxtaposed to the capitalist and militarist subtext of the Kraftzentrale (Power Station) and the Gebläsehalle (Blasting Hall), that have been powerfully activated by directors including Peter Brook, Arianne Mnouchkine, Heiner Goebbels and Robert Wilson.

**Figure 4.1** Kraftzentrale Duisburg-Nord: regional park as *Ausstellungsraum*. Photo showing performance space in the mega-region. Photo courtesy of Planinghaus Architekten BDA, Darmstadt.

By intervening through the reinterpretation of industrial space, the Landschaftspark Duisburg-Nord may be an illustration of what Rosalind Krauss has termed the 'expanded field' of Modernism (Krauss 1979). Krauss bemoaned the 'sitelessness, or homelessness, an absolute loss of place' (34) in modernity and suggested constructing programmatic urban environments and transformative performance architecture. In this spirit, Latz expanded the industrial wasteland into a cultural forum with plazas, nature parks, walkways and theatres. Latz restricted himself to interventions that linked the remaining ruins and wastelands but left the industrial architecture of the buildings intact. Following the blueprint of the railroad tracks used for transportation of materials, the park develops along the old railway lines to 'secure the coherence in the 230 hectares of the park' ('Duisburg-Nord – The Railway Park' n.d.).

In this newly established urban environment, the power station, the former engine of the industrial site, has been converted into performance venue (see Figure 4.1). Like other large industrial halls in Bochum and Essen, it produces an expanded field as a *Bildraum* in performance. While the visitor was to experience 'visible decay' in the park, Latz designed the venue's interior to activate the memory and experience of industrial power. Historically, the power station was an integral part of the mighty Thyssen Corporation, a major player in Germany's industrial war machinery that remained important in the post-Second World War economic miracle. Its military and economic potential has literally been hollowed out by replacing machinery with cultural events. Latz preserved the physical shell and the scale of the power station's interior space. Much like a skyscraper, the building's massive scale was achieved by a repetitive sequencing of smaller units on a wide horizontal level mirroring the expansion of urban areas. As a venue, it provides a vast open space that allows for the flexible unfolding of large-scale performances such as *Schlachten* (1999), directed by Luk Perceval, which combined several Shakespeare history plays. One of the most effective productions staged in such a hollowed-out archive was the 2006 production of Bernd Alois Zimmermann's opera *Die Soldaten*, directed by David Pountney. Based on Jakob Lenz's eighteenth-century play, it premiered in the Bochum Jahrhunderthalle (Century Hall). Zimmermann's critique of military power, in which the soldiers turn the daughter of a middle-class merchant into a prostitute, unfolded within a structure of historical experience archived by these industrial halls. The orchestra was integrated into the audience seating, and the action played on a runway spanning the entire hall with audiences on both sides. The division of the space echoed the complex collaboration among the components of the gigantic industrial machine and allowed the audience to contemplate its mechanism. Motorized units moved the spectators, inscribing them in an invocation of the original industrial function of the halls that configured the performance event.

## Urban interlocutor in the financial district

Urban site dramaturgy, and performance space as urban set piece, have generally played a subordinate role in New York and US theatre. New York City developed rapidly along the famous Manhattan grid of equal blocks after its inception in 1811. The grid system neglected to plan for any public spaces, such as squares, parks, public buildings and theatres. The result was a city in which individuals and businesses competed to develop empty blocks, eventually turning to skyscrapers to maximize land use. Semi-public spaces emerged only in some areas, such as where Broadway, the original north–south thoroughfare predating the grid, crossed one of the avenues. The original Metropolitan Opera on Broadway and the Lincoln Center Complex are notable exceptions to the general rule that Broadway theatres move with and cluster around the business district (Henderson 1973: 169–170). The facade structure of Broadway theatres vanishes among more impressive hotels or office buildings, and for the most part even the interiors lack any significant social space that would mark them as urban gathering spots. The signs of the global city are visible in the construction of the World Financial Center: following the example of Rockefeller Center and the World Trade Center, it takes the form of an edge city – or out-of-town commercial development – constructed on top of landfill, complete with office towers, shopping and the Winter Garden for entertainment.

Cesar Pelli's Winter Garden – not to be confused with its namesake theatre on Broadway – represents a paradigm shift that illustrates the changing nature of both financial practices and the structure of the performance event in the global economy (see Figure 4.2). It is not a traditional theatre but an open performance space that displays various traditions of Western commercial culture. Socially, economically and culturally, Pelli's complex amplifies the scale and ambition of the Parisian arcades. It conjoins commerce and performance in a way that makes it a key example for unfolding Benjamin's perspective. Developed by international mega-developers Olympia and York, the Winter Garden is an integral part of the World Financial Center on the West Side in lower Manhattan: a glass-domed pavilion situated between two skyscrapers of the financial centre near the former World Trade Center site. Severely damaged when the Twin

**Figure 4.2** Winter Garden: urban interlocutor and *Spielraum* negotiating the global city. Photo courtesy of Jill Clardy. Licensed under CC BY-SA 2.0.

Towers collapsed on 11 September 2001, the building was reconstructed. Like other large-scale urban developments such as Canary Wharf in London or Century City in Los Angeles, the World Financial Center consists of a group of skyscrapers providing millions of square feet of office space for thousands of workers. Entertainment and high-end shopping are integral to these cities within cities, and the space creates a hybrid of public space within a privately managed business site. Instead of regular theatre offerings, the space provides a home for commissioned works, concert events and site-specific installations such as the recent *Luminations*. This programming provides a constant stream of presentations analogous to the centre's raison d'être of seamlessly delivering high-end financial products.

When the building opened in 1988, it was generally hailed by critics as a major architectural achievement. The *New York Times* critic Paul Goldberger proclaimed its glass structure, 200 feet (61 metres) long and 125 feet (38 metres) high, 'the grandest public space built in New York since the Grand Central Terminal' and the architectural climax of the World Financial Center, making it 'the finest grouping of skyscrapers since Rockefeller Center' (Goldberger 1988). Pelli was the sole architect for the entire commercial area; he made a conscious effort to integrate the new area visually with the existing skyline at Battery Park (Pelli, Gandelsonas and Pastier 1990: 92). Pelli's four towers created a dual image: the material covering the lower floors reflects the form of traditional Manhattan skyscrapers, while the glass covering of the rising floors sports a very modern texture. Until the destruction of the World Trade Center and the extensive damage to the Winter Garden, Pelli's group of skyscrapers accompanied the twin towers like cruisers sailing alongside a massive battleship.

As the centrepiece between skyscrapers, which are so often self-contained boxes without any real urban functions, the Winter Garden plays a mediating role, becoming 'Pelli's barrel-vaulted homage to Paxton's Crystal Palace' (Darton 1999: 116, 123, 181) and the quintessential Benjaminian exhibition space. The building performs as a public gathering place, bringing the massive scale of the skyscrapers into a proportionate relationship. Pelli deployed the Winter Garden as an urban interlocutor in an otherwise rather predictable development, positioning the Winter Garden so as to produce a more unified scenography of skyscrapers with the twin towers as centrepiece and a very pronounced axis linking the Hudson River to the Twin Towers. By creating a 'vertical port' in the image of Venice, including a market square, fabled columns and an echo of the Venetian Molo, the water entrance to the piazzetta that greeted the traders in the Renaissance, Pelli's urban site dramaturgy revived the narrative launched decades ago by city stakeholders such as Nelson Rockefeller and Austin Tobin when envisioning the World Trade Center.[6]

The academically-trained Pelli thereby renewed urban site dramaturgy by intimating a *Spielraum* of multiple historical spaces. The Grand Entrance orientation towards the Hudson River creates a sense of both arrival and perspective for those inside the building. Channelling the view from the west into the canyons between the skyscrapers lends the monolithic towers some limited urban coherence, and the glass shell puts a lively scene on display for the thousands of workers in the financial sector. The building connects to the economic power of the past, recalling the glass and iron construction of the grand train stations of the nineteenth century and acting as a visual surrogate for the loss of the old Penn Station. Furthermore, the Winter Garden recalls the nineteenth-century Parisian arcades on a grander scale. In contrast to the small shops comprising an urban block in Paris, it has turned into a gigantic food court with adjacent luxury shops, fittingly called 'le district'.

The performance space inside the encasing glass shell offers a conflicting image-space that merges traces of classical theatre with current event culture. The food court and the event experience clash with the allure of a grand theatre to create a contested site. The space's overall event structure foregrounds the by-now prevalent so-called culture of gathering, shopping and eating experiences, exhibited and 'performed' for passers-by and tourists. The space includes a large atrium where the consumer/performer sits under palm trees and watches other performances at either end of the building. There is space for a stage against the glass facade facing the Hudson River that, like the ancient Greek theatre, allows an enjoyment of both the staging and the spectacular views. The more remarkable stage is set up on the opposite side. Here, Pelli has created a complex image of theatricality drawn from history and set into today's shopping environment. At the centre of the eastern third of the space is a circular platform raised halfway between the auditorium floor and the back wall. This very simple spatial configuration can be turned into a Greek-inspired arena-type space – albeit with the audience seated below the performance space. Alternatively, it suggests yet another theatrical configuration. Pelli has placed a set of raised semicircular tiers for spectators with a set of loggias behind them, recalling the layout of the early indoor Renaissance theatres – a fitting image, since the Winter Garden serves the very affluent movers and shakers of the financial industry. Juxtaposing Renaissance and classical theatrical spaces with traces of railroad station facades and nineteenth-century arcades, Pelli's Winter Garden conjures up a complex *Spielraum*, a performing space that serves as a set for contemporary high finance.

# Skyscraper theatre: Urbanism and the global arts park

Dallas exemplifies the new type of networked global American city. Stretched out on the plains of the southern United States, it has grown exponentially since it became an oil and transportation hub in the 1960s. Until the 1970s, central Dallas was basically a business district without any significant residential neighbourhoods and without established cultural destinations. Beginning in the mid-1970s, the city planned an extensive arts district to house existing arts institutions. A commissioned report by Kevin Lynch and Stephen Carr suggested that a clustering of facilities would 'benefit the organizations involved while also helping to revitalize the central business district' (Dillon 1985: 168). On the basis of the report, city leaders planned an urban exhibition space of cultural institutions. Reviving controversial US urban renewal practices that used art edifices as neighbourhood-clearing programmes and accentuated racial divides,[7] the Dallas Arts District has become the world's densest exhibition space of art venues. In addition to the building I discuss, it features an I. M. Pei symphony hall, a Norman Foster opera house, a sculpture garden by Renzo Piano and an art museum by Edward Barnes.

Koolhaas shares Benjamin's enthusiasm for making architecture and cities legible as image-spaces. Working in traditional American cities taught Koolhaas how to create *Bildraum* through block configurations. In his 1978 book *Delirious New York*, Koolhaas argued that the key historical moment for structuring New York was its decision to organize Manhattan in a grid of 2,028 equal blocks (Koolhaas [1978] 2004: 20). A widely accepted urban layout with roots in ancient civilizations, the grid became the organizing principle in many US cities, where streets run at right angles. The grid can easily be expanded in all directions. Emphasizing the potential for the grid to act like a dramatic plot that structures multiple episodes, Koolhaas argued that the desire to make each city block more fantastic becomes the major force in the spectacular game of 'Manhattanism'.

In Dallas, Koolhaas encountered a different system, where floating blocks constituted the site for the art venues. As a quintessential global city, Dallas addressed the need for arts venues with a Haussmannesque flourish, by creating a new edge city. A seventeen-block section just outside of the downtown area was cleared and designated by city planners for the Arts District. As in other suburban redevelopments, this area was landscaped and developed without the constraints of a well-defined urban area. The urban planners organized the arts district as a pedestrianized area along Flora Street, which forms the 'front door to major cultural institutions and to private and semi-private developments' (Sasaki

Associates 2014). The street was subdivided into sub-districts along an east–west orientation: 'Museum Crossing is a collection of boutiques, galleries, and art shops, Concert Lights centres on the Dallas Concert Hall with theater-oriented restaurants and clubs, and Fountain Plaza creates an artists' quarter ambience with gourmet shops and open air markets' (Sasaki Associates 2014). Koolhaas's theatre building was assigned to the 'Concert Lights' subsection, where Pei's Symphony Hall and Norman Foster's opera house each also occupy a block.

In contrast to the traditional challenge of placing a performance venue into an urban configuration, Koolhaas (like the other 'starchitects' designing venues for the Arts District) faced an emblematic issue of the global city: designing a

**Figure 4.3** Dallas Theater Center: skyscraper as performance space. Photo courtesy of the author.

building that was part of a themed perimeter city. In contrast to other Koolhaas projects such as the CCTV building in Beijing, where Koolhaas has created 'hyper-buildings' (Spencer 2016: 96), Koolhaas's strategy for the Dallas building was to integrate the building into the downtown area. In this case, he generated a 'graphic image' for his building's composition that corresponds to Benjamin's critical strategy of making historical forces visible in *Bildraum*. In their data analysis for Dallas, Koolhaas's firm OMA produced three such images, which formed the basis for designing the Dallas theatre. The first, featuring tall upward columns and small downward columns, visualized the appearance of Dallas's downtown as peaks in the midst of a flat region. The second image drew on the city as a network of centres comprised of the historic West End, financial district, arts district, market centre and exchange mall, and separated by railroad tracks, freight yards and freeways. The third image visualized how Dallas's various districts may be experienced as a periscope, with other districts forming a system of mirrors and lenses that focus on the arts district.

Synthesizing those images, Koolhaas conceived the new Dallas Theater Center (DTC) as an eleven-storey skyscraper. Visually, Koolhaas has integrated the building into the Dallas skyline where it functions as a gateway from the business to the arts district. The building's shell is divided into two distinct parts in contrast to conventional theatres: the actual performance area on the ground floor is completely visible from outside through large glass windows, while most of the remaining floors are veiled in what looks like a grey curtain. This curtain is punctuated only by a few windows: one window in the upper left-hand corner of the building recalls the window in the Dallas Book Depository from which it is believed that President Kennedy was assassinated; together with the building's size and shape, this feature links it visually to the architectural shape of the much smaller skyscrapers in the old downtown.

By designing the theatre as a skyscraper, Koolhaas rethought the entire concept of the theatrical event and the production process: instead of wrapping shops, rehearsal rooms and lobbies around the performance space, all spaces are stacked vertically. Furthermore, Koolhaas changed each floor composition, varying their size, height and length. Through the transparency of the surface and sectioned space, Koolhaas celebrates the culture of congestion by allowing the public to experience the performance as a dynamic event from the outside and the inside. The actual performance space itself can be transformed into a wide variety of audience–stage configurations including proscenium, thrust, flat floor and traverse. These configurations are inscribed vertically: a hydraulic system can lower them into the space, reducing the theatre's operating costs when changing the format. Unlike the repetitive glass surfaces of skyscrapers that shut out the public from the interior space, the DTC's glass surface at the ground level suggests a creative theatrical exchange: a director may choose to keep the windows open and integrate the downtown silhouette into the show; conversely, the theatre may decide to keep the stage permanently visible from the outside. It is a building for highly innovative directors and designers.

The skyscraper design enabled Koolhaas to generate a *Spielraum* that unmoors the building from its essentially non-urban arts district context. Audiences enter from below the theatre emulating the vertical movement of the skyscraper. Unlike the district's other architects, Koolhaas abandoned the conventional horizontal orientation of theatre facility and, above all, erased visual traces of the theatre as cultural monument. While the auditoria of the other venues are concealed from the public, the DTC presents itself as open to the city. Drawing on the urban convention of window-shopping, city dwellers can look inside the theatre. Koolhaas invokes the density of skyscrapers as an exciting and desirable condition, producing a contested space between the verticality of modern urbanism and conventional theatre architecture; that is, he reimagines a modern theatre building in a US downtown landscape even as, by veiling most of the skyscraper floors with the same cladding, he acknowledges the model of traditional horizontal orientation in the theatre.

## Theatre as performing space in the post-industrial city

Among the current examples treated here, Jean Nouvel's Guthrie Theatre is perhaps the most elaborate intervention into the global city and the most ambitious effort to create an urban site dramaturgy. Replacing the beloved old centre of the Minneapolis theatre scene in a new location, the new Guthrie visualizes a critical *Spielraum* in which the theatre building negotiates multiple urban relationships. Minneapolis is a mid-sized US city with a long industrial heritage since its location on the upper banks of the Mississippi River made it an important transportation hub for grain. It too faced the challenge of revitalizing the sites adjacent to areas with decaying industry in the age of globalization.

Minneapolis has also been one of the United States' most hospitable cities for the arts, supporting venerable national institutions such as the Walker Art Center and the Guthrie Theater. Beginning with the founding of the original Guthrie in the early 1960s, Minneapolis played a key role in the Regional Theatre movement. Its original building – planned by Ralph Rapson in accordance with

**Figure 4.4** The Guthrie Theater in downtown Minneapolis: creating a *Spielraum* in the industrial city. Photo courtesy of drbcoaster. Licensed under CC BY 3.0.

director Tyrone Guthrie's wishes, and housing a 1,441-seat thrust stage designed by scenographer Tanya Moiseiwitsch – stood as a symbol of civic pride and alternative artistic vision to the commercial theatre in New York City. In 1995, then artistic director Joe Dowling began campaigning for a new theatre, arguing that the old Guthrie's signature thrust stage was too limited for contemporary American plays – shorthand for a perceived need for a proscenium stage to enable musicals and design-heavy productions. Dowling and his board started a capital campaign to build a venue that included a thrust stage – a nod to the old Guthrie – as well as a traditional proscenium and a studio theatre for an actor training programme. The Guthrie leadership retained French architect Jean Nouvel after witnessing Nouvel's reconstruction of the Lyon Opera House, which sported, besides a beautifully renovated interior, spectacular views of the city.

Like Koolhaas, Nouvel was fascinated by American cities, but according to him, they lacked depth, historical reference points and aesthetic form. Indeed, Nouvel thought of American cities as a 'primal scene of space' (Baudrillard and Nouvel 2002: 13), desert-like spaces without aesthetics or art history. Still, he recognized that urban life in American cities is structured by social, cultural and economic realities, which he successfully blended into a *Bildraum* through the theatre's architecture. Nouvel had a reputation for having an 'obsession with technology; and a magician's bag of optical tricks' (Ouroussoff 2006). Nouvel's first US project, the Guthrie vindicated the future Pritzker prize winner, who developed a visually appealing architectural language rooted in very site-specific, practical considerations. For Nouvel, blending real space and images is a deliberate strategy for expanding the observers' perspective. He explained his architectural space by drawing on analogies to landscaping and cinema: like the deceptive effect of the vanishing points in a Japanese garden, 'we don't know whether the garden stops or continues' (Merrick 2010). Like a film director who creates a sequence of spaces, Nouvel designs architecture as a Benjaminian *Spielraum* that must be comprehended as a sequence of images. In his urban scenography, various images converge in the visual field, providing the spectator-citizen with a new kind of architectural experience. Depending on where the observer situates himself or herself in relation to the building, these separate viewpoints can indeed be isolated or perceived as staged.

Nouvel's blending of urban and theatrical space is precisely the type of intervention Benjamin suggested with his concept of a *Spielraum*, and the chosen site provided a great opportunity for a performance venue to create an urban site dramaturgy. The new Guthrie is located on an open stretch of land along the Mississippi between the northeast section of downtown and the University of Minnesota campus, which the city developed into an upscale residential area. Located outside the grid of the business district or the art district, which included the original Guthrie and the Walker Art Center, the theatre now anchors the mill district, the former industrial heart of Minneapolis. The mills are now defunct, and many of them have been transformed into condominiums. The building functions both as a connective tissue between different layers of the Minneapolis urban landscape and as latter-day cultural monument, inscribing past historical forces into the industrial city.

Nouvel conceived the Guthrie as an urban agent, a building that suggests an urban site dramaturgy via the power of its *Bildraum*. As in the high-tech version of his 1987 design for the Institut du Monde Arab in Paris (Curtis 1996: 672–673), Nouvel blends perceptions of performance and reality, using the building to stage the city and turning it into an urban event. The Guthrie consists of three large, distinct components, whose composition allows for a fluid transition between interior and exterior space. The thrust and proscenium stages mark the opposite ends of the complex. Both theatres are elevated off the ground, leaving space for cafes and bookstores underneath them. In between, Nouvel built a rectangular block devoted almost entirely to public space, allowing pedestrians to penetrate deeply into the building without attending a show. This central space, featuring large lobbies on the first and second floors, has a twofold purpose: it connects the street with the riverfront and sports spectacular views of Minneapolis from the second floor. This staging of the city is completed by a cantilevered bridge that extends towards the river from the second floor of the public space, only to be cut off abruptly by a terrace that provides another breathtaking view of the river and the city.

Nouvel has conceptualized the Guthrie's visual field through what he calls 'a series of filters' (Baudrillard and Nouvel 2002: 6). The spectator needs to go around the building to synthesize the series of views that deconstruct the potential perception of the building as a conventional urban monument. Unlike most theatres, which have clearly defined facades within the city context, the new Guthrie blends multiple images from different vantage points, which transfers the experience of a cinematic or virtual space into the three-dimensional urban arena. First, approaching from the south, its dark, deep blue colour evokes a range of echoes from a conservative business look to a prominent religious monument such as the Black Stone of Mecca (see Roulet 2015: 84–151). Second, for the visitor arriving from the business district, the building resembles a regular theatre with the high massive outline of the signature thrust stage and the proscenium's fly space behind it. Third, a series of large-scale images of playwrights line the first-floor wall of the thrust stage like a film sequence, chronicling the illustrious history of the theatre. Fourth, if viewed from the river, the theatre's silhouette suggests a grain silo, perfectly situated in the mill district – with the cantilevered bridge blending with the image of a conveyor belt. Nouvel's filters allow cultural and industrial space to converge, drawing in the spectator's view and integrating the space from multiple directions through different systems of references. Nouvel intervenes in the sprawling city with a building visually stunning enough to compete with skyscrapers, airports and museums, to act as an urban agent and as an anchor to a previously defunct area.

## Conclusion

Walter Benjamin's theory of the city as a complex visual field materialized from his research on nineteenth-century cities. Benjamin's theoretical framework encourages us to think historically, critically and practically about *urban site dramaturgy* in today's global cities, where the dissolution of the urban fabric and ensuing expansion into hybrid geographies he described has only intensified. From this perspective, I examined a phenomenal series of performance spaces located at dramatic and contested sites that illustrate four nodal points of the regional urbanization process today. Each building generates a *Spielraum* that draws new and old street patterns and other structures into a scenography (or 'scenographic performance'; Spencer 2016: 92): the industrial ruin of the Duisburg Power Station is converted into a gathering spot for the entire region; Pelli's Winter Garden revives urban design inside a global development that reinscribes theatre as a version of privately managed urban public space; and Koolhaas's skyscraper asserts its presence in downtown Dallas, modelling architectural innovation for theatres in new dense urban areas. Jean Nouvel's Guthrie Theater is perhaps the most complex urban intervention, employing architecture and siting to craft an urban dynamic of its own. The imaginative configurations generated by these performance spaces revive the experience of urban site dramaturgy in the global city, reurbanizing the global city as they stage it through the architecture and creative urban design.

# Notes

1 This process also crosses national borders, transforming cities from social, political and cultural centres in an interstate economy to nexuses in a global market served by international hotel chains and mega-developers (Sassen 2005).

2 Architectural theorists who adopt theatrical language include Douglas Spencer ('compositional logic' and 'scenic performance') and Cathy Turner, whose *Dramaturgy and Architecture* (2015) brings plays, buildings and event structure into conversation.

3 This trend also requires an updated analytical model. Marvin Carlson's pioneering semiotic study *Places of Performances* (1989) was published at the beginning phase of international neo-liberalism.

4 I discuss these issues in my current book project *Image Space: Walter Benjamin and Cultural Performance.*

5 For an alternative approach that focuses on the historical development in one global city (Toronto), see McKinnie (2007).

6 Never mind the irony that Manhattan had turned its back on the railway and shipping piers of the Industrial Age to clear the way for the World Trade Center (Darton 1999: 122–124).

7 The Lincoln Center in New York is probably the best-known example of displacing African American and Puerto Rican residents.

5

# The Play of Place: Producing Space and Theatre near Mumbai

Himanshu Burte

## First sight

In March 2012, The Company Theatre (TCT), a small, Mumbai-based theatre group headed by award-winning Indian actor-director Atul Kumar, moved into its own 'dream space', a five-acre residency by a lakeside in the hills three hours from Mumbai. Kumar and TCT's work is widely admired in India for its energetic and skilful experiments involving foreign, traditional and unconventional theatre forms and spaces. The residency represents a decade's work of fundraising, finding land close enough to Mumbai and Pune to be accessible to urban audiences there, navigating the tangle of regulations and putting up the first buildings; all this while producing and touring nationally and internationally with many devised and scripted performances.

Anticipation mounted as I drove through beautiful hills around sunset, during my first trip to the residency in February 2014 for the night-long Kamshet Theatre Festival hosted by TCT. Car parked in the lit playground of the village school, I followed the suspended paper lanterns from the gate in a curving walk till a house came into view. Set on a plateau sloping down to the dark trees, it looked like an outsized, big-boned bungalow. The scale was a bit 'off' to my architect's eye. The concrete sloping roof was also too thick and inadequately visually-anchored to the mass below. The detailing was patchy. And the building did not seem to embody TCT's ethos or the vision of the larger project tied to the residency. As an informal collaborator with Kumar during the conceptualization of the project, and having enjoyed the spatiality of his theatre, I was disappointed. As I began walking towards the friendly crowd milling around the steps of the house, I wondered: had architecture let down theatre once again, this time in a space for *making*, rather than *presenting*?

# Introduction

In this chapter, I am interested in the dialectical tension between the everyday and the extraordinary that is central to the spatiality of theatre and architecture. Both practices are grounded in everyday spatiality – involving bodies, social encounter, things, physical space – which they seek to sustain and transcend at the same time in artistic practice. Both seek to coax out their own 'exceptional' from the soil of the everyday. As spatial theorist Henri Lefebvre says, 'It is in everyday life and starting from everyday life that genuine creations are achieved' (2002: 44). This tension is most relevant to the production of spaces where theatrical works are incubated and produced. Debates about theatre architecture usually concern spaces where a performance is formally presented to an audience, the stages and seating areas of theatre auditoria (see, for example, Breton 1991; Leacroft 1973, 2011; Mackintosh 1993), although the fundamental importance to theatrical production and reception of backstage and 'other' spaces within the theatre building has begun to attract attention in recent years (see Filmer 2006; McAuley 2000). The space for *making* theatrical works, however, is relatively neglected, even though, in urban India at least, it is the most pressing infrastructural lack threatening the development of theatrical practice (Rao 2009).

I approach the tension mentioned earlier as playing out in contradictions between multiple Lefebvrian productions of space (1991) through a case study of TCT's residency. Methodologically, a focus on contradictions between architectural and theatrical productions of space (in the context of those related to everyday life as well the broader political economy) allows me to approach them together fruitfully. The contradictions intrinsic to and born of TCT's desire to produce a secluded space in which to make theatre, and newer productions of space they spur in turn, offer new insights into both theatre and architecture. Contrary to expectation, theatre is revealed to be a practice that *produces*, not just occupies, space at different scales. Architecture, on the other hand, is temporalized; rather than the conventionally static end-state of design, it is revealed as a generative but pliable *iteration* within the process of making a place for 'producing' theatre. Everyday life, creative work and performance are seen to be entangled with, and driving, the endless spatio-temporal dialectic to which architecture is a constantly performed response, and not a final solution.

The broadly Lefebvrian theoretical framework has three prongs. Lefebvre sees space as always being produced – and thus always entwined with time – in at least two broad ways related in a dialectical contradiction. On the one hand, bodies and social groups (like TCT) produce their own space in realizing an integral socio-spatial existence. On the other, opposed to the above but coupled to it, (already) dominant social formations – like feudal structures, state and capital – also seek to constantly impose their own space to reproduce their power and control. Another dialectic in Lefebvre, that between 'work' and 'product', helps map the results of the ensuing contradictions (Lefebvre 1991: 70–75). Works are relatively unique, unpremeditated, exploratory creations that emerge organically out of a living practice. Nature's unselfconscious, non-instrumental creations are the purest 'works', like the rose that does not know that it is a rose (Lefebvre 1991: 74). Products, on the other hand, are the result of goal-oriented human intention, not organically emergent from their contexts, and tend to become commodities and instruments of control. Lefebvre's dialectical conception, of course, assumes that every concrete space embodies both aspects to different degrees: their conflict is the motor of change, as we will see with the residency.

The two framings above map the production of the residency conceptually from the 'outside'. But to elucidate the encounter between architecture and theatre, we need a way of distinguishing between physical spatiality and social practice. Therefore, I return to my dialectical conceptualization of 'place' – place being understood here as the particularized, localized and valued aspect of the broader dynamic of social space (Merrifield 1993) – proposed elsewhere (Burte 2008). I see place as a field of three forces: physical or 'natural' space (*site*), the formal and informal laws, cultural-historical rules and conventions that organize action in it (*protocol*), and the actual *practice* that occurs in the context of *site* and *protocol*. Neither of these forces is necessarily privileged, nor do one or more predate the other, in principle. Any particular conjuncture of the three forces must be considered a distinct place (even if it occurs in the same space, or *site*), and conversely, every place presupposes such a distinct conjuncture. Thus, a particular stage or everyday space can be considered a *site* that is turned into different *places* in different moments of performance. The physical space (or *site*) remains the same across performances, as does the *protocol* of behaviour and functions, but since a different 'world' is being created through *practice* on stage in different performances, a new place is being produced as a totality every time.

This conceptualization of place ties each of the three forces relationally to the other. The three are not absolute categories. Thus, for example, an architectural space is a *site* in relation to certain *protocols* and *practices*. It is seen to emerge from the larger project underlying a place – home or residency – through the practice of dwelling. John Turner's famous argument that what a house does is more important than what it *is* (Turner 1976: 53) can thus be interpreted as privileging the *practice* a *site* enables, over the latter's independent objectality (for a similar argument linking theatre and architecture, see Rufford 2015).

The rest of the chapter is broadly divided into three sections, thematically connected by TCT's pursuit of seclusion. I assume that the history of the residency's emergence, as well as its relations with the 'external' socio-spatial context, is integral to understanding its internal dynamics. Accordingly, in the next two sections I provide Lefebvrian accounts, first of the incubation of the project of the residency in the city and then of its current relations with the village it is set in. The third section enters the residency proper to outline the interplay between the spatial practices of architecture and theatre in the making (or production) of the residency as a place devoted to making theatre. Given the newness and changefulness of the residency, the concern here is with changes in the practice of making theatre, and not with outcomes in terms of new theatrical form or content which, anyway, are not immediately noticeable. The chapter draws on two short visits to the residency, interviews with different people involved in running and using it, and my long-term personal knowledge of its evolution as an early collaborator of Kumar's.

## Room for work

Serious modern theatre, often commercially unviable, has always lacked rehearsal spaces in urban India, especially Mumbai. In Lefebvrian terms, the political economic production of urban space in Mumbai obstructs the theatre practitioner's lived need and desire to produce his or her own space of theatre, by simply denying access to physical space for creative work. A few, relatively small and scattered physical spaces released over decades to some practitioners by wealthy or institutional patrons have yielded most of the city's theatrical legacy (Gokhale 2016). Thus, turning everyday spaces – artists' homes, hallways in colleges after hours, public gardens and footpaths, even city buses (Rao 2009: 31) –

against the grain of their *protocols* into rehearsal and play-reading spaces has been the tradition. However, over the last twenty years space and everyday life are being more tightly programmed, instrumentalized and commodified in Mumbai. Real estate prices (including rents even for hourly use, where available) have spiralled up unbelievably (Mumbai's relatively upmarket Bandra comparable with New York's posh Brooklyn Heights), apartment sizes have shrunk and the sociability of residential and public spaces has weakened in step with the privatization of everyday life. Simultaneously, every square foot of urban space is increasingly scrutinized through police presence, security guards and CCTV cameras, narrowing openings for uses not coded formally into it.

Kumar has felt the pinch particularly sharply, given his commitment to spatial and bodily explorations, and to experimentation with diverse theatrical forms, both relatively unusual in the Indian context. His artistic roots lie in the modern theatre that evolved after Independence (1947) in New Delhi. TCT's theatrical practice – broadly, devised performance – has moved away from many features common to that tradition: ready-made sole-author scripts, conventional narrative structures, a single (or even a comprehensible) language, realism, the proscenium stage and a direct address to social issues. Kumar, who moved to Mumbai in the mid-1990s, has drawn inspiration from diverse performance traditions and practices based on training or experience with the classical south Indian form of Kathakali; European traditions of clowning; and Philip Genty's performance practice. Following the critical and commercial success of *C for Clown* (1999), a devised performance in gibberish directed by Rajat Kapoor in which Kumar had acted, TCT took clowning to Shakespeare's *Hamlet* (*Hamlet the Clown Prince*, 2008) and *King Lear* (*Nothing Like Lear*, 2012). The group was also commissioned to perform Shakespeare's *Twelfth Night* at the Globe Theatre for the London Olympics in 2012, and Kumar turned to a genre he had never worked in: the musical. Refracted through a folk form called *nautanki*, the play was staged in a dialect of Hindi under Kumar's direction as *Piya Behrupiya* (*Beloved Impressionist*) and had a successful national and international tour, which helped fund the construction of part of the residency. TCT has also stepped off the stage into everyday spaces, modulating actor–audience relationships in subtle but significant ways. Faced with a paucity of technically sound performance spaces that enable meaningful engagement between actor and audience in Mumbai, from 2000 to 2004 TCT also moved into friends' homes to stage performances, bracketing out the everyday *protocols* and producing a new space in living spaces through bodily gesture. One stylized and psychologically charged performance I remember turned on the tension between the everyday social and spatial intimacy between audience and actor in a living room, and the exceptional space of affective significance that the extraordinarily presented body of the actor created. For TCT, therefore, theatre has clearly meant producing new lived spaces infused with meaning, to coax out the 'new from the repetitive' and the exceptional from the everyday (Lefebvre 1991: 203).

Understandably, Kumar (who leads TCT with wife Rachel D'Souza and Sujay Saple) concluded by the late 1990s that the group's constant reinvention of its practice required room to produce its own space through theatre. Such room – as lived conjuncture of inspiring and supportive physical space, open time together in a group for serious exploration and consolidation, and seclusion – is being choked off in Mumbai's urban dynamic. This external contradiction is matched by one internal to Kumar's personal creative practice today, underlining the importance of a space for creative renewal. Over the last decade, certain modes of TCT's experiment – like taking clowning to *Hamlet* – that once yielded unpredictable and personally exciting 'works' have begun to feel, for Kumar, like templates for predictably successful cultural 'products' for a sophisticated paying audience.

This is the context in which Kumar and TCT decided to move out of the city to produce their own lived space in the hopefully less contradictory social space of the village, while remaining connected to Mumbai for sustenance and in contact with national and international audiences and networks. As we will see, this paradoxical emplacement – in and out of the city and village at the same time – appears to have given rise to TCT's often tense relationship with a section of the village, and insinuated an unresolved tension at the heart of the residency between its 'work' and 'product' aspects.

## Product of seclusion

Kumar developed his vision for the residency as a space for his loosely and flexibly knit group to stay and work together while in Mumbai. It would consolidate everyday activities in a single space, overcoming the fragmentation of resolve and creative intent that spatially dispersed everyday life in Mumbai causes. It would also be a secluded space, immersed in an inspiring natural landscape, preferably beside water, possibly in the hilly rural landscape between Mumbai and Pune. Thus, the residency was conceived independently of the actual social context in which it would ultimately be set, possibly coding contradiction with the village into its very script. Tensions with a section of the village have played out in small things and have also obstructed Kumar's plans for engaging the broader village public. He is regularly pressured to buy construction material only from specific suppliers in Kamshet, the nearest town. At other times, there are demands for continued access to the land even though it had been private property – not commons – before being bought legally by TCT. Kumar says he was ready to quit at least on two occasions, in spite of the monumental effort that had got TCT there, because of the severity of aggression.

Immediate causes for the conflict are difficult to isolate. Cultural contrasts between city and village, as well as linguistic barriers (Kumar is from north India and not a native speaker of Marathi, the local language), are probably involved. Those who sold Kumar land also possibly resent losing out on the sudden eightfold rise in land prices in the intervening period. But a more plausibly fundamental cause may also be traceable. Today, the residency stands literally as an exceptional enclosure within the relatively continuous everyday social space of the village. It is physically cordoned off and generally inaccessible to villagers, though give and take is increasing. Moreover, those living in, running and visiting the residency are disconnected from village society. The residency sits as an abstract, preconceived, spatial 'product' imposed on the incommensurable social space of the village with which it shares no genealogical history. Thus, the contradiction with the village may be traceable to the generic seclusion from surrounding social space (and time) that TCT has been able to secure on the basis of an economic power generated in the city. The contradiction thus expresses the broader inequality of socio-economic power across the social spaces of village and city.

Fortunately, TCT has also managed to engage other publics in the village. From the first edition I attended, the Kamshet Arts Festival has been open to villagers. Now, every six months, TCT also organizes a ten-day theatre workshop for village children, led by specially engaged professionals, which culminates in a performance. At the villagers' request an English teacher has been hired by TCT to come from Pune and teach in the village school twice a week. The initiative of individual performers working with TCT has also helped. One actor-singer regularly joins in the devotional music sessions at the village temple. Another is initiating a project to use applied Theatre in Education techniques in the village school. If that succeeds, apart from the benefit for the children, the contradiction between the village and the residency could potentially catalyse new directions of socially engaged creative work by TCT. Equally, a more enduring everyday relationality may yet resolve the conflicts related to the 'product' aspect of the residency.

Lefebvre's dialectical conceptualization implies, of course, that 'products' can become 'works' over time through creative everyday practice. As we will see in the next section, inside the residency the 'work' aspect is already ascendant.

# Place, work and *practice*

The imagined payoff of secluded 'room' has sustained TCT through the founding contradictions above. We enter the residency in this section, to explore the new everyday and creative practice it catalyses. The agency of bodily theatrical practice and the temporality of this particularized space it drives is discussed below in terms of three different developments, each centred on a contradiction or paradox.

## House of work

The small commune – deliberately sited outside the everyday social space from which it arises – is a familiar mode of critical social and artistic practice in India, possibly following Gandhi's ashrams and Rabindranath Tagore's Shantiniketan early in the twentieth century. Two small recent examples, Adishakti (founded in the 1990s near Auroville by theatre director Veenapani Chawla) and Nrityagram (founded in Hesseraghatta outside Bangalore in the 1980s by dancer Protima Gauri), offered models and insights for TCT's project. Given the paucity of architects specializing in theatre spaces in India, Kumar concluded from a meeting with Nrityagram's administrative head that he should keep full control over design and building, leaving a relatively secondary role to the architect. This power hierarchy between client and architect is common in India, especially when performers build their own spaces (Burte 2007). Further, Chawla convinced Kumar that TCT should only move in once the first structure was ready to house the team, with at least one good space for living in, and another for rehearsal.

The residency was planned to have permanent living quarters for core artistic and administrative staff, and guest houses for visiting practitioners. The combined building footprint is quite small. The master plan includes the approximately 145 square-metre Big House which has a 'studio' with a wooden floor, the residency's main work space; a couple of existing lime-washed,

**Figure 5.1** The 'Big House', Uksan village, Kamshet. Photo courtesy of Atul Kumar/ The Company Theatre (TCT).

rough brick cottages, one that Kumar and D'Souza eventually moved into, and another as a guest house for the moment; a more formal guest house for sixteen people to stay; and a dining-cum-performance space for fifty (both now nearing completion, thanks to the money *Piya Behrupiya* brought in). As a place for making theatre, the residency currently has only one relatively formal performance space: an open-air stage at the foot of an unpaved natural slope loosely approximating an amphitheatre in the Greek tradition. The stage is being fitted out with demountable screens and a roof to enable daytime use for practice. The indoor studio has also hosted smaller performances. TCT sees every space on the site as a potential performance space, and certainly one for rehearsal and practice. D'Souza says that performers often choose a particular tree to think under. However, a separate, formal indoor performance space is likely to be initiated in the next five years.

TCT did not have money to build separate living and working spaces initially, so the Big House was planned as a combined facility following Chawla's suggestion. Consequently, an unresolved tension between three conflicting programmes marks the space. The design brief expected it to be, by turns, a house for a couple (Kumar and D'Souza); a guest house for visiting actors and team members; and a work space. In India such flexible space-use – changing the use of the same space (*site*) by changing its *protocols* through *practice* – is common, as is cross-use between relatively public and private, indoor and outdoor spaces. However, the contradictions between programmes demanded acknowledgement which is absent in design, sometimes challenging the integrity of theatre practice. The plan follows the conventional configuration of living room, kitchen and one bedroom (the last larger than normal to accommodate mattresses for eight people on the floor). An early design drawing even shows the 'studio' as a living room with sofa sets!

Not surprisingly, the house has failed and succeeded at the same time. D'Souza had been away in London for theatre training while it was being planned and built. When she saw the house in 2012, she decided she could not live in it – it was too big to be home – so the couple immediately moved to a much smaller, rougher cottage where they continue to live happily. Other programmatic conflicts were soon revealed. As a singer launched into the first song at an early rehearsal of *Piya Behrupiya* in the studio, the pressure cooker in the adjacent open kitchen suddenly blew its whistle long and hard, to Kumar's mortification. The kitchen was, of course, promptly moved out to a temporary structure, now made permanent, next to the Big House.

But the studio, 6 by 11 metres, with a semi-sprung teak wood floor (over plywood and one layer of teak framing, without foam) for intense physical work,

**Figure 5.2** Action in the studio of the Big House. Photo courtesy of Atul Kumar/The Company Theatre (TCT).

has been a 'success' as a space for practice, according to at least four practitioners I spoke to. With a veranda on either end (the rear framing a spectacular view of lake and hills), wide doors and even a modified bay window, greenery outside and lots of light and breeze, it has been a 'joy' to work in say Kumar and D'Souza. Even with twelve people working in it continuously, D'Souza says, it has never felt crowded, possibly due to the verandas and the expansive landscape outside. There are practical reasons for the promise and pleasure of the studio too. The sloping roof, a symbol of domesticity and a practical response to heavy monsoons, rises to almost 5.5 metres and promises to accommodate a lighting grid in the future, ensuring that TCT can develop performances at its roughshod, rural retreat to the same technical standards as are expected by the urban theatre venues to which the work will travel. Currently, it also offers a wooden floor for rehearsal – a luxury in Mumbai's make-do spaces of practice. This symbolically also marks the space as dedicated (not impersonally allotted) to creative work.

The combination of contradictory spatial *practices* in the same *site* – the Big House – has had the unintentional, yet potentially useful, effect of coding tension into TCT's live/work/show space. The tension between programmes may well be that between the everyday and the extraordinary aspects of place, tightly woven into this unusual house of work. This tension may not always be evident to external observers. A house is perhaps the most everyday of building types. Training and creating performance involves spinning an extraordinary space of gesture and meaning out of the matrix of the everyday materiality of the house. It may well require a secluded space to better focus body and consciousness on creative work, in spite of pervasive Indian protocols of dwelling that partially help: for instance, shoes are kept out of the house by habit and the interior of the home thereby rendered sacred. Walking barefoot to the wooden floor over the smooth stone floor becomes, subtly, a passage to a space thereby set off from the profane everyday outside.

Nihaarika Negi, a live art practitioner recently returned from performance training at the University of Exeter and collaborating on a project with TCT, values the ambiguity and continuity between work and living space:

> That it is not a definite space – 'this is where the studio begins and ends' – has been very useful, since the space in itself helps open up your mind. Because it is always in flux it allows you different points of view. We use the studio when we are training, for practical reasons – it is cooler and more comfortable inside. But immediately, we take what we make outside. The nature of that space [Big

House] allows you to do that very easily. If it was very rigid – that you had to take off your shoes, close the door etc. – it would inform the work differently. It would make the studio more sacred. Right now everything is always changing and evolving, like our work.

Negi's observation suggests that everyday spatial forms – the 'house' type – may be capacious, complex or flexible enough to incubate 'works', possibly because theatre itself fashions an exceptional place and time out of everyday realities – gravity, bodies, voice, gestures, emotion and possibilities of encounter. *Practice*, for Negi, can mine these possibilities, while subverting informal protocols (Negi may not necessarily remove shoes going into the house). D'Souza thinks otherwise: 'I like a bit more sacredness to my workspace.' She plans to modify the *site* by building a wall to separate the studio from the bedroom and former open kitchen completely. House and work space would thus have independent entrances from two different sides. Negi is waiting to find out what that would do to her more pliable *practice*. Whatever happens, it could be argued that the unique combination of everyday *practices* of dwelling while making theatre are reshaping the Big House from a preconceived spatial product ('house') into a spatial 'work' responsive to, and evolving with, their demands.

## Temporal landscape

Making a definitive distinction between space and time is unwarranted for Lefebvre (1991: 95). With a new space comes the possibility of a new time. This can imply a new consciousness, and possibly new directions for creative work, especially through the mediation of the body and the rhythms of everyday life. At Uksan, secluded space implies a fully owned time held slow by a lakeside landscape enclosed by hills in the distance. Here, new rhythms of creative practice are incubated in the new rhythms of everyday occupancy. According to D'Souza:

The format of rehearsing in Mumbai is like this: you rent a space and have a four to five hour shift. After coming here, for the first time we have uninterrupted access to space. For the first time, we have a separate time slot for *riyaz* [daily practice], the way repertories have as a tradition. We realized that TCT does not have its own 'practice', like say Adishakti has, where irrespective of the production they always do certain exercises. Now we have begun to ask: what is our riyaz? Do we do Yoga, do we work on voice? This is exciting. When you have that kind of time, you begin to confront important questions about your work.

When I watch Atul [Kumar] at this age, it is like he is going back to school. Now we have the whole day – morning to evening – so what do we do with it? Life becomes connected with work, eating, sleeping … you live with your colleagues. I feel that the stages of rehearsal reached in one or two months in the city, you sometimes reach in 15 days here.

More time also implies a deeper, more integral consciousness. Negi elaborates:

That quietness and slowness of life allows you to enter a different state of consciousness from which you can create work that is informed by the ideas of what you see around, but you look inside and see what is emerging. It is very hard in Mumbai to be able to sustain that. We can focus very hard for a month and a half for a project in Mumbai. But to repeat that becomes very difficult. Partly because the performers go back and then forget all that was created, the rigor that was created. That becomes tiring.

Thus, the project of building a new quotidian in seclusion does not just yield *more* time, and a more penetrating self-consciousness; it yields *continuity*, a continuity of consciousness between the quotidian, and moments of its artistically refracted intensification, the extraordinary work of creating a performance.

The continuity of consciousness extends outwards to other people, but also to the landscape. In Negi's live art aesthetic, 'the stones are collaborators'. The body emerges as a medium of this extension, while its memory spurs new theatrical experiment. Negi conducted most of a recent fifteen-day workshop for a collaborative production outdoors. A dip yielded unexpected results:

For me, being in the lake was incredibly terrifying: I have swum in pools, but there was something about the density and strength of the water. If you are in one spot for thirty minutes it feels like you have been beaten up – it is exhausting and draining! It was a revelation, the fear of water that emerged. When we returned to Mumbai and began working on our pieces, mine developed around that experience.

On another plane, everyday rhythms of dwelling and maintenance – not just *using* space for creative work, but producing it out of dwelling – have deepened D'Souza's sense of place. New connections with land emerge in planting food, or in experimenting successfully with the traditional North Indian practice of 'drip irrigation,' which allows water to percolate continuously through a filled earthen pot that is buried beside every sapling. Though indeterminate today, the consequences of this new everyday rhythm, for creative work in place, might be significant for creative work over the long term.

## Architecture as iteration

To count as a creative gesture, architecture is conventionally expected to aspire to the immutable finality of an exceptional presence. But at the residency it has been absorbed into the process of placemaking (or the production of a lived residency space). Architecture emerges as an iteration – a step that is initiated, retraced and modified in the unfolding of a process leading to a valued rhythm of *practice* – in two complementary ways: *practice* spins new and fantastic places out of ordinary architectural spaces; and architecture, in the form of specific buildings or built spaces, effectively becomes one iteration in the larger cycle of realizing the residency as an extra/ordinary place.

Devoted to enabling the *making* of theatre, the residency has minimal architectural provision for performance. An open-air stage – rudimentary, thus inviting later modification – was built in a fortnight for the inaugural Kamshet Arts Festival. It was designed for a historical play about a social reformer battling caste discrimination, performed by municipal sanitation workers from Pune. The siting of the stage implied an auditorium into existence on the slope leading down to it. Cloth partitions – a popular device of temporary enclosure – marked off a backstage area. During performances, thick rugs near the stage for floor-seating, and portable chairs on the gentle, natural slope, accommodated a few hundred guests from across the country, to forge a memorable event. The broad stage framed the actors (frequently arrayed across it following the traditional *kirtan* form) appropriately, and the slope and stage geometries interlocked comfortably. Later that night, a similar conjuncture transformed the already-transformed wooden-floored studio – now a temporary sleeping space – into an intimate, end-stage auditorium, charged by the conversational yet literary wit of a *Dastangoi* performance (an old Urdu storytelling form). In both cases, a tiny piece of everyday architectural space – the stage without a formal amphitheatre, the studio – was amplified into a memorably performed place, an affectively intense conjuncture of *site*, *protocol* and *practice*. The fact that *practice* effected such a transformation of everyday *sites* into exceptional places provided the edge to the experience.

Architecture itself is also approached implicitly as an iteration – never a culmination – within the bigger project of making an extra/ordinary place. There is a master plan, of course, but everything could not be built in one go – there simply was not enough money. The gaps in building activity have allowed evaluation, learning and modification of the already built, and the planned. Within a week of being occupied, the Big House began to be modified. First, heeding the pressure cooker's whistle, the kitchen was shifted out, thereby making it less of a house. Later, a small courtyard was enclosed and the studio floor extended into it for more working space. The wall D'Souza intends to build between the studio and the rest of the house will complete the transformation of the building, though it might look the same externally. The outward form – that of an integral house – may well contradict the divided place inside. Kumar is clear: 'I have no hesitation pulling down walls, or the building, if it is required for creative reasons,' he says, in spite of the daunting challenges surmounted in putting them up in the first place. Architecture is thus valued for the *practice* it makes possible, and expected to be pliable to its drive: use is creative of a spatial 'work', the preconceived design only of a spatial 'product'.

Across the three thematic discussions in this section, theatre practice is seen to produce space in different ways, drawing on the creative capacity of the performing body. The lived body demands seclusion for creative work and pushes against the walls of the Big House till a conventionally implacable architecture yields. The body also *lives* (and thus produces) a continuum across house and landscape and transmutes experience into performance. Seclusion, the source of external contradiction with the village in the previous section, enables this *practice*: the new time in which the residency immerses artists hinges on its seclusion as much as on the beauty of the landscape. It thus fosters an everyday in which the artist can discover the immanent matrix of an exceptional theatrical moment. In the process, the ordinary architecture of everyday space – of house, open land, trees and water – is revealed as potentially pregnant with the extraordinary.

## Conclusion

To recap, Lefebvrian spatial contradictions are seen to spur, shape and emerge out of multiple, conflicting productions of space related to the residency. Prompted by TCT's project of fashioning a new theatrical practice, these dialectical productions of space have yielded the residency as an often contradictory 'work'-in-progress. One source of contradiction is the fact that the residency is an urban theatre artist's dream of secluded space for creative exploration planted in a rural social space with which it has no shared genealogy. Seclusion itself is thus revealed to be a paradoxical ideal, enabling creativity while spurring conflict, in this case borne of a structural socio-economic inequality between village and city. We are thus compelled to view the creative productions of space and theatre inside the residency against this context. At another level, the body, as a spatialized and spatializing consciousness, consistently emerges as a creative force producing space in the course of theatrical work. Through theatrical *practice*, it temporalizes architectural space.

From a Lefebvrian standpoint, theatre emerges as the more thoroughly spatial art at the residency, since it avowedly integrates physical space, everyday time, the body and social encounter. The implication for architecture is clear. If it seeks a similarly thorough-going spatiality, it must be reimagined as the unfolding scaffold for the production of lived space. It must seek the seeds of the exceptional and the poetic within that quotidian spatio-temporal matrix. And its value must always be judged in relation to how it participates in, and enables, the social project that produces it in the first place. Such a view implies that visual or plastic qualities of architecture – my initial disappointment at the form of the Big House – are not as important as its pliability to *practice*.

## In the event

The event of place unfolded slowly over a sparkling night after the disappointing initial encounter with architecture. A leisurely rhythm of performances, food and sleep – around the openair theatre, on the grass, in the Big House – filled the night as it grew colder. Many mini reunions had occurred over a dinner eaten flitting between inside and outside; then, the play in the openair theatre, and after a break, *Dastangoi*, in the studio of the Big House. Just before the latter performance, I had been asleep right there for an hour or so, one in a row of blanketed bodies. Within minutes of being woken up from a deep sleep, I was led bleary-eyed into a delightful realm of anecdote and irony in which Urdu's aristocratic irony met street-smart storytelling. Throughout the night, people and action moved smoothly and informally within and between the grounds and the Big House. The 'place' configurations of the openair theatre – itself an event – and the festive night landscape kept changing. The night started running out and a classical singer began unfurling a composition to welcome the day. As dawn broke, the open-air theatre was revealed – through the curtain of trees surrounding it – to be nestled in the curve of the lake behind that had been invisible throughout the night. Architecture, and disappointment, was lost to view in the play of place.

# 6

# *KHOR II*: An Architecture-as-Theatre Project by TAAT

Breg Horemans and Gert-Jan Stam

As a theatre maker and an architect, we discovered how much our respective disciplines can challenge and enrich each other when we collaborated on the design and construction of a wooden theatre pavilion, *KHOR I*, at Floriade 2012, in Venlo, the Netherlands. We founded TAAT (Theatre as Architecture Architecture as Theatre) as a collective that works at the intersection of theatre, architecture, the visual arts and design. Taking the complex relationship between theatre and architecture as a starting point, our work explores how the arrangement and sequencing of physical spaces can serve as a means of stimulating interaction and encounter. We also emphasize co-creative processes. All TAAT projects are about dialogue and making connections. In our work there is no distinction between actors and audience: according to our principle of Do-It-Together co-creation, participants are always equal. Because TAAT's artistic practice includes different experts, artists and students as well as audience members, we consider it a collective. Following *KHOR I*, our projects have included the building kit *KHOR II*, the long-term artistic research project *HALL33*, the curatorial design programme *Bokrijk Sengu* and, in collaboration with Bow Arts London, an interactive and participant-led project for play, performance and learning, *PlayGround*.

KHOR II appears as a monumental building kit on the central square of a neighourhood, village or city. In *KHOR II*, people are provided with a manual ('*KHOREOGRAPHY*') which tells them exactly how they can BUILD the pavilion, how they can PLAY a Do-It-Yourself theatre piece in it and how they can use it to SHARE ideas and initiatives for community building. It was first created for Festival Cultura Nova in Heerlen, the Netherlands, in 2014, and since then it has been constructed for festivals in the Netherlands, Flanders and Europe.

*KHOR II* is best understood by experiencing it first-hand as a participant: building, playing, sharing or being in close proximity to the pavilion. The following texts and images evoke something of the experience of the project.

KHOREOGRAFIE ᴺᴸ                                                          KHORÉGRAPHIE ᶠᴿ

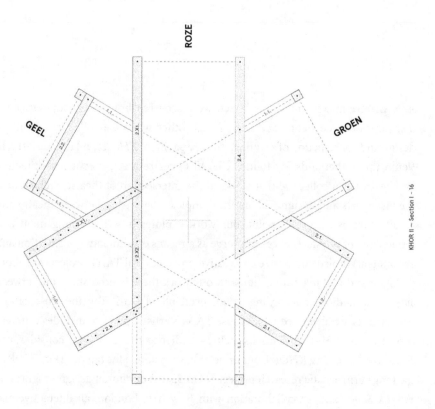

## LAYER 2

KHOREOGRAFI ᴰᴷ                                                           KHOREOGRAPHY ᴱᴺ

**Figure 6.1** Floorplan showing Layer 2 of the *KHOR II* installation. Plan courtesy of TAAT.

# BUILD KHOR II

In *BUILD KHOR II*, volunteer participants have one day to erect the theatre from a kit of parts. This text is composed of short excerpts from the *KHOR II* manual, *KHOREOGRAPHY*, providing a flavour of the instructions given to participants and the way in which the building process is organized. *BUILD KHOR II* places an emphasis on collaboration, respect, communication and fun.

## 1. Introduction

Thank you for participating in *KHOR II*!
*KHOR II* is an architecture-as-theatre project that appears as a building kit. This manual explains exactly how the theatre is built. The challenge is to solve this theatrical puzzle in one day.

## 2. Teams and Tools

You will work in three teams: PINK, YELLOW and GREEN. On the construction site you will find three boxes – one for each team. First, pull straws to decide who is on which team.

## 3. Construction Zones

Each team has its own construction zone, the specific area in which to work. The zones are marked pink, yellow and green.

## 4. Stacking and Coding

*KHOR II* consists of fifty layers. The theatre arises from stacking one layer on top of the next.
Each team has a number of pallets with wooden beams. Each beam is marked by a colour coding that corresponds with the drawing.

## 8. Roles

Each team has three different roles or functions: the Supervisor, the Suppliers and the Stackers. Decide together who takes which role. On agreement anybody can change roles at any time.

## 10. Layer Drawings

Action time!

On the following page you will find the construction drawing for the first layer (Supervisor). Find the corresponding beams (Suppliers) and start stacking (Stackers). A building process is never constant: sometimes things proceed quickly, sometimes a little slower.

The first six layers are the most important and therefore the most difficult. After that things get more regular.

Make sure you never forget: you're not alone in this!

**Figure 6.2** Participants in *PLAY KHOR II* (Festival Boulevard, Den Bosch, Netherlands, 2015). Photo courtesy of Saris and Den Engelsman/TAAT.

## *PLAY KHOR II*

In *PLAY KHOR II*, up to thirty-six participants are provided with a script and invited to perform a Do-It-Together theatre piece in and around the installation, exploring interpersonal relations and notions of community and leadership. The following text is based on a transcript of the documentary *PLAY KHOR II* by Evite Ancarola. The documentary was filmed in Den Bosch (the Netherlands) during the run of *KHOR II* at the Boulevard Festival 2015.

## Participant:

You get a script. So it's not the case that somebody tells you what to do. And you read it. And you read it at your own tempo. And you encounter people while you are on your way through the script.

## Participant:

You notice how you are forced to stand close to people, because you're in a limited space. And you actually think, 'I don't feel like it.'

## Participant:

You're very curious what will happen with every page, so you want to reach the end of the script.

## Festival Director:

In the moment that you have a common goal everything becomes easier. So, for me it is interesting – in the place where you are at or the environment you're in – to search for what you want to accomplish together.

## Participant:

You look at who is opposite you: you have to make eye contact with this person for a very long time and, if it feels right, to hug each other.

## Participant:

So then all of a sudden you are embracing a stranger! Well, that's making contact with somebody in a way you normally wouldn't do on the street.

## Participant:

As soon as she was standing in front of me I thought, 'Oh, she actually looks a bit like me.' Considering her appearance I mean. But she took in everything and offered it very fast. So I found it very loving and, somehow, in a strange way, it connects people straight away.

## Participant:

On the very essential level of how you meet people and how you present yourself to others, as generous or very closed, the play touches these mechanisms and makes you aware of them.

## Participant:

If I wanted to establish a group I would give everybody a hug straight away and look them in the eye, really looking at who you have in front of you. I'd start with that.

## Participant:

It often is the case that people stand in a group but have never really looked at each other, or they just pick out one or two people. If you really give attention to each other, personally, for a few minutes, then it's always very nice.

## Participant Reading the Manual:

People on tribune A, you decide who of us will keep his or her script open to lead you through the next scenes. Choose your leader, by standing next to him or her.

## Festival Director:

Being together as a factor, in a place, a place in time and space, helps of course. That contributes to the pace at which such a community can come into existence. And to the intensity of the experience of that group of people.

## Participant:

You have to have something in common for a community. And I think the commonality here is this building. And everybody gets a script.

## Participant:

I think it also concerns how you share an experience with each other, with a group. And what that does to the group but also to yourself as an individual.

## Participant:

I thought it wasn't going to work out, but the feeling of getting through this together … it's as if you have known each other for three days and say, 'Let's go to a bar together!'

## Festival Director:

A community, of course, suggests commonality. But the interesting thing in a community is what is not the same. And if, together, you find a way to let what is not common exist, to disagree with each other, then I think you have organized your community in a good way.

## *SHARE KHOR II*

*SHARE KHOR II* examines the possibility of generating a longer-term community initiative that might continue after the KHOR II installation has gone. This text is an excerpt from *KHOREOGRAPHY*, the *KHOR II* manual.

Welcome to *SHARE KHOR II*.

This part of *KHOR II* deals with the question: How do we build our community?

The 'we', in this case, are the participants of this *SHARE KHOR II* session. So if we're talking about 'our community' we're talking about the small, temporary community formed by all of us here present. The community of this *SHARE KHOR II* session, one could say.

As in BUILD and PLAY, this SHARE-session involves a manual. The SHARE-manual however is not so much a script as it is a catalogue containing exercises and tools that could help or support us over the course of this session.

The manual for BUILD was very strict and the end result very clear and specific: a wooden pavilion. The manual for PLAY was a crafted script as well but it was open to interpretation, allowing for a more unpredictable end result. The manual for SHARE is just an aid and the end result is completely open. Following the Do-It-Together philosophy, we therefore determine what this session will look like.

We have 2 hours maximum.

# Part Two

# Practices

# 7

# Living Between Architectures: Inhabiting Clifford McLucas's Built Scenography

Cathy Turner and Mike Pearson

In March 1996, Welsh theatre company Brith Gof staged *Prydain: The Impossibility of Britishness* in an empty industrial building in Cardiff's docklands; it was restaged in May that year at the Tramway in Glasgow. The challenging production aimed to rectify diverging aesthetic approaches in the company. This chapter traces the ultimately irreconcilable tensions involved in making *Prydain* – between architectural and performative approaches, individual and collective stances, and 'major' and 'minor' dramaturgies. In doing so, it identifies both the productive potential of an architectural dramaturgy and some of the possible limitations inherent in its containment of human interaction.

In the late 1980s and early 1990s, Brith Gof created several large-scale, site-specific performances in disused, often semi-derelict, industrial buildings and large public spaces: a car factory, ice rink, railway terminus, iron foundry and swimming pool (see Pearson 2010: 68–72). Designer Clifford McLucas, who trained as an architect, supposed that the particular properties of such sites – their extent and height, ground plan, layout of integral features and distribution of vernacular details – might offer unique opportunities for scenography: to create installations at the scale of the building itself, employing materials unusual in the auditorium but commonplace at such locations; and to construct another architecture within the existing architecture (Pearson 2010: 112–115). In *Gododdin* (1988), he employed hundreds of tonnes of sand and dozens of trees and wrecked cars in a formal setting of circles, avenues and cones, which was gradually flooded with thousands of litres of water during the performance (see Pearson and Shanks 2001: 102–108); in *PAX* (1990), he built a section of a Gothic cathedral from metal scaffolding (see Pearson 2010: 68–70); in *Haearn*

(*Iron*) (1992), new tram tracks and an existing gantry crane allowed stage elements to approach and recede along the full length of the 100-metre iron foundry, while a performer sat on raised chairs above the audience.

After *Haearn*, lack of opportunity and diverging interests led McLucas and co-director Mike Pearson increasingly to engage in personal projects within Brith Gof: a division in the company's work, therefore, predates 1996 and the production of *Prydain*. The work was moving increasingly in two directions: towards multi-layered architectural composition (McLucas) and towards an enquiry into the embodied relationship between performers, between performers and audience, and between audience members (Pearson). McLucas's approach was evident in several video works for television broadcast, including *PAX TV* (1992) and *Y Pen Bas/Y Pen Dwfn* (1995); and in *Tri Bywyd* (1995), staged at a ruined farm in a forest outside Lampeter in west Wales using two 16-metre scaffolding cubes – effectively two new buildings – that intruded into the existing building and each other, and within which three narratives could be advanced on various levels simultaneously. Pearson's approach was apparent in the *Arturius Rex* project (1993–1994) – four separate productions staged in nondescript warehouses, all focusing upon the physical activity of the performer, all involving rudimentary scenic designs and all including examination of the spatial and corporeal relationship between performers and audience.

These two distinct explorations could coexist, but not without tensions. McLucas's previous designs had created sets of material circumstances as much to be endured and countered by performers as forming a backdrop for their activities. In the effort of inhabiting them and functioning within them, performers subjected their bodies both metaphorically and in reality to the demands and contradictions of physical and cultural conditions, while struggling to express other possibilities. The scenic configurations placed the performer (sometimes the audience member) under duress: this could become a means to produce an urgent physicality. To some degree this tension and demand from space/system to human body propelled the dramatic action, and contributed to the scope and power of Brith Gof's middle-period performances.

But while *Prydain* was intended to unite, and perhaps resolve McLucas and Pearson's ostensibly diametric approaches, the difficulty of this undertaking was to signal the end of their collaboration.

In one diagram in McLucas's working notes for *Prydain*, he positions 'Architecture' between two poles representing 'object, unity and formality' on one side, and 'informality and field' on the other (see Figure 7.1). In doing so, he is informed

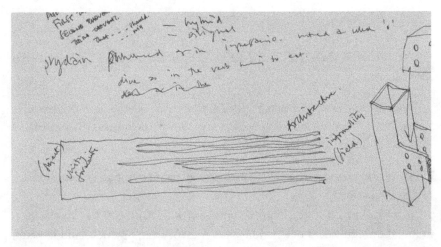

**Figure 7.1** Page detail from Clifford McLucas's working notes for *Prydain* (PK2). By permission of Llyfrgell Genedlaethol Cymru/The National Library of Wales.

by the thinking of architect Bernard Tschumi who describes architecture as an 'event-space' in which the informal and the formal collide (as 'space, movement and what happens in it' (Hannah and Khan 2008: 53)). However, the detailed, self-generated expressivity from and between performers might not always require, or be supported by, such an architectural framework.

Tschumi describes this meeting between movement and architecture as implying violence: 'the logic of objects and the logic of man […] inevitably face one another in an intense confrontation' (Tschumi 1996: 121–122). In Brith Gof's most successful work, the 'field' of performance meets with architectural object, unity and formality to produce visceral, emotional effects; however, the individual performer, voice and body can become dominated and subsumed by difficulty, volume and scale. Pearson's interest in the dynamics of interpersonal communication was sometimes compatible with an architectural dramaturgy yet potentially frustrated by or independent from it. This potential for indifferent, conflicting and reciprocal relationships between movement and architecture (and between architectures) is theorized by Tschumi, and these ideas influenced both directors of Brith Gof (see, for example, Tschumi 1983: 67–69). Though Tschumi regards the power relationship as complex and essentially symmetrical – 'ultimately a deep bond is involved' – he often describes architecture in terms of authoritative and even oppressive figures such as guards, police, hunters and doctors, and confirms the possibility for architecture to become 'spatial torture' (Tschumi 1996: 122–124). The conflict here produces dynamic effects, but not necessarily sustainable ones.

## *Prydain*

The subtitle of *Prydain* is an ironic acknowledgement of Welsh historian Gwyn Alf Williams:

> Wales is impossible. A country called Wales exists only because the Welsh invented it. The Welsh exist only because they invented themselves. They had no choice. (Williams 1985: 2)

If this is the case for Wales, what degree of labour might be required for Prydain – Britain?

In 1995, Pearson states: 'Our big ambition with Brith Gof has always been to found the equivalent of a nation state. A theory and practice hand in hand, which is a complex being' (Morgan et al. 1995: 4). The company's ambiguous identity within Wales was a significant factor in this ambition. As McLucas expresses it in his notebooks, 'Living and working on the periphery of Britain which is itself on the periphery of Europe, the company lays no claim to the centre', which made it possible to 'problematize' the idea of Britishness from that perspective (McLucas c. 1995–1996). The fact that both artistic directors were English by birth also troubled that Welsh identity, creating a hybrid perspective: neither inward-looking Welsh nationalism nor externally – located cultural colonization. While some reviewers considered these English roots problematic in themselves, accusing them of 'making Wales an English invention, creating an artificial Wales' (Adams 1996a: 55), the company consciously sought to exploit the complexity of a dual position, and without accepting an essentialist view of Welsh cultural identity, saw theatre as a place in which identities could be performed in conflicting, reciprocal and multiplicitous ways.

The essential problem in making *Prydain* was the lack of obvious thematic material. What might elaborate the complexities of the rhetorical title? What could be the substance of performance? A tentative link was drawn between the London Cymmrodorion (founded in 1751) – including poet and forger Iolo Morganwg, instigator of the Gorsedd of Bards of the Isle of Britain in the early 1790s – and their invention of Welsh-ness, the visionary texts of William Blake and the writings of other period revolutionary writers who were assumed to have inhabited the same intellectual milieu. And text did appear:

> Text was everywhere – on the floor, on clothes, on bodies. Books and burning books were much in evidence. As most of it was in Welsh, I could only receive it as polemical attitude. What emerged was a sense of a chronicle. Its subject was

the theatre of politics, clashing against the supposed politics of certain kinds of music. The redundancy of rhetoric. The forcible silencing of the underclass. (Thorne 1996: 30)

But the narrative shortfall led to a fundamental dramaturgical decision – that *Prydain* would be a work in-the-making, that it would involve audience volunteers in acts of making, that it would demonstrate and embody 'impossibility' through its own provisional attempts at theatrical *and* political coherence. Volunteer audience participants, each dressed in industrial jackets with coloured shoulder panels, would be given physical performance tasks – being rehearsed in plain view moments before being called into action.

*Prydain* does not *represent* Prydain/Britain, but in effect attempts to model and to reflect upon the effort towards unity that is implied in the very concept of 'nation'. Within the performance structure, audience members blur with performers and the work is constituted through a collective act of creation and a system of organization. The difficulties and possibilities for a hybrid and shifting Britishness (as well as its impossibilities) are addressed through the organization of disjunction and heterogeneity, the conscious assemblage of bodies and spaces. Pearson describes it in an interview with Andrew Houston:

> Instead of making a performance which is meant to be *about* something – about the conflict of this many different opinions and perspectives of Britain – we decided we had to make a performance that *is* something, that *is* the experience of this situation [...] to try to 'embody' what is going on in Britain. (Houston 1998: 255)

In this sense, the generation and *arrangement* of contents, rather than 'content', in a conventional sense, is the focus of *Prydain*, combining architectural system and dynamic audience–performer relationships. Spatial and temporal structures order these dynamics, or attempt to, and create a multiplicity of frames and hierarchies within which the movement takes place. Some of the most optimistic reference points in the work are derived from club culture and dance – bodies taking over, renewing space together, in ad hoc, euphoric modes. This involves an audience's active involvement in space-creation, seemingly chaotic, but potentially multi-textual. On the other hand, the ecstasy of rave culture could appear hollow in the cold light of day; the surface unity gives way and the imposition of spectacle, hierarchy and exclusion, facilitated by architecture, presents an ultimately bleak prospect. The role of music is integral to the work, conceptually, dramaturgically and experientially. The rave or club night as counter-cultural utopianism is evoked here, although the abstraction of music could tend towards an only abstractly communal situation.

One might describe this microcosmic approach to nation in terms of the relationship between 'major' and 'minor' dramaturgies, using Flemish dramaturg Marianne van Kerkhoven's terms (Van Kerkhoven 1994b). She speaks of the difference between the 'minor dramaturgy' of 'that zone, that structural circle, which lies in and around a production' and the 'major dramaturgy' of 'its interaction, through its audience, and through what is going on outside its own orbit':

> And around the production lies the theatre and around the theatre lies the city, and around the city, as far as we can see, lies the whole world, and even the sky and all its stars. The walls that link all these circles together are made of skin, they have pores, they breathe.

This curious metaphor, of breathing walls of skin that 'link all these circles together', is potentially confusing. The 'walls' here do not seem to 'link all these circles' in a literal sense, but rather, are envisaged as living bodies, through which the connections between the theatre and its ever-expanding circles of reference are mediated, allowing the exterior world to enter into and be interpreted in the theatre event (and vice versa). Van Kerkhoven does not differentiate between the human bodies within the theatre and the walls of the theatre building, but instead her image makes bodies and architecture equivalent (as the word 'theatre' itself, both a word for building and for action, might imply). She does not mention the concept of 'nation', but in so far as *Prydain* is concerned, the minor dramaturgy of the event exists in relation to the major dramaturgy of nation – a relationship mediated by porous structures and experiencing bodies.

What Van Kerkhoven does not examine, though no doubt she would have recognized them, are the tensions in these relationships between the minor and major dramaturgies, and internal to them.

## Host and ghost

After *PAX*, McLucas characterized the overlay and interpenetration of the *found* (the site) and the *fabricated* (the production) as the coexistence of *host* and *ghost* (see early notes in McLucas c. 1993–1994). The 'host' is the extant building with its fixtures, fittings, ambiance; that which pre-exists the work; all that is *at* site, while the 'ghost' is that which is temporarily brought to and emplaced at site, that which remains spectral and transparent (see Pearson 2010: 34–38).

It is once more useful to refer to Tschumi's categories of spatial relationship in terms of 'indifference', 'reciprocity' and 'conflict', this time with a focus on the relationship between 'host' and 'ghost'. If one sees *Prydain*'s site, the 'host', as an evocative detritus of the deindustrialized city and nation, thus part of the 'major' dramaturgy, the scenographic 'ghost' is deliberately oriented to cut across it, suggesting a 'minor' dramaturgy in conflict with its context.

The site for *Prydain* in Cardiff was an empty warehouse, lacking the rich histories of the old Rover car factory (*Gododdin*), the iron foundry (*Haearn*) or the rural site of Esgair Fraith (*Tri Bywyd*). In so far as the site itself held significance, it resembled the kind of space that might be requisitioned for an illegal musical rave – in an industrial part of town and providing an empty shelter for a temporary event-space. This bleak, industrial nothingness itself became an object of transgression – a gap to be filled by, and rebuilt by, performance.

An immediate point of reference for McLucas's design was Tschumi's preliminary concept for the Parc de la Villette project in Paris. At the intersections of a hypothetical grid laid on the park, Tschumi placed *folies*, small 10.8 metre cubes 'divided three dimensionally into twelve cubes forming "cases"' (Tschumi cited in Lang 2005: 106; see also Tschumi 2014: 20–37) that could then be decomposed in fragments or extended through the addition of other elements to develop independent architectural features.

The design for *Prydain* refers back to the earlier cubes of *Tri Bywyd* (1995) and to McLucas's initial work on NVA's *Sabotage* (1993) in Glasgow (McLucas c. 1995–1996). The idea of the tension between private space and shared street space was resonant in both *Sabotage* and *Prydain*, together with a concern to overlay found spaces with incongruent performance architectures. In relation to the first possibility, *Sabotage* began with the idea of cubes placed diagonally across a space, as in the initial *Prydain* concept: here, McLucas emphasizes an attack on 'the notion of "congruence" in the development of architectural responses to a given site (the "host" and the "ghost")' and continues: 'Site-specific stagings of event succeed inasmuch as they generate an interjection into the site that is not of the site, thereby setting up an architectural difference and dialogue, a charged space within which "event" may crystallise' (McLucas c. 1995–1996).

These notes are included in the Devising Notebook for *Prydain* and appear to be a starting point for that work's ideas, too. Thus McLucas suggests that the spaces of performance are transgressive, rather than indifferent, and that the 'event' is partly produced by the charged conflict between spaces.

Three cubes were installed for *Prydain*, but in the relatively small building only one was complete and had structural integrity. The other two could not be ascended or even stood beneath, and it was impossible to insert 'movement vectors – ramps, stairs, and so on' (Tschumi in Tschumi and Walker 2004: 124) in the partly-built structures. They occupied space in a dogmatic but exclusionary manner: difficult for the physical action to work with, impossible to avoid. This led to another dramaturgical decision to create physical activity adjacent to them at ground level in a relatively narrow street-like strip.

Adding to these difficulties, the site was entirely insecure – the production's amplification system was stolen twice – leading to a further dramaturgical decision, resulting from expediency. All performers and mobile scenographic elements, such as sound equipment and wheeled platforms, would enter in vehicles at the beginning, be unloaded and set up in an ad hoc manner as part of the performance itself. Only the scaffolding structure would be set up in advance.

## 'Space, movement and what happens in it'

Tschumi identifies the violence implicit in architecture as occurring in two ways, the first of which is that of form, a metaphorical violence of design (Tschumi 1996: 132–133). In this metaphorical sense, the stage space of *Prydain* violates the found space.

Yet not only could McLucas's built architectures deliberately transgress the layout of the host site, but, as we have noted earlier, the performers and audience could respond reciprocally, indifferently, or could conflict with both sets of material architectures. In the first section of *Prydain*, which emphasized the industrial, colonial past, the performance was to be aligned with the horizontal and vertical lines of the warehouse, indifferent to the diagonal lines of the performance architectures, then transitioning through a period of conflict between movement and structure to a more reciprocal relationship between performers and built scenography. This movement was mirrored in the shifts in music and atmosphere.

The actions of the human beings in the space, therefore, move from an engagement with the cultural and material architectures found at site (representing Welsh industrial history), through a tussle with them and the possibility of a different orientation (the present?), to a new space that is entirely produced through the performance and its own material structures, bodily and built (the 'special world' (minor dramaturgy) that might hint at the future of a 'nation' (major dramaturgy)).

Heike Roms clarifies that in *Prydain* a shift has taken place in Brith Gof's approach to site. Here, the company does not primarily treat the site as already full of cultural resonance, but finds in it the potential for new, 'heterotopic' spaces to be created (minor dramaturgy as counter-proposal to the world outside). There is still a friction with the connotations of the site itself, but the site is not excavated for content, as is partly the case in *Tri Bywyd*, for example (Roms 2001: 171–172). For Pearson, such heterotopic spaces were formed through performance and interaction. This idea existed in parallel, at times in conjunction, but potentially in conflict with McLucas's understanding of architecture as the shaping of not only a new space, but a new 'event-space'.

Tschumi's work, while not utopian, is haunted by architectural conceptions of a transformational *Gesamtkunstwerk*. Inspired by the Situationists, he was clearly informed by Constant Nieuwenhuys's experimental 'New Babylon' and the work of the Russian Constructivists who preceded him. Yet, in Tschumi's *folies*, the earlier utopian search for an architecture that would not merely allow, but rather tend to *enforce*, a new way of life has changed to an acknowledgement of the potential for rupture between architecture and movement. Architecture still implies order, but the relationship is acknowledged as potentially ambivalent.

McLucas, after Tschumi, both acknowledges tensions in and with architecture and simultaneously conceives of the event-space as an orchestral complex, or as a fractured, but total work of art. For McLucas, dramaturgy *is* architecture. Tschumi himself expresses it in these terms: 'The architect designs the set, writes the script, and directs the actors' (Tschumi 1996: 128). However, this very statement, like so many others Tschumi invokes, hints at a relationship of authority and dominance.

McLucas had come to regard all dramaturgical components as 'architectures'. He explicitly articulates dramaturgy in this way for the production of *Haearn*, where the 'seven architectures' comprise: the configuration of audience and choir; layered narratives; layered time periods; the body; climate; mechanical grid structure; and two solo voices. In *Y Llyfr Glas* he expresses this idea again, clarifying his understanding of architecture:

> It's basically about spatial relationships but it's also the relationships between different bodies of material. [...] to me these constitute another kind of architecture. Now, it may be that I'm being very cavalier with this term 'architecture', but I can't think of any three or four dimensional word or metaphor

that does it for me. [...] 'Architecture' – the inner structures – the shape of the piece. (Morgan et al. 1995: 19)

Temporal structures were part of this 'architectureeventspace' (McLucas c. 1998: 9). *Prydain* exhibited the structuring familiar from earlier Brith Gof productions – twenty-seven sequences occurring across nine named sections, given titles in McLucas's notebook and apparently to have been subdivided into two (Pearson notes eighteen sections). These nine (or eighteen) sections were divided into three sets, each underscored by a live musical soundtrack – Slovenian Robert Merdzo providing an intense guitar and drum-driven soundtrack for the first part; the Welsh band ReuVival providing the sampled 'drum n' bass' for the last three (six) sections, with a period in between the two where they overlapped. A tight temporal and musical structure thus held the disparate aspects of the performance together throughout the process, while signalling the ultimate impossibility of sonic resolution.

During work on the large-scale productions of the late 1980s, Pearson and McLucas had begun to characterize the components of performance – generated from different starting points and processes within the company – as horizontal layers of varying relative thickness that might be mixed against each other at a stage late in the production process, in a dramaturgical structure of vertically differentiated named and timed sections. In McLucas's conception of *Prydain*, the layers are 'sound, music, text, scenography and [...] action'; or otherwise, conceiving this more thematically, 'climate, culture [...] politics', represented variously by the spatial conditions, the performers and the organization of the audience (McLucas c. 1995–1996).

Tschumi writes that 'it is not a question of knowing which comes first, movement or space, which molds the other, for ultimately a deep bond is involved. After all, they are caught up in the same set of relationships, only the arrow of power changes direction' (Tschumi 1996: 128). However, it might be that Pearson and McLucas's apprehensions of performance are best regarded as located at either end of Tschumi's 'arrow of power' – McLucas working from space towards event and Pearson from event towards space – rendering further collaboration difficult.

Pearson describes McLucas's process: 'He always works from the building inwards, unlike most theatre design that works outwards from the performers. The building's architecture tells him many things that may be invisible to us' (Cousin 1992: 45). McLucas repeatedly distinguishes his work from 'stage design', which exists to serve the performance. But if all dramaturgical components are rendered as architectures, what is the substance of performance? And are all the unstable and profligate flows of action and chance occurrence effectively harnessed when considered as rigid frames?

The presence of McLucas's third element, the 'witness' (the audience), also troubles the relationship between 'host' site and 'ghost' performance. Is the audience also held by the architectural frame? Is the audience also rendered as architecture? In the interview with Houston, Pearson comments of this production that in fact, 'the event creates the space', and that the 'fluidity of the event' is 'difficult to arrange formally' (Houston 1998: 252). His interest in the spontaneous movements of a crowd, often forming circles around an action, is not easily reconciled with the lines and diagonals of McLucas's staging (working from the building inwards).

Tschumi's second category of violence is not metaphorical, but involves violence towards the body, taking place within architectures that exist in service of constraint. While the structures of *Prydain* do not represent prisons or torture chambers, they do offer limitation, discomfort and some degree of danger, particularly in their conjunction with the always-in-process constitution and dissolution of space through interaction and performance.

In his notebook, McLucas writes:

> There is no Arena where you can see/know (command) everything. There is an Architecture (both 'sculpture' and 'field') depending on your point of view. This architecture is both continuous (one system) and discontinuous (many separations). We can force unity/oneness. But not for long – it is too difficult. Discontinuities + fractures + intertextual in nature. But 'held' (even if in abeyance) (1) by the gaze of the external audience (2) by the systematic systemic nature of the architecture. (McLucas c. 1995–1996)

Architecture is both continuous and discontinuous, a system in which 'unity' can only be temporarily 'forced'. It 'holds' the discontinuities, fractures and texts ('in abeyance') through the gaze, and through its doubly systematic qualities.

The performer appears in McLucas's plans only as a small block, one architectural element among many (McLucas 1996). The object space includes the object body, at least in terms of representing the production on paper. In *Y Llyfr Glas*, McLucas comments that Brith Gof's performers 'don't have to pretend to be under some duress [...] they don't have to pretend anything! I mean, the environment, the task at hand, is carrying all the metaphors and the meanings, really' (Morgan et al. 1995: 61). Yet performance's necessary resistance to systematization, made more urgent here through a deliberate decision to work with unrehearsed participants, results in violent collision, not always metaphorical. Pearson recalls hearing John Rowley tell a story of this performance within another (Forced Entertainment's *The Travels* (2002)), in which he describes injuring himself with a Stanley knife as he hurries to perform an unrehearsed action within a demanding time frame with no potential for pause or medical attention.

Pearson, listening to this anecdote, recalls that next phase – Rowley would blindfold himself and walk, carrying burning books. Later,

> he would blame me for directing him into a metal pillar and that would cause bad blood between us for some years. (Pearson 1994: 2)

Pearson writes in an 'unpublished letter to the *Prydain* performers' that, 'No architectural diagram is available to plan the field: we are operating at "ground-level", face-to-face' (cited in Roms 2001: 177). This, Roms suggests, implies that 'Pearson puts forward a new dramaturgical concept for *Prydain* which replaces spatial-architectural structures with the phenomenology of spatial experience and perception.'

Within this event-space, the relationship between performers, technicians, musicians and audience members was integral to the work. Brith Gof performers were engaged in putting up and dismantling set elements and moving platforms into different configurations; the musicians were present on the provisional stage, and the spectating audience was at times addressed as a group, at times subdivided and moved around the space. Roles were therefore somewhat fluid, and the potential transition from spectator to performer was implicit, if not always realized. Performers, too, might become spectators. Pearson comments on the difficulty of rehearsal, when so much of the show depended on working with participants who were absent until the night itself. How could one rehearse what could only be created with the presence of an unprepared crowd?

In photographs of the later Glasgow performances, the lines of McLucas's scaffolding cubes rise with elegant, mathematical precision, at an angle to the metal pillars, above the crowd of audience members and donkey-jacketed participants gathered around a narrow runway.

Perhaps one might say that Rowley is injured by the conjunction of unpredictable lived experience with the rigidity of a systemic, 'architectural' dramaturgy, where neither performance nor architecture takes the lead. Risk was part of this performance. The Cardiff warehouse was at near freezing temperatures; flames flared close to the spectators; 'precarious elevation' made performance difficult.

The *Glasgow Herald* comments that, 'As the punter who was injured last night will attest, there's an all too palpable sense of danger about the show' (*Glasgow Herald* 1996, cited in Pearson 2004: 11). Houston, who suggests that such precariousness creates 'psychosomatic "force"', describes the way in which, in the latter part of the performance, Richard Morgan, playing an outcast figure, enters to disrupt three established playing spaces, yet suggests that neither controlled meaning nor revolt against it ultimately holds sway (Houston 1998: 259–260). The body is caught between order and disorder: evocative and dangerous.

## Architecture and performance

Extant descriptions of the performance overwhelmingly focus on the opening sequences, describing the effect as the audience entered the warehouse, to be confronted only by space, two scaffolding cubes on a diagonal, the space in front of them divided by fencing. A van then entered from the other side of the fence from which technicians began to assemble a platform for the musicians, speakers and other equipment. Another van drove in; Rowley exited and came towards the audience speaking words written by William Hodgson in 1795, beginning 'All men, when they come out of the hands of nature, are equal and free.'

He then began to rip his clothes (the moment of his injury), exposing skin marked by text in ornate letters – text by the poet William Blake. Once he was blindfolded, Pearson placed two books in his outstretched hands, setting fire to them, dowsing them in fuel as Rowley stumbled across the space and into the crowd, speaking lines from Blake's 'Four Zoas' (1797–1807):

> What is the price of Experience? Do men buy it for a song?
> Or wisdom for a dance in the street? (Blake 2008: 325)

What is it about this opening section that means it is so vividly recalled by Pearson, Rowley, Roms and Houston, as well as evoked by a reviewer from the *Glasgow Herald*? It could be the sheer sense of danger, made real by the accidents mentioned previously. It could also be that this opening section set the tone of the narrative in its arc from hope to despair, as a 'forced' unity of structure gave way to movement, 'held' fractures 'in abeyance', confining, elevating or excluding performers, then gave way once more. The suffering body of the actor, the vehemence, vulnerability and ubiquity of text, its material fragility (going up in flames) and the uncertain position of the audience were themes that ran throughout the work. While it is evident that this production played with the friction between structure and chaos, it is difficult to say whether it finally spun out of control, or to what extent this was indicative of the limits of reciprocity between architecture and performance.

*Prydain's* apparent staging of hope and failure met with a mixture of responses, many uncertain how to read its ambiguous creativity. In Cardiff, *Prydain* was for some difficult, confusing, cold and unwelcoming, even resembling a personal affront: 'Boring first night leaves me cold' (Adams 1996b). At the restaging in Glasgow – in the same space as *Gododdin* in 1989 – it was received as

> mighty, messy, spectacular [...] a kind of exhausted lament for all the collectives
> we have known, for the British state, for socialism, for the collective experience
> of theatre itself [...] makes words largely indistinguishable [...] sometimes loses
> all sense of impulsion and organisation. [...] But at its best [...] a magnificent,
> angry and superbly well-acted tribute to the spirit of British rights-of-man
> radicalism, its struggle and its ultimate failure to create the egalitarian Utopia of
> which it dreamed. (McMillan 1996: 10)

For some in the crowd, the show was urgent, passionate, 'chaotic, vigorous, exceptional and quite, quite impossible', akin to 'the feeling you would have got stumbling accidentally on a Sex Pistols gig in 1976, or having your first art class with Pablo Picasso in 1910' (*Glasgow Herald* 1996, cited in Pearson 2004: 11).

The work might, as the *Glasgow Herald* reviewer suggests above, have been staging its own limitations, theatre's limitations, as well as those of nationhood. *Prydain* was to some extent utopic, to some extent merely heterotopic: it modelled an attempt at systemic inclusivity, yet it also demonstrated the fracturing of such attempted unity.

If architecture, as McLucas implies, played the role of the system that held – or forced – other elements together, the production raises the question as to whether this is symptomatic of the architecture–performance relationship. Does architecture inevitably tend towards organizing macro structures that cage the living energies of performing bodies, or render them as movable objects? Architecture is a way of articulating a form of life; so is performance. Where the arrow of power begins with architecture (as in theatre at the Bauhaus or in some of Robert Wilson's work, for example), there often seems to be a tendency to reduce the status and agency of the individual. On the other hand, such work does facilitate an approach to system, environment or *Gestalt*, which might be essential to a political theatre.

Pearson, regretting the lost qualities of this performance writes, 'From this point, theatre in Wales would only ever be *instrumental* in servicing policies of social inclusion' (Pearson 2004: 16). This implies a non-instrumental attempt to create, or offer the possibility (or maybe the impossibility) of a social space (an 'event-space'?) which always knew it couldn't 'work', at least not in current circumstances.

The 'major dramaturgy' of a stateless nation concerns the tension between the concept of 'Britain', as systematizing, homogenizing, ordering force (architecture), and the reality of Welsh experience (performance). This theatrical experience may have been less a representation of such tensions than an analogous experience of them.

Human skin, volatile, suffering, unpredictable and individual, would not, finally, be synonymous with, or subject to the same ordering logic as wall, text or diagram. The violence of the encounter between different orders of material was no longer sustainable. The tensions that had helped to make Brith Gof would now resolve into independent trajectories.[1]

# Note

1 Clifford McLucas's archive and that of Brith Gof are now housed in the National Library of Wales in Aberystwyth.

# 8

# Occupying the Scene: Architectural Experience in Theatre and Performance

Andrew Filmer

On a freezing November day, I'm seated on a low wooden stool in the interior of a huge Gothic church in Ghent, Belgium, waiting to participate in *HALL05* by Dutch-Belgian collective TAAT ('Theatre as Architecture Architecture as Theatre'). An attendant approaches and asks me to follow him to a sliding door at one end of a large plywood-clad installation. Opening the door, he asks me to step inside and wait until I see someone else enter at the other end. *HALL05*, he explains, is a 'Do-It-Together' performance installation that I will experience with another person, who is a participant like myself. I am to follow a few basic rules: stay together with this other person, don't talk and close all the sliding doors behind me.

Once inside the installation I look down a long corridor that is split in the middle by horizontal planks. I can see to the far end, but when the other participant enters and stands facing me, he is revealed only in silhouette. We are each framed by the corridor, but held apart in separate spaces. We slowly approach each other and look through the gaps between the planks. Then we turn – I to my left, he to his right – to face sliding doors that will allow us to move deeper into the installation. Already the experience is theatrical: inside the defined space of the installation we are each performer *and* spectator, appearing before the other, and jointly responsible for animating the work. The experience is also architectural: the structure and materials of the installation surround and shelter us, mediating our encounter, and articulating its theatricality. As we progress through the installation, my companion and I begin to play, exploiting its various affordances: panels in the floor shift and creak; the sliding doors scrape softly as they open and close; planks and boards bend, transmitting pressure and movement between our respective rooms; and gaps in the walls frame the appearance of our shoes, legs and hands, inviting us to look, to reach out and to touch each other. Then, at the furthest point from the entrance, we enter the same long narrow space, separated only by a black curtain which bisects the corridor at an angle. Passing close by on either side of the curtain, we move back through the installation. Having crossed paths we now move through the same sequence of rooms in reverse and on the side previously traversed by the other.

*HALL05* is part of *HALL33*, TAAT's long-term research project into architectural dramaturgy that aims to construct 'a theatre play that is a building and a building that is a theatre play' (TAAT 2016). The project explores how architecture might operate as a means of communication, framing and articulating spaces of encounter between participants, and it is motivated by a desire to generate creative frameworks for furthering social interaction and exchange. As Breg Horemans of TAAT states, 'In our age of hyperconnectivity, the importance of real people meeting each other in real space and real time is becoming more and more relevant' (Horemans in Poláček and Pokorný 2015: 120). TAAT's work is one example of how theatre and performance are engaged in an expanded interdisciplinary field of critical spatial practice (see Rendell 2006), generating new social and spatial possibilities through contact with practices and critical languages from art, architecture and urban design. This engagement is spurring experimentation into how theatre might be (re)positioned in the public realm, coupled with experimentation into how relations between spectators, performers, spaces and locations can be creatively reconfigured. As a corollary, much contemporary theatre and performance now invites spectators to engage in diverse forms of aesthetic labour through engaging with the productive slippages of site-specificity, or playing with logics of participation, intimacy, immersion or mobility: spectators may be implicated or made complicit in situations and scenarios, asked to negotiate meetings and interactions with others or called upon to do 'double-duty' as both interpreters/ witnesses and role players/aides (Zaointz 2012: 167). Peter Boenisch (2014) has identified how the development of relational or reflexive dramaturgies provide spectators with 'the blurred sense of being at the same time opposite and still within, even right in the middle of the performance' and in so doing 'throw us back onto our own actions: they force us, the audience, to take ultimate responsibility as "acting agents", for our own agency, for our actions *as spectators* in this world' (240).

In this chapter I discuss how relational or reflexive dramaturgical logics offer a site of engagement between theatre and architecture through the way they construct spaces for reflection and encounter. Architecture is directly connected with the concrete shaping of the built environment through its concern with the processes of designing and constructing buildings, and the purposeful articulation and organization of meaningful spaces. But, as Cathy Turner (2015) argues, despite its more temporary, mutable and dynamic nature, the practice of dramaturgy can be considered analogous to that of architecture because both share a concern with the composition and construction of structures in space and time and both activate social spaces of possibility. Architecture, like dramaturgy, operates as a relational practice, concerned with the construction of relationships between objects, subjects, materials and actions and the construction of spaces that are mental as well as physical. 'Architecture is not simply about space and form', asserts Bernard Tschumi, 'but also about event, action, and what happens in space' (Tschumi 2005). Tschumi's introduction of the concept of 'event' to architectural discourse and his contention that there is 'no architecture without event' has been influential in challenging dominant architectural understandings of the relationship between form and function (Tschumi in Read 2000: 174). In particular, by arguing that the disjunctive and confrontational relationship between the 'concept of space' and the 'experience of space' is central to architecture, Tschumi has brought into focus the ways in which users of architecture produce and experience space (Tschumi 1996: 15–16).

The agency of users is a creative and disruptive force in architecture: through action users occupy and appropriate architecture; they inscribe it with their own narratives of use; misuse it in ways that cannot be anticipated; attribute meaning to features and spaces; and literally, over time, reshape and alter built form. Because of this, architectural theorist Jonathan Hill asserts that, 'Architecture is made by design and by use' (1998: 11). Countering the tendency for architectural discourse to lay claim to the experience of architecture, Hill has challenged architectural authorship through his exploration of the creative action of users. And he offers what he calls 'a more appropriate definition' focused on the concept of occupation. Architecture, he argues,

> is, primarily, a particular relation between a subject and an object, in which the former occupies the latter, which is not necessarily a building, but can be a space, text, artwork or any other phenomenon that displays, or refers to, the subject-object relations particular to architecture. (1998: 6)

This expanded relational definition foregrounds architecture's habitational affordance and its basic function as a shelter, while also stressing its availability for appropriation. The concept of occupation carries with it the sense of ownership and possession, but also the sense of making use of something. In Hill's usage, it suggests the mutual entanglement of architecture with the performance of action and the possibility of examining the architectural nature or operation of cultural forms that are not, in themselves, immediately recognizable as architecture. For instance, in her discussion of Louise Bourgeois's sculpture *Spider* (1997), cultural theorist Mieke Bal perceives an invocation, exploration and contestation of architecture in the way that work requires the viewer to construct a performative narrative through the act of viewing it. In her viewing of *Spider*, Bal perceives an 'architectural sense of *habitat* that shelters us while we contribute, in real time, to building it' (1999: 126). The work shelters the viewer, but the viewer also constructs the work through his or her performance of it. This complicates the strict subject–object divide referred to by Hill and suggests the doubled nature of architectural occupation: in occupying a building, a text or an artwork, we too become occupied by it.

The sense of habitat and shelter noted by Bal, combined with the invitation to the viewer to construct performative narrative through acts of aesthetic perception, seems pertinent to the way contemporary theatre and performance constructs and configures aestheticized spaces. Relational and reflexive dramaturgies – part of a broader postdramatic reworking of conventional dramatic representation – generate performance environments that are distinctly architectural in this sense; event-structures that allow for occupation and inhabitation without prescribing or fixing a spectatorial relation. Such dramaturgies commonly operate by *retheatricalizing* a spectator's relation to what they are seeing, dislocating them from a position opposite or outside a work and implicating them in the process of representation (Bleeker 2008: 7). Reflexive dramaturgies also frequently call attention to the gap between the figure of the spectator and the spectator's own identity, 'between the spectating "I" which the performance addresses and the perceiving I (or maybe better: "eye") of the spectator' (Boenisch 2014: 239). The interplay between theatrical representation and presentation in reflexive dramaturgies frames spectators' encounters with dramatic representation and 'establishes coordinates' for their experiences (233), providing spectators with a theatrical experience that invites them to inhabit and occupy the scene physically and/or mentally, engaging with it perceptually and intellectually. The theatre event therefore operates as a framework for encounter, a dynamic spatio-temporal construction through which the spectators engage with the materiality of the spectacle and their own acts of spectating or sense-making. Reflexive dramaturgies establish a virtual reality that is experienced through the duration of a performance, in order that we might think with and through them, analogous to the ways in which built architectures provide the grounds and conditions for action and relation. The environmental quality of reflexive dramaturgies derives from the way spectators are positioned within the mise-en-scène. For instance, Toneelgroep Amsterdam's *The Roman Tragedies* (2007) rescripts the assumed spectatorial conventions of the theatre venues that house it by inviting spectators to move between the stage and auditorium at will for much of the performance, taking up their own spatial positions and viewpoints, and eating, drinking, reading newspapers and using social media. In National Theatre Wales' *Coriolan/us* (2012), the sophisticated use of media technology, including headphones for audience members and the remediation of the dramatic action through multiple live video feeds, denied any closure of the fictional world (see Filmer 2016).

In what follows I trace out the architectural dimensions of two recent productions by National Theatre Wales (NTW): *Mametz* (2014) and *Iliad* (2015). Rather than interrogate existing physical architectures, the performances discussed in this chapter engage with architecture in an oblique way through the construction of situations and experiences for spectators to occupy. *Mametz*, while largely operating according to a dramatic logic, offered a fleeting moment of reflexivity in which a mental space opened up. By contrast, *Iliad* constructed its own architecture of relations within the extant physical architecture of a theatre building. My focus in discussing the first rests on the experience afforded the spectator. In my discussion of the second I focus on the dramaturgical logics that facilitated a more sustained occupation of the work. How did these performances manifest differing architectural senses of occupation? And what might be gained by considering theatre and performance in such architectural terms? Having noted Turner's suggestion that dramaturgy and architecture are analogous practices, here I want to think specifically about how the design and construction of dramaturgical environments or event-spaces can produce architectural experiences through inviting the spectator to occupy the scene.

## *Mametz*: Encountering and commemorating the historical past

Since its opening season in 2010, the English-language NTW has existed as a non-building-based company, seeking to develop the legacy of site-specific performance making in Wales and echo the approach taken by the National Theatre of Scotland. In setting out the vision for its inaugural season, founding artistic director John E. McGrath proposed that NTW would focus on 'place' as a means of exploring nation, language and history without asserting identity. Outlining plans for a 'theatrical mapping' of the country, McGrath stated that NTW would 'explore the land through theatre and theatre through the land' (2009: 10). Through this emphasis on location and community, NTW has sought to function as a 'theatrical meeting place' (11) by staging site-located productions, running an associated programme of community-based performance and debate events, and hosting an online social platform. But one of the tensions it has encountered in manifesting this vision has been the way theatre possesses its own normative architecture, encompassing modes of production, reception and behavioural conventions. In NTW's work the theatrical apparatus has been deployed as a means of encountering and experiencing a variety of locations – from beaches to libraries to urban spaces, military sites and mountains – with the dramaturgy of each event serving to locate and orient spectators. But rather than unsettling space or articulating the ongoing contested nature of particular places, this site-located staging has often served to settled space and place by prescribing how spectators are able to move, how and what they attend to and what constitutes appropriate modes of response (see Schmidt 2010: 289).

When theatre 'leaves the building', the dramaturgy of an event constitutes an architecture that facilitates encounter, being the means by which relations between site, work, performers and spectators are mediated. NTW's 2014 production of *Mametz* – a large-scale site-responsive production performed in the farmland and woodland of Great Llancayo Upper Wood near Usk, in South Wales – manifested an unresolved tension between a more disciplinary normative dramatic architecture and moments of more reflexive theatrical architecture.[1] Produced as part of the 14–18 WW1 Centenary Art Commissions, *Mametz* depicted the experiences of the 38th (Welsh) Division in the bloody Battle of Mametz Wood during the Somme offensive of 1916. The drama, written by Owen Sheers, recounted the experiences of the troops involved through the remembrances of survivor and novelist Llewelyn Wyn Griffith and the ruminations of Dutch physicist Willem de Sitter on the implications of Einstein's then newly postulated theory of relativity. A key thematic of the dramatic narrative was the coexistence of the past in the present, expressed through the blurring of temporal frames and the overlap of characters from spatially and temporally disparate settings. As theatrical event, the audience's entry onto the site was facilitated via the trope of the battlefield experience tour. Led by a knowledgeable professor, spectators were first firmly figured as tourists and pedagogic subjects. Standing in an open field at the beginning of the performance, the figure of a lone soldier running across the hillside suggested a blurring of distinctions between here/there and past/present, reinforced by our walk down a narrow trench, constructed from sheets of corrugated iron, to an open-sided barn. Here, spread around a central stage area – delineated by cattle barriers – we witnessed a scene of choreographed fraternization between British soldiers and French women, followed by a short lecture from our tour guide which outlined the historical context and literary significance of the battle (Robert Graves, Llewelyn Wyn Griffith, David Jones and Siegfried Sassoon all wrote poems or novels in response to their experiences in and around Mametz Wood in 1916). The professor's direct address reinforced the dramatic geometry of the performance – and its pedagogic logic – before we were led into another adjacent barn. This barn was fully equipped as a theatre with stage, auditorium and production machinery (lights, amplification and black curtains forming a rear wall for the stage). Seated in the darkened quietened rows of a specially constructed auditorium, our position was further fixed within a rigid dramatic architecture. The stage before us depicted the wall and fire step of a trench, allowing us to witness scenes of trench life with its fears, forebodings and boredom, interspersed with the direct address of women from the home front. Beyond the trench, the curtains could be drawn back to reveal an expanse of grass and a distant tree line, the 'real' of the field beyond serving as scenic backdrop.

A key trope of many First World War narratives is the moment of attack when troops go 'over the top', exposing themselves to the ferocity of enemy fire. In *Mametz* the inevitability of the battle loomed, and its eventual representation offered the key reflexive moment in the performance. Prior to the moment of attack, as the soldiers prepared, we too were ordered onto our feet. As the soldiers climbed over the trench wall and walked out of the barn into the field beyond, a section was removed to reveal steps, and we were ordered out into the field as well. Leaving the enclosure of the barn and entering the open air once more, we turned to see that the field had been marked out in a grid of wooden poles, linked with LED light strips and lined with flickering fluorescent tubes. Large speaker stacks pulsed with a metallic soundtrack and the amplified impact of shell explosions. Lined up horizontally behind a sergeant (the same actor who played the professor) we were ordered to advance across the open ground towards the tree line at the far end, meeting and passing a line of placard-carrying suffragettes travelling in the opposite direction.

It was in this moment that the dramaturgy of the performance shifted, introducing a new reflexive logic. Walking across the field we, the spectators, were positioned within the mise-en-scène for the first time by being asked to re-enact the role of Welsh soldiers crossing no man's land and, in so doing, to construct the representation we were also witnessing. My experience in this moment was one of exposure after the enclosure of the barn – suddenly I was walking across an open field, subjected to a pulsing and jarring soundscape, and on view to others. Implicated in the scene for the first time, I found that the gap between the role I was being asked to perform and my own identity as spectator opened a kind of mental space where thought could finally reverberate. As I advanced across the field, my thoughts filled with images of trench warfare I had encountered in literature and film. Paul Virilio's evocative description of 'military space' came to mind; the First World War's creation of a 'steel-vaulted heavens' and a 'sky of fire'; warfare assuming the status of natural forces (Virilio 2009). Rather than merely witnessing this moment, I was invited to co-produce it through the action of walking, producing space and time for thought. The moment, and the spectatorial mode it enabled, closed with our arrival at the edge of the woods. Here we were once more firmly figured as witnesses to the staged representation of battle and death. Entering the woods, we were directed to yet another constructed theatre in the form of a semicircle of logs placed opposite a lit stage, to witness the final scene of the drama.

In *Mametz*, a predominantly normative dramatic architecture gave way to a moment of reflexive occupation and reflection. The moment was fleeting – largely serving as a means of transitioning and transporting the audience from one location to the next – but it produced, in theatrical terms, the possibility of presencing the past in the present that elsewhere was only gestured to representationally. The moment was memorable because it enabled me to locate and orient myself in relation to other representations of trench warfare, and it was architectural because it structured and articulated a mental space for reflection, opening up perspectives on a wider cultural-historical landscape. The tension between the representational and relational aesthetic modes evident in *Mametz*, and the dynamic of spatial enclosure in the barn followed by exposure in the field, was clearly intended by the makers of this event. But a more thorough consideration of how the dramaturgy of the event functioned in specifically architectural terms – how it articulated spatial relations of distance, volume and direction to position spectators in a particular relation to the dramatic action – could have allowed other opportunities for spectators to appropriate and co-produce the space of the event, generating a more genuinely troubled and unsettled encounter with history.

## *Iliad:* Constructing a theatrical architecture of relations

*Iliad*, staged in 2015 and directed by Mike Pearson and Mike Brookes, constructed a theatrical architecture of relations within the spatial envelope of an existing theatre. Here spectators found themselves implaced in the mise-en-scène for the duration of the event. Staged as a series of separate parts and two 'marathon' eight-hour performances, *Iliad* was performed in Y Ffwrnes (The Furnace), a 504-seat adaptable multipurpose theatre in the South Wales town of Llanelli.[2] As a new purpose-built theatre, constructed as part of a five-acre commercial and cultural redevelopment of the eastern end of Llanelli town centre, Y Ffwrnes was a departure of sorts for Pearson and Brookes, lacking the locational uniqueness of their previous productions with NTW. In 2010, their staging of Aeschylus' *The Persians* took place in the uncanny and exposed environment of FIBUA (Fighting In Built Up Areas), a replica German village in the British Army's Sennybridge Training Area in the Brecon Beacons. In 2012, *Coriolan/us*, based on a textual adaptation of Shakespeare's *Coriolanus* and Bertolt Brecht's unfinished *Coriolan*, took place in a large concrete 1930s aircraft hangar adjacent to the Ministry of Defence's St Athan Airbase in the Vale of Glamorgan. By contrast, Y Ffwrnes was a contemporary theatre, a spatial machine designed and equipped to facilitate theatrical appearance through its articulation of the familiar theatrical divisions between outside and inside, stage and auditorium, and the visible and the invisible.

In *Iliad*, the theatre auditorium was the site of critical address and intervention. This was effected through bringing to bear many of the dramaturgical features of the previous two productions, particularly the overt use of audio technology and the integration of live and pre-recorded elements. The auditorium was emptied – 'evacuated', to use the term of one reviewer (Dickson 2015) – and what was on show as the audience entered was the spatial envelope of the room itself, its attendant technologies (light, vision and sound), and piles of car tyres, white plastic chairs and lengths of timber. The seating bank in the theatre was retracted and its flat floor covered in a uniform expanse of medium density fibreboard (MDF), blurring the spatial division between stage and auditorium. Down the middle of the space an arc of car tyres and pieces of board constituted a low barricade of sorts. At one end a vast cinema screen, suspended at an angle in what would usually be the void of the stage, displayed the title of this first part – KINGS – in large white capitals. At the opposite end, a temporary wall of MDF, shored up with timber supports, cut across the auditorium beneath the line of the balcony masking the retracted seating bank. Flat screen televisions were installed around the space at the level of the unused balcony, piles of identical white plastic chairs were stacked around the walls and a number of microphones on yellow cables hung loose from the grid, just above the floor.

The radical reconfiguring of the auditorium rendered it a shared space, denying a clear sense of orientation for the audience, who spread out around the perimeter of the room at the beginning of the performance, encircling the arc of tyres. From the beginning, others were also present – performers dressed in matching austere black – walking watchfully. As much as we, the audience, were watchers, we were also being watched in the uniform light of the room, already constituted as a key scenographic element of the environment. The signal to begin came in the form of performer John Rowley depressing the buttons on his watch, setting the performers about their allotted tasks. This revealed a division not only between them and us, but between some of the performers as 'speakers' and others as 'constructors'. The former gave voice to Christopher Logue's epic adaptation of Homer's *Iliad*, the text of which remained present throughout as a relentlessly scrolling autocue on the multiple monitors. The latter began to rearrange the tyres and loose pieces of board, erecting platforms and redistributing chairs (see Figure 8.1). Their labour was logistical, task-based and unhurried, but also open to representational possibilities through the images formed by constantly evolving combinations of bodies with materials. Against a ceaseless stream of spoken language, encampments, temporary shelters, defensive positions and palisades, troop movements, massed assaults and the prone bodies of the slain were evoked by the bodies of the constructors as they sweated through the real labour of rearranging of timber, tyres and chairs, as well as please through the range of forms they constructed, their shifts in tempo and rhythm, and their invitations and requests to the audience to leave their chairs, to move over here or over there, or to lie on the floor 'like this'. Importantly, the images did not offer a mimetic representation or suggest a contemporary referent; rather, they arose through the way in which sequences of action and compositions resonated with and against the text. Throughout the performance, real-time acts of material construction created a temporally contingent and mobile architecture of platforms and towers that articulated a shifting array of positions from which to speak or to watch.

**Figure 8.1** The constructors: Ffion Jones, Richard Huw Morgan, John Rowley and Rosa Casado in *Iliad* (National Theatre Wales, Llanelli, 2015). Photo courtesy of Hide the Shark/National Theatre Wales.

A key aim in *Iliad* was to stage the whole of British poet Christopher Logue's epic adaptation of Homer's *Iliad* – often referred to as *War Music* – in an environment where its performative dynamics could be experienced. Written and published as a series of poetic texts between 1959 and 2005, on the page *War Music* is a hybrid text, manipulating visual media and using typography inventively to 'cue' a reader's performance (Greenwood 2009: 506). It is also distinctly cinematic in its shifts of scale and point of view, and its use of sound effects, while the subtle ironies in its anachronisms and imagery and its direct address to the reader/listener make frequent appeals to 'see' and 'think', 'notice' and 'consider'. In the opening moments of the performance the narrated text shifted the focus from the actuality of the room and the certainties of clock and task time to the endlessness of geologic and mythic timescapes. Limestone plates shift and the formation of the Greek archipelago takes place under the watchful eye of Zeus, accompanied by the song of the gods:

> In the beginning there was no Beginning,
> And in the end, no End

This was followed by the first of many requests during the hours of performance in a shifting fibreboard world: 'Picture the east Aegean sea by night.' The invitation was to participate in the construction of a shared fictive world within the enclosure of the auditorium. Logue's text contains many of these direct appeals, inviting reflection on the sensorium of battle, and suggesting how a spectator's body might react, or suggesting that they may not be able to imagine the scene adequately. 'Think of the noise,' I was asked, and then later, 'Think of those fields (As your heart skips a beat)'. Later still, 'See if you can imagine how it looked.' Christopher Reid identifies that the conscious use of cinematic terms within the poem allows 'movie-literate (i.e. most) readers to register certain scenes quickly and vividly', drawing on 'cinema's rapid alternation between the small, isolated detail and the big, general effect' (Reid in Logue 2001: xii). In performance, the presence of a huge cinema screen, the constant rhythmic and musical underscoring of the action, and the placement and movement of sound within the auditorium served to orient and re-orient us within the ever-evolving perceptual and imaginative field of the event. In each of the four parts of the marathon performance the screen offered a single slow pan across a Welsh landscape devoid of overt human presence. This almost imperceptibly shifting landscape gestured towards an everyday 'outside', against which the text, the actions of the performers and the presence of the audience 'inside' were juxtaposed (see Figure 8.2).

*Iliad* was structured as multiple simultaneously and continuously available tracks of activity. These included the vocality of the speakers, the labour of the constructors, the musical scoring, the projections and the pre-recorded performances of the gods – played by teenagers – which were displayed on the flat screen televisions. Operating durationally, the parameters and behaviours for each of these tracks were established from the very beginning of the performance and then operated in a remarkably consistent fashion throughout. While the text offered a sense of sequential narration through the constant recitation of Logue's *War Music*, the performance itself constructed a narrative architecture in which the text was only one element. As a spectator, I found myself situated within an associative framework of meanings that communicated connotatively in an unstable and unpredictable fashion as I navigated it (see Coates 2012: 15). The dramaturgy of *Iliad* denied me a fixed position outside and opposite the performance, instead implicating me within a shifting space-time composition in which the spoken text and its violent roiling imagery of battle was encountered as a visceral pulsing force, assaulting my ears and impacting my body. Across the duration of the marathon performance the physical and mental effort to stay with the work, and to endure its sheer relentlessness, became ever more pronounced.

**Figure 8.2** Audience and performers in *Iliad* (National Theatre Wales, Llanelli, 2015). Photo courtesy of Hide the Shark/National Theatre Wales.

In their programme note for *Iliad*, Mike Brookes and Mike Pearson stated that the production's unifying concept was to construct

> a combination of performers and projections and sounds and architectures and behaviours organized in time and space that together resembles a 'theatre machine' – the mechanism that embodies war music as Iliad. (Brookes and Pearson 2015: 3)

This metaphor of the 'theatre machine' emerged during their production of *The Persians* and has subsequently served as a central dramaturgical and conceptual conceit in *Coriolan/us* and *Iliad*. Through their use of the metaphor Pearson and Brookes have sought to conceptualize the operation and functioning of the entire theatre event in its totality as an apparatus of appearance while also attending to the multiple operations within it. This figures the theatrical event as a hybrid mix of interdependent elements and operations, encompassing not only those related to production, but also the spectator and processes of reception. The metaphor of the 'scene as machine' has, of course, been a key conceptual driver of scenographic innovation in the theatrical avant-garde of the twentieth century, placing an emphasis on 'the inner mechanics of the place of performance rather than surface and pictorial detail' (Baugh 2005: 47), and focusing attention on the architectural void of the stage rather than on the creation of pictorial illusion. Pearson and Brookes draw implicitly on the close association between the theatre, machinery and spatiality and the way in which theatre buildings have long functioned as 'building-machines', their stage machinery providing the structure and framework for the construction of the theatrical scene. The concrete manifestation of theatrical machinery reflects the machinic nature of theatrical representation itself and its reliance on the configuration of different spaces to produce appearance.

For Brookes, the machine metaphor reflects a fundamentally structural conception of the theatre event, organized through the establishment of 'parameters' and 'infrastructures' (Filmer 2015). Through these Brookes seeks to trace threads of material and define the behaviours of different elements, allowing for what he calls 'control with flexibility'. Rather than orchestrate specific acts or moments of significance within a linear timeframe, Brookes seeks to deploy multiple layers of simultaneous and continuously available activity, and to compose the performance from the accumulation of distinct tracks that can be actively navigated and negotiated by spectators during the event (see Brookes 2014: 13). The 'theatre machine' therefore generates and sustains a situation or event-space within which a spectator's focus can shift from one element to another across the duration of the event as they interact with it perceptually. Within this situation the interplay between location, media technologies and the performance of the dramatic or poetic text is the locus of resistance or tension as each of these elements constantly recontextualizes or remediates the other in the spectator's shifting perception. This conception of the dramaturgy of the theatre event extends the approach to large-scale architectonic site-specific performance pioneered by Pearson and Clifford McLucas with Welsh theatre company Brith Gof in the 1980s and 1990s by combining it with the intermedial and multisite techniques subsequently developed by Pearson and Brookes since they began collaborating in 1997.

The machine metaphor conceptualizes a relational and reflexive dramaturgic framework with a strongly architectural dimension. In Pearson and Brookes' hands the 'theatre machine' generates a relational narrative architecture, characterized by constancy, which a spectator inhabits for the duration of the event and navigates perceptually and cognitively. The work offers an experience that is sensorily and cognitively immersive, but within which the conditions of visibility and the shifting constructions encourage an awareness of oneself as spectator within the mise-en-scène, co-constructing the work through one's physical presence and thoughtful engagement. Similarly, the obvious presence of mediating technology – scrolling text, pre-recorded performances, vocal amplification – encourages reflection on the apparatus through which representation is produced and one's implacement within that representational apparatus.

## Concluding remarks

This brief discussion of dramaturgy and spectatorship in *Mametz* and *Iliad* suggests how architecture can serve as a productive frame for analysing and critiquing the performative dynamics of these works. Both afforded spectators opportunities to occupy or inhabit the event-structures they created, orienting them towards an encounter with, or an opportunity to reflect on, aspects of history, memory or myth. In *Mametz*, the opportunity to occupy the scene and the experience of a parallax gap between the spectating 'eye' and the perceiving 'I' was only fleeting because of its adherence to traditional dramatic logics, while the relational theatrical architecture of *Iliad* allowed a more durational inhabitation of a narrative environment as it was continually constructed and reconstructed.

The critical potential of identifying these sorts of architectural experiences in theatre and performance is that they help us think in more detail about what different theatre events do, and what can be done with them, especially at a time when theatre and performance are increasingly participative and interwoven with, or distributed through, various locations and landscapes. Importantly, they also help us conceive of theatre not just as a practice of representation, but as a site of habitation, a material site where – as in the example of TAAT's *HALL05* which opened this chapter – practical experiments in living and being can be explored.

## Notes

1  *Mametz* ran from 24 June to 5 July 2014 at Great Llancayo Upper Wood near Usk, Monmouthshire (writer Owen Sheers; director Matthew Dunster; designer Jon Bausor; lighting designer Lee Curran; sound designer George Dennis).

2  *Iliad* consisted of four two-hour parts: 'Kings', 'The Husbands', 'Red/Cold' and 'War Music'. These were each performed twice over a two-week season that ran from 21 September to 3 October 2015. An all-day 'marathon' performance of all four sections was held on 26 September and a corresponding all-night marathon on 3 October (directors Mike Pearson and Mike Brookes; composer John Hardy; costume designer Simon Banham; sound designer Mike Beer).

# 9

# Housing Acts: Performing Public Housing

David Roberts

In December 2015, Tower Hamlets Council approved plans to refurbish and privatize Balfron Tower, a twenty-six-storey high-rise of 146 flats and maisonettes built in 1965–1967 by émigré architect Ernö Goldfinger in Poplar, east London (see Figure 9.1).

In this chapter, I describe my collaborative work with the tower's current and former residents from 2013 to 2016. I draw on performance in three ways: as a mode of analysis to interrogate cultural, academic and archival material; as a method of engagement to build collective knowledge through site-specific re-enactments; and as a means of activism using this material and evidence to campaign for Balfron Tower to remain a beacon for social housing. The chapter is structured around a series of site-specific performative workshops I led with residents, re-enacting Goldfinger's unique methods of gathering empirical evidence about Balfron in 1968.[1]

Through the chapter, I expand on an emerging interdisciplinary terrain by forging new connections between, in turn, the work of architectural historian Adrian Forty, performance theorists Rebecca Schneider, Jen Harvie and Heike Roms, and architectural designer Jane Rendell. Each operates with a different site of enquiry, but the practical and ethical questions they pose proved inspirational for a collaborative project which attended to the rapidly diminishing possibility for social tenants to return to their homes. In reflecting on this project, I advance an argument that research and practice into the history and future of public housing estates must not only pay tribute to the egalitarian principles at their foundations – it must enact them.

**Figure 9.1** Balfron Tower, Rowlett Street, 1971. Photo courtesy of RIBA Library Photographs Collection.

## The chorus of failure

In 2013, I was invited by Felicity Davies, a resident of Balfron Tower, to assist her in conducting an oral history project as her neighbours were leaving their homes to make way for refurbishment works. The refurbishment was part of an urban regeneration scheme that had begun in 2008 following stock transfer of the Brownfield Estate from Tower Hamlets Council to Poplar Housing and Regeneration Community Association. The plans detailed that approximately half of Balfron Tower's 146 dwellings would be sold to cross-subsidize costly 'heritage standards' refurbishment of the Grade II listed building, which had degraded under a piecemeal approach to maintenance and repairs (LBTH 2006: 23).

However, in 2010, the housing association informed tenants of the ninety-nine socially rented households in the tower, approximately half of which had registered their intention to stay, that it was 'possible but not probable' they would have a right of return to their homes following the works, citing 'the impact of the global financial downturn' and planning setbacks on the estate as the reasons for this uncertainty (LBTH 2010: 2). Before we began working together on the project, and before I had even set foot on the estate, I searched for the tower online.

*My cursor flickers under six bright letters. If you want to know a building now, you do not actually go to the building first; you enlist the help of a search engine. BALFRON TOWER: 75,900 RESULTS. For most people, this is where the building is. RELATED SEARCHES: BALFRON TOWER SALE; BALFRON TOWER CRIME. A list of results guides me to encyclopaedias, articles, blogs and videos that sing an online chorus.*

Balfrons
The Balfron
Balfron Towers is a

big brutalist
demonic
decaying tower block in

east London
in the shadow of Canary Wharf
in the Olympic fringe, which stands

25
27
26 storeys high.

Its 145, 146 post-war flats were built
in 1963, in the 50s,
in late 60s by an architect who moved in to the tower for a week

a few weeks
a couple of months
a week or two but that was it, and left

flooded walkways
cockroaches in the concrete
and residents fuming.

He was a tall and powerful man
married to an heiress and a Marxist to boot
precisely the sort of person to have strong and arrogant views
about how to reorganize society.

The tower positively shouts his clear
but flawed view of the future:
verticality as the cure.

But why make the service tower separate?
Why make the whole lot so high and thin that it looks as if it might fall over?
I'm not proud of my next thought, but I found myself wondering
how come such a fantastic view has been wasted on the working classes and the destitute?

I was so startled by the quantity of spurious fact, dissonant opinion and rhetorical questions I discovered online that I made a performance text entirely from found phrases. The first one hundred search results argue over simple details – Balfron Tower's height, age and even name – but agree on a complex one: its failure.

Twenty years ago, architectural historian Adrian Forty (1995) reflected on some of the reasons why the architecture of the post-war period absorbs our interest and some of the things that stand in the way of our understanding it. He notes that the first, and most awkward, 'fact' faced by the historian is that it is widely considered a failure (1995: 25). This label of failure, he observes, is reserved almost exclusively for social housing schemes. Forty suggests that the mistake historians make is to look in the wrong place for the causes of this failure. Historical attention is primarily dedicated to vindicating the architects or buildings by stressing their aesthetic qualities and honourable intentions, overlooking social issues or proposing causal explanations for their failure on technical or cultural grounds (1995: 27). Forty contests that it would be better to 'examine the minds of those who judge these works' (1995: 28). We should not, he said, be troubled by whether they *actually* were a failure but that they have been *perceived* to be.

How might this chorus of online commentators have arrived at the damning conclusion of failure? To answer this, I considered the body of cultural material that performs a certain perception of the tower to the public. The most famous representations are in feature films that go beyond the typical kitchen sink dramas set in housing estates to fictive dystopian wastelands. In Danny Boyle's harrowing sci-fi horror *28 Days Later* (2002), a virus spreads to humans turning them into 'the infected', frothing zombies that scale the tower in vicious bands. In Elliott Lester's crime thriller *Blitz* (2011), Balfron stars as the home of a strutting psychotic serial killer who murders members of the police force. These films, and countless others, use Balfron as a backdrop to invariably frightening incidents. They embellish Balfron's material neglect and exploit its height and style as inherently unsafe and violent. As Charlotte Bell and Katie Beswick observe from similar dramatic and theatrical representations, they reinforce the popular belief that there is 'a correlative relationship between the council estate environment and "pathological" behaviour of estate residents' (2014: 132); in this case an architectural determinism so extreme that a brutal building might even breed brutal murderers.

Balfron's architect came to have an equally strong hold on the popular imagination. By accident of a peculiar set of circumstances that brought his exotic name to the attention of *James Bond* author Ian Fleming, Goldfinger was fated to exist as much in spy fiction as in the flesh-and-blood world of architecture (Warburton 2005). Indeed, almost every article repeats the trite contention that he provided the inspiration for Fleming's villain. The *Architects' Journal* reports, 'A large part of Goldfinger's iconic status rests on his name itself, with all its bizarrely descriptive resonance and its filmic associations with evil desires for world dominance' (Cameron 2004: 44). The other part of Goldfinger's iconic status rests on his forceful character. An imposingly tall, life-long Marxist with an unmistakable Hungarian accent, he was known for his explosive temper. The same articles associate Balfron's dramatic proportions and Goldfinger's dramatic personality with a way of life for the tower's residents that is equally stark and severe, prompting a politician to declare Balfron 'the benchmark of post-war architectural failure' and Goldfinger 'as wicked as his fictional namesake' (Golds 2013; Stungo 1991: 17). The architect stands as his creation – a terrifying, flawed tower of a man.

I came to realize how easy it is to be seduced by this dominating story; to conflate, without any available evidence to the contrary, these perceived experiences with lived ones and assume tenants have been clamouring to escape. Having dwelt in the speculative and the fictional, I too wish to escape, leaving behind the sofa strewn with popcorn kernels to enter the civilized spaces of the library and archive.

Balfron Tower has been the subject of decades of careful scholarship that recognizes its qualities of design and its social ideals as symbolic of a public-spirited collectivity largely absent today. In terms of its design, historian Bridget Cherry and colleagues (2005: 656–657) recognize 'superior quality is at once apparent' in Balfron's attention to detail and quality of materials. Its most expressive invention is to separate its 146 homes from the services (lifts, rubbish chutes and boiler room) as well as communal facilities for different age groups (laundry rooms, 'jazz-pop room' for teenagers, hobby room for older residents) in a detached circulation tower, symbolizing and generating new possibilities for communal interaction. In terms of ideals, former employee James Dunnett (1983) traces Goldfinger's 'social idealism' and 'spatial interest' to his adherence to the moral and aesthetic tenets of the Modern Movement: high-rise housing offered 'sun, space and greenery' to its urban inhabitants. Critic Owen Hatherley (2013) describes the tower as a fragment of a 'better, more egalitarian and more fearless kind of city than the ones we actually live in'. This scholarship advances a case that Balfron's social aspirations and use are an intrinsic part of its architectural heritage; moreover, it suggests that these vital qualities would be lost if the tower were to be privatized. Yet it is important to consider the views of those who have not been able to participate in these academic debates. Balfron's residents have been passed over by decades of research, an omission that does not make these accounts invalid but does make them incomplete. Scholars can justly claim the tower's distinction compared with the environmental and technical deficiencies that have afflicted other high-rise blocks. But without engaging generations of residents in discussions on Balfron's social life, persistent accusations of social unsuitability remain unchallenged. The perception of failure that Forty observed still haunts the tower.

## The sociological experiment

Davies and I began our oral history project at Balfron with one-to-one interviews to draw a more nuanced story from first-hand accounts. Her neighbours spoke frankly about the problems of living in the tower – the lack of sufficient funds for repair, unreliable lifts – as well as wider changes in the area. They also spoke eloquently of details and experiences they cherished – the well-proportioned flats, the generous sense of light and space and the importance of the view that had become vital to their sense of belonging, identity and engagement with the city. Without fail, and without prompting, every interviewee referred to the most famous resident forty-five years earlier: the architect himself.

The tower was constructed during a decade when council housing reached new peaks in provision and height, but the majority were system-built and engineer-designed, cheap and characterless, without the same invention and care in details. This prompted Goldfinger and his wife Ursula to move from their home in Hampstead to a flat at the top of the tower for its opening two months in what he termed a 'sociological experiment'. He did so to demonstrate his faith in high-rise living and to gather empirical evidence from the new tenants by speaking to them individually as well as inviting them in groups, floor by floor, to his penthouse for regular champagne parties where the Goldfingers mingled with guests, collating opinions on the new homes in notepads in order to document and remedy design issues.

Goldfinger's act generated considerable press, noted in almost every national newspaper and even reaching Chicago. He announced, 'I have created here nine separate streets, on nine different levels, all with their own rows of front doors. The people living here can sit on their doorsteps and chat to the people next door if they want to. A community spirit is still possible even in these tall blocks, and any criticism that it isn't is just rubbish' ('East End's Tallest Block of Flats Make "Ideal Homes"' 1968). Goldfinger used the building and its residents as evidence, yielding a very different narrative from that available online or on screen, and his act of research became a public performance itself. The longest-serving residents we interviewed remembered meeting Goldfinger at his parties. As our ambitions for the project developed, we became interested in how to re-stage this archival material and these conversations on-site, and brought in two other practitioners to collaborate: oral historian Polly Rogers and theatre maker Katharine Yates. Together we conceived of a series of performative workshops running in parallel with oral history interviews, re-enacting Goldfinger's empirical methods to share collective knowledge and experience. We discussed how to stage this: how to dress the room, what to serve, who else to invite, what to wear. This prompted further research, rather than relying on stereotypical descriptions of Goldfinger which, like Balfron, seemed all too one-dimensional. We attended community events and bingo afternoons to inform residents of our work and elicit their participation, inviting them to meet their neighbours of forty-five years ago.

In preparation for the events, I was drawn to performance theorist Rebecca Schneider's scholarship (2011), which investigates re-enactment as a term that has increased in circulation in art, theatre and performance circles. My interest in bringing her mode of *acting out* and *thinking through* re-enactment into my practice was twofold. First, Schneider describes how Civil War re-enactors 'play across their bodies particulars of "what really happened" gleaned from archival "evidence" such as testimony, lithographs, and photographs as a way, ironically, of "keeping the past alive"' (2011: 10). I was interested in keeping alive the sense of purpose and idealism present in Goldfinger's archives. This involved a shift from preserving documentation of the past as correct, to the suggestion that it could become script or material for future instruction. Second, 'They also engage in this activity as a way of accessing what they feel the documentary evidence upon which they rely misses – that is, live experience. Many fight not only to "get it right" as it *was* but to get it right as it *will be* in the future of the archive' (Schneider 2011: 10). I wished not only to draw inspiration from the archive but also to augment it with residents' voices today, believing that the early ideals of public housing require thoughts and activities to be embodied. I turned to performance to enact this double gesture forward and back, to scrutinize the intentions of these future ideals and historical methods in new time and space and reactivate their affective possibilities together.

## The champagne party

*A party is held for thirty guests in a two-bed flat on the top floor of Balfron Tower.*
*The rooms are dressed with an array of photographs, sketches and letters.*
*I flit from room to room acting as waiting staff, cloakroom attendant, photographer and gallery invigilator, explaining the exhibited material to guests if they enquire. As the first guests trickle in, a couple emerge from the bedroom to mingle. Ernö Goldfinger, a dark-haired man in his mid-thirties, wears a lightly striped three-piece suit and a bow-tie. His wife Ursula wears a roll-neck and A-line skirt. She pours glasses of champagne to guests, her hands clasped around the base of the bottle, concealing the label 'Tesco Cava Brut Sparkling Non-Vintage'. He holds a small dictaphone, recording conversations with guests.*

> ERNÖ    So did you live here?

> RESIDENT    Yes, 21st floor.

> ERNÖ    How was the flat?

> RESIDENT    Beautiful. I had a one-bedroom flat. I now just live in a tower over there...

> ERNÖ    I am very interested in your impressions of the building and how it was to live in.

> RESIDENT    My first impressions when I knew I had to live here and I didn't have any choice: I wanted to run away, I didn't know anything about the tower. As soon as I moved in I just totally fell in love with it, everything about it.

> ERNÖ    Why did you want to run away?

RESIDENT   It just looked like some big – I've never lived in a high rise before – big concrete thing, I hadn't known the history of it, all that.

ERNÖ   So the image of the tower was intimidating?

RESIDENT   Very intimidating and obviously that kind of – people jacking up in the stairwells – that kind of thing that you think of inner-city tower blocks, but actually I found it to be a very different experience when I moved in. It was very very friendly which I was surprized at.

ERNÖ   If you could change something about the flat?

RESIDENT   Well, it was quite old, the windows were draughty, that sort of thing I would have changed. Not a lot else really, not a lot else.

ERNÖ   Was there enough space for you?

RESIDENT   Oh plenty for one. It was beautiful. I became very, very inspired by the whole story of it. Everything sort of, something happened, and it opened up a new world to me.

In September 2013, we hosted a champagne (actually discount cava) party in a neighbouring flat to the Goldfingers' on the top floor. I scripted the dialogue of the actors playing Ernö and Ursula Goldfinger based on archival excerpts as well as other brief exchanges between the couple available in oral history recordings (see Figure 9.2). The Goldfingers mingled throughout the evening, asking current residents the same questions about their everyday experience of the tower as they did forty-five years earlier, using audio recorders rather than notepads to record conversations in a dialogue between past and present. I had dressed each room of the two-bed flat with archival material in situ: isometric sketches alongside press cuttings in the study; the many letters he had written to members of the public in the bedroom; and early photographs of the tower in the living room.

In each of the oral history interviews we conducted, residents lamented the lack of opportunities for communal interaction in the tower today. The workshop opened a social, discursive and imaginative space that brought different residents from different tenures together into one space to talk to one another. In this sense, our restaging touched on the spirit of the original endeavour; a community wasn't just re-enacted but, if only temporarily, reconstituted. There was a considerable level of engagement with the material on display. Dressing a flat that is identical to residents' homes as an archive makes it estranging and uncanny. It forced people to see their own flats differently and acted as a trigger for memories. Accompanied

**Figure 9.2** Actors playing Ernö and Ursula Goldfinger during a workshop at Balfron Tower, 2013. Photo courtesy of David Roberts.

by the informal theatricality of the actors, it created a setting where people stepped outside their daily routine into a mode of critical reflection, re-examining their estate, their flats and themselves.

The event was free, and open to all current and former residents. Without funding from cultural institutions associated with the regeneration of the area, it created a fleeting space in which residents spoke to each other freely and in their own terms about their homes and the process of regeneration. Residents engaged enthusiastically with the performative premise, telling the actor portraying Goldfinger that he was an inspiration to them or telling him off for the things that didn't work. The re-enactment encouraged comparison of the past and present on the same footprint to understand changing values and priorities then and now. As the evening progressed, the architecture became more of an active participant in the conversation, being the site and object of collaborative discussion. There were, however, barriers to participation. The live nature of the regeneration processes limited the diversity of participants by privileging those who were still present in the building at that time, and the use of a single language impacted on our ability to encourage Bangladeshi and Somali residents to engage in our workshops.

Critical reflection on that first event was useful in highlighting a range of tenants' responses to the past and future of the estate and revealing a potential problem with the project. When I listened back to the recordings, I witnessed how knowledgeable the residents were about the process of refurbishment and the design and quality of their homes. Despite this, they bemoaned the lack of clarity and certainty about the regeneration and their own place within it. One former resident said:

> On the 23rd floor we felt magnificent. I think for social housing tenants to lose the view is such a terrible theft of experience. You live in the space in a different way. It affects your being. And that's critical to your entire existence. And for poorer folk like myself it's a great loss.

I also reflected on the fact that some of the residents had described the evening as a release, providing relief from the frustration about the regeneration plans that they had felt in recent years. But as I learnt more about their shared anger at the potential privatization, I worried about the catharsis my work could entail. I was reminded of an interview in which Theatre of the Oppressed director Augusto Boal proclaims: 'I don't want people to use the theatre as a way of not doing in real life' (Taussig et al. 1990: 60). This echoed my concern about whether this workshop had diffused anger that would otherwise be taken into the next meeting with the housing association or channelled into constructive protest. To address the political and practical issues this raised, I returned to performance, and to theorists Jen Harvie and Heike Roms.

## The Tenants' Association meeting

Harvie's monograph *Fair Play: Art, Performance and Neoliberalism* (2013) was written in response to the recent proliferation of performance and art practices that engage audiences socially by inviting them to participate, act, create or simply be together. These practices raise important questions, including 'what they say about contemporary culture, what they can actually do for audiences, and what they can offer contemporary social relations' (Harvie 2013: 1). Harvie identifies how well-meaning engaged artists working in formerly working-class areas can, albeit unintentionally, exclude resident populations and, even worse, contribute to the marketing and colonizing of urban spaces in ways that risk breaking up local social networks and moving people physically and economically into greater deprivation.[2] However, Harvie also outlines the tactics of artist-activists who critically reflect on their own implication in processes of regeneration and gentrification to reclaim space for less advantaged communities and model modes of engagement that challenge forces of segregation (2013: 136).

I asked myself the same questions that Harvie (2013: 2) poses in relation to the social efficacy of art, architecture and performance practices; specifically, how could my practice help understand forthcoming changes at Balfron and their effects on social relations, as well as protect and extend the equality of these relations? It seemed essential to make public the emotional consequences of regeneration experienced by the tower's outgoing community of residents. I became interested in creating a collective platform in subsequent workshops to directly interrogate current regeneration plans. In this instance, I would use engaged practice not to distract from or wallpaper over social conflict but to expose it.

If Harvie warned of the treacherous path into engaged practice in neoliberal times, Roms offered clear methodological tools to help. For her project *What's Welsh for Performance? Beth yw 'performance' yn Gymraeg?* (2014), Roms conducted a series of oral history interviews with artists, breaking with the convention of conducting interviews as one-to-one conversations in the intimacy of private, domestic settings. She proposes the oral history interview itself performs as a scene of historical evidence, and can be regarded as an instance of site-specific performance (Roms and Edwards 2011: 176–177). As such, Roms stages conversations in different ways to generate different insights, from interviews with public audiences to re-enactments in original locations drawing on documentation as prompts.

I had already begun to gather residents in-situ around archival and academic texts, but Roms offered more focus on the embodied and dialogic dimensions of this act. From her work I could develop new ways to stage archival material and conversations. As Roms attended to her historical research, she increasingly engaged in archival practices herself, 'cast into the role of a custodian' as people placed material in her hands and trusted her to care for their legacy (Roms 2013: 39). In doing so, she also drew my attention to another responsibility in these performative workshops: how could I care for the legacy of Balfron's public housing?

*Two dozen people and a baby sit around a large aged oak table, its curled ironwork legs too ornate for the vinyl flooring of the community centre. Darts boards are partially obscured by scattered images of Balfron Tower. In one corner sits the barman, drawn out behind his dark wood bar by a discussion of his former home, but reluctant to leave its side; protecting it, not from this group of residents with whom he is familiar, but from the besuited man portraying Ernö Goldfinger, and us, his colleagues facilitating the discussion.*

*Having introduced ourselves, Felicity, Katharine, Polly and I ask residents to recite twice from the sheets we have handed out, comprised entirely of residents' words we have gathered in interviews and events. The first time we read every line together like a church congregation. The second time, we ask residents to only read the words with which they agree.*

When they showed me Balfron I said, oh ain't it lovely.
Like islands in the Mediterranean catching the sun.
I was watching it being built and I thought then what a mess.

Imposing.
Architects think it's a marvellous thing but it's just another building to me.
A bit brutal, scary, but kinda nice.

There ought to be more lifts.
Like a battery chicken in a box.
I wouldn't change it for Buckingham Palace.

It's much more like a street than a typical tower.
There was such a friendship.
Where are the meeting spaces?

The view is gorgeous, I'll miss that.
The sunrise in the morning waking you up.
Why do they want to make so many zombie films here?

The horizon is closing in.
The little bits of this area that make it like London will probably be eroded away.
If Goldfinger was still alive he would listen to people living here. Ernö would listen.

Our final workshop was held at the community centre at the foot of the tower in March 2014. We used the occasion to announce that the RIBA board had approved our proposal to add our work to their Goldfinger collection, updating their records with decades of residents' lived experience. We had chosen to perform this construction of evidence with the intention of making the subjectivity and staging of it explicit. This was reinforced by the act of reciting, which invited residents to act individually and to reassess their words in concert with others, in an exercise borrowed from the art collective Freee's Manifesto Choir. In only reading the attributes they agreed with and falling silent at other times, residents' participation is restricted to agreeing with others or remaining silent (Freee 2010: 80).

The event re-enacted an occasion when Goldfinger attended an early Tenants' Association meeting but, according to the archival record, contributed to the agenda only once, letting the residents share their thoughts openly and without interruption. The actor playing Goldfinger returned to recount his solitary line and it then opened to a group discussion between this community of outgoing residents who shared emotive stories and opinions, particularly about the renovation and decant of the tower, as they negotiated the array of archival material available around the room and on tables.

To fit with the enactment of a Tenants' Association meeting, and because of the sensitive nature of regeneration, we drew up an agenda of topics to discuss. Throughout the discussion we acted as facilitators, seeking individual responses, but also remaining aware that the timing of this event (during the regeneration process) would shape the content and scope of discussion. I came to realize how much of the proposed privatization had escaped media, cultural, intellectual and resident scrutiny, in part because of the difficulty of accessing and understanding material related to these complex and contested processes of change. This chimed with the experience of other campaign groups in London where information had been withheld or legislative definitions invoked ambiguously to cover a chasm between the promises and the realities of social housing provision (Wainwright 2015). Although it was late in the regeneration process, if there was still a potential opportunity to intervene and protect the provision of social housing in Balfron Tower, as so strongly desired by current tenants and essential to its original principles and purpose, then inaction, to me, seemed unethical.

## The campaign

The processes of regeneration that had begun during my engagement with residents accelerated in the year leading up to the submission of the refurbishment proposals that would transform the character and tenure of Balfron Tower. As tenants and I feared, these would usher in the privatization of Balfron's ninety-nine homes on social rent. The design approach to the regeneration appropriated and commodified Goldfinger's vision and ideals as a cultural cache to be marketed, instead of principles and homes to preserve: 'We want to invoke Goldfinger's original optimistic spirit and sensitively refurbish Balfron Tower to be a shining exemplar of contemporary living again, this time for the 21st century' (Studio Egret West 2015: 18).

Before I turn to the actions I took leading up to the release of these plans, I wish to introduce the final theorist from which I drew inspiration. In her praxis of site-writing, architectural designer and historian Jane Rendell suggests the critic always takes up a position to art objects, architectural spaces and theoretical ideas, and that this needs to be made explicit through the process of writing. She argues that such a project involves 'rethinking some of the key terms of criticism, specifically judgement, discrimination, and distance' (Rendell 2008: 83; see also Rendell 2010, 2017). By repositioning the work of criticism itself as a site, 'site-writing' investigates the site of the critic's engagement. 'Rather than write *about* the work', Rendell proposes, 'I am interested in how the critic constructs his or her writing in relation *to* and in dialogue *with* the work. The focus on the preposition here allows a direct connection to be made between the positional *and* the relational' (Rendell 2008: 83).

Over the course of my research, and in unanticipated alignment with it, the focus of Rendell's praxis has moved further and deeper into the history and future of public housing in London. A key move on Rendell's part is to locate the political imperative at the heart of public housing; how Modernist ideals 'of social community and progress' in the post-war period, providing housing based on need, have been driven out by successive governments promoting the ideology of home-ownership, and imposing a market-based housing model (Rendell 2015). She asks, 'What does it mean, now, to turn back and examine these icons of modernism at an early moment – a spring time – when hope for a better future was not viewed as a naïvely misjudged optimism?' (2011: 127). Rendell posits 'precisely because an aspiration for social change remains [...] we are being presented, continuously, with an image of modernism as a project, which has collapsed – this is the myth-making of a capitalist ideology' (2011: 127–128).

Like Rendell, I wished to draw attention to how these development partners have personally and ideologically addressed public housing in their site of writing. I, too, wished to address my anger at the loss of public housing and question how my work could feed into legislative processes. In this ethos, I embarked on a long-term campaign working at the service of fearless and tireless local groups Balfron Social Club and Tower Hamlets Renters – to preserve social housing in the tower, drawing on documentary evidence from our work to reassert architecture's performative, political and social dimensions.

In August 2014, over a year before the planning application was submitted, I assisted James Dunnett in writing a Grade II* listing upgrade nomination to try and safeguard the estate's original design and designation as social housing (Dunnett 2014). The principles and grounds of our argument explicitly emphasized the importance of Balfron's social context as integral to the vision and function of the building and as an intrinsic part of its architectural heritage. Dunnett produced a rigorous history of the tower which I accompanied with a supplementary document devoted to residents' experiences gathered from performative events to identify the aspects of the building they cherished (see Figure 9.3). I also produced an online archive in the hope that access to the full range of information on the history and future of the tower would enable the regeneration process to be subject to the force of public scrutiny (Roberts 2014). I collaborated with designer Duarte Carrilho da Graça to make *www. balfrontower.org* – an impossibly tall tower of 120 documents spanning five decades.

Tower Hamlets' Development Committee met to consider the planning application in December 2015. By this time, Historic England and the Culture

**Figure 9.3** Workshop with residents at Balfron Tower, 2013. Photo courtesy of David Roberts.

Minister had ratified our upgrade to Grade II*, recognizing the social ideals and purpose of the tower as a key component of its heritage (Historic England 2015). I had been driven by the conviction that if all the empirical and historical evidence from archives and our performances was presented alongside relevant policy, guidance and precedent, councillors could not help but demand accountability for their socially housed constituents and demand a more informed approach to heritage. Devastatingly, and unanimously, the vote to refurbish and privatize passed.

## Concluding remarks

Balfron Tower represents a microcosm of what, at the beginning of my three years of work with residents, was described as the 'housing question', then 'housing crisis', and now 'housing catastrophe' gripping London. It is a story of loss at all scales: personal loss of home as estates are sold-off or demolished; a collective loss of our neighbours as low-income communities diminish and disappear from London; and a societal loss of ideals both in what these homes stood for and also the type of city in which we want to live.

Facing this loss, I asked what recovery might look like. Interdisciplinarity was key to the creation of engaged practice, interleaving oral history gathering and telling, architectural historiography, archival research, applied performance and political activism. I turned increasingly from architecture to performance to develop a robust and constructive methodological approach to questions of dwelling, redevelopment and housing crisis. I used collaborative methods of engaged practice not to distract from social issues at the heart of regeneration but to expose them through discussions around critical material. Our re-enactment of Goldfinger's methods during his 'sociological experiment' and restaging of this material acted as a prompt to bring residents together, share knowledge as peers and establish a dialogue of trust.

We have a duty to put our work at the service of those whose lives we seek to improve. Maintaining an ongoing relationship with buildings and their users is all-too-often overlooked by architects and academics today. Encouraging more playful and unusual ways of engaging residents with their homes can help us to better understand the spatial relations that architecture and policy constructs. Social and lived aspects of the built environment are not only valid but vital in oral history and architecture writing. Making residents' testimonies about life at Balfron Tower was important. Their experiences challenge overwhelmingly negative cultural and media representations that distort understanding.

By sharing documentation of these performances we contributed to a more informed public debate and fed this evidence into legislative frameworks. Our campaign neither reinforced stereotypical images of housing estates nor hid their faults. Instead it displayed the liveliness, diversity and vibrancy of this estate community. In doing so, it advanced an argument for the continued and urgent need for public housing as these communities and the qualities they bring to London are diluted or dispersed.

## Notes

1    I have written elsewhere in more length about my research into Balfron Tower as part of my broader interest in the past and future of east London housing estates undergoing regeneration (see Roberts 2017).

2    There is a vital, parallel story of the strategic use of cultural activity at Balfron Tower to maximize financial value which writer Feargus O'Sullivan (2014) has labelled 'artwashing'. The implications of this have been critically and urgently exposed by artist and former resident Rab Harling and campaign group Balfron Social Club (2015).

# 10

# Double Visions: Architectural Models in Performance

Natalie Rewa

*If architecture is a veritable genre of space creation, then the model is functional. If architecture serves to stabilize, reinforce and build up the structure of the real, models can be understood as the architecture of the imaginary. If architecture can structure our sense of reality, models can loosen and disrupt that structure – revealing the freedom that we have.*

Topalovic 2011: 38

In architectural design, models have assumed several significant purposes: the most publicly evident are the exhibition models that appear in many urban centres as part of a now familiar material vocabulary miniaturizing large projects. In the architectural atelier, models serve as a mode of research, testing materials and design hypotheses, and elsewhere architectural historians turn to detailed models to study unrealized projects which may exist only in archival drawings. In design for performance, scale models have often been part of the process of pragmatic dialogue between a scenographer and a director, and later as part of an orientation for the cast. In this chapter, I consider the dramaturgical contribution effected by the presence, and often by the onstage assembly, of an architectural model as an active element *within* performance. Practical engagement with a scale model, rather than an adaptation of a ready-made object, or a two-dimensional pictorial or projected depiction, acknowledges a distinct scale in relation to actorly presence and animates the 'traffic of the stage'. Such models instantiate a kind of knowledge within the performance that invites active analysis of the event-space. In effect, the model by its rhetoric of scale remains autonomous, but by virtue of its assembly and manipulation becomes a kinaesthetic presence which introduces a lively interplay of associations; as an object on the stage the model takes up immediate space, while at the same time it spatializes a concept that might not be actually realized by or within the performance. By maintaining this double focus as integral to the performance, the model on stage multiplies the possibilities of performance by augmenting the *modalität*, the manner of seeing, in the enclosed space of the stage.

Models have been singled out within the architectural design process for their three-dimensional materiality in contradistinction to two-dimensional perspectival drawings and plans. In the late 1960s, Marcial Echenique reinvigorated the discussion of the typologies of architectural models according to *their* design and conceptualization in response to distinct functions; he emphasized how aspects of their three-dimensionality serve as a form of exploration. His taxonomy begins by drawing attention to the model as it describes, predicts, explores or investigates an architectural feature within a planning process. His second category concerns the proposed emphasis on the use of materials or the development of concepts and testing materials as iconic or analogous. The third aspect, perhaps the most relevant to performance, concerns the manner in which the model establishes static or dynamic temporal relationships (Echenique 1970: 27–30). Such miniaturization of a project has long been recognized for its contribution to appreciating a comprehensive perspective, specifically as it establishes an autonomous exhibition value for the model aiming to identify context (see the inquiry into models as autonomous objects in Jacobs 1958: 106–111, 196), at the same time, these same qualities have also been recognized as integral to a critical discourse of architectural design. The exhibit *Idea as Model* in 1976 under the auspices of the Institute for Architecture and Urban Studies in New York City featured various kinds of models by twenty-two architects as conceptual and artistic expression and probed metaphysical questions of architecture that emerge in a material form (see Frampton and Kolbowski 1981; see also Busch 1991; Morris 2006). Subsequently, the exhibition 'Modernism in Miniature: Points of View' (2011–2012) at the Canadian Centre for Architecture in Montreal looked back at Modernism's distinct relationship between architectural models as objects and as the subject for architectural photography between 1920 and 1960. The artefacts and images rephrased the question regarding two-dimensional representation by probing the mechanical reproducibility of architectural design and how we have come to see architecture. The energy of exhibiting a materialization of a concept as performative as well as visual is evident in performances which use architectural models; in these instances models architecturally rephrase the dramaturgy of the architecture as they remap cultural relationships.

Locating architectural models beyond the atelier, gallery or museum has thrust them into the centre of debates regarding public space. While models in a condominium sales office coax desire from prospective customers, models of large urban projects reimagine shared spaces and often elicit strong engagement. In March 1992, the models of the three finalists for the new Vancouver Library Square were anonymously exhibited in the City Hall, in the existing library and at a shopping mall with a questionnaire regarding preferences. Of the 7,000 questionnaires returned (only 500 were initially printed), Moshe Safdie's model captured the public imagination, to the consternation of architectural pundits. Respondents reacted to the bold proposal that would provide their city with a new and distinct library reminiscent of a Roman colosseum with its interlocking elliptical shapes, bordered on one side by a seven-storey urban room, with colosseum-like window openings, and a green roof. Similarly, the model for what would become Toronto's first opera house since the nineteenth century was exhibited over several seasons (2003–2006), and it represented architect Jack Diamond's promise of superior acoustic quality by showing the continental (horse-shoe) configuration of the house. It was a material response to patrons' greatest complaint regarding the limitations of the current municipal facility. So the performativity of the architectural model, in itself, needs also to be taken into account in this discussion.

Bradley Starkey argues that models productively challenge the privileging of architectural drawings as an intellectual 'equivalent to the process of writing, doing mathematics or philosophising' (2005: 266). He proposes that while drawings offer an undeniably durable record of an architectural design, the potential to explore the functionality of architectural details materially shifts the focus of a model to an 'ideological performance' (265). Modelling the phenomena of the mechanisms of the architectural programmes not only investigates kinaesthetic structures but also, as John Monk observes, engages the observer in processes of cognition that serve as 'triggers' to elicit an explanation (1998: 40). Such investigatory reduction of a larger project plays out the relationships of the components, and, moreover, makes material the abstractions of a theoretical position. The details that guide model making illuminate the 'grammar of accounts of what can happen' (Monk 2012: 3). This act of translation or animation is germane to my discussion.

As production design, an architectural model evokes an analogous narrative by its scale and becomes an ineluctable element of the visual and spatial dramaturgy. The miniaturization intrudes on a geometral vision by reorienting spectating simultaneously in three scales of magnitude. Initially, a model appears as an object on the stage that takes up a role between set and prop, with the potential to renegotiate the physical flow of the narrative. The arrival of a model on stage brings it into a second level of spectatorship, since it necessitates a distinct form of behaviour, often labour, a ceremonial effort or choreography to assemble the stage environment. Moreover, its location becomes an event that draws attention to the differently meaningful interaction with non-human elements as an 'association between entities which are in no way recognizable as being social in the ordinary manner, except during the brief moment when they are reshuffled together' (Latour 2005: 64). Qualities of a model potentially link it to recognizable structures and demonstrate a desire to apprehend a cultural entity. In performance, such fleeting moments trigger the need for explanation that John Monk notes. Finally, once assembled, situated or placed on the stage the architectural model contests a social-cultural context that is a purely human 'landscape' of the stage. Once the stage environment assumes the qualities of an experimental space, social relationships can be mediated through objects rather than exclusively human characters, so that even when directly referred to in the mise-en-scène the architectural models disrupt mechanisms of performance.

Bernard Tschumi's early confrontation of the limitations of modelling spaces in two dimensions in his *Manhattan Transcripts* (1976–1981) is helpful to this discussion. He challenged the diagrammatic quality of architectural drawings in contradistinction to the fluidity of human motion. His spatial scenarios propose to re-evaluate an architectural interpretation of place and space by presenting ground plans and photographs that either direct or 'witness' events (architectural 'functions' or 'programmes'). Running counter to these designated functions are the traces of the movements of the 'protagonists' who follow their own narrative which intrudes upon the order of the architectural 'stage set'. As Tschumi migrates through Henri Lefebvre's triad of perceived, conceived and lived spaces of the twentieth-century city, his emphasis on the latter becomes a theatrical nexus of modes of being and persons. For his part, Tschumi explores architectural programmes here and in his practice, as delving into forms of knowledge and not simply a knowledge of forms (Tschumi 1990: 88). Attention to 'event-spaces' accommodate as yet unplanned social interactions; they are the liminal zones of shared spaces that link architectural form to social relevance.

The use of architectural models in performance takes this energy of the form of knowledge of spaces that is present in an architectural model and introduces it into the stage space with all *its* accompanying programmes, but now held up for inspection within the parameters of human choreographies.

The potential to intervene in a performance recasts the architectural model as dynamic and encourages inquiry as to *how* models contain information, of what kind, and how they are animated and animate. In this discussion, I show the expansion of the manner of seeing in three productions which make extensive use of performing *with* an architectural model as a component of their dramaturgical architectonics. Crucially, these models conceptualize the aspirational processes of creating a built environment, rather than accepting its inevitability. The first example is introduced as a mnemonic device – a memory palace – by Robert Lepage in *887* (premiered in 2015); the model is of 887 Murray Avenue in Quebec City, where his family inhabited apartment five when he was a child. This model is narrativized as part of his effort to memorize 'Speak White', a seminal poem by Michèle Lalonde, for a national commemorative event in 2014. The materiality of this model is juxtaposed with the yet more miniaturized and capacious digital memory enabled by the screen of his cell phone. Switching between the two devices enacts a syncopated rhythm between the specificity of the architectural spatial language and the generalized sense of knowledge and acts of memorialization. The second example is taken from Canadian designer Michael Levine's architectural *leitmotiv* for the first full production of *Der Ring des Nibelungen* by Richard Wagner produced by the Canadian Opera Company in its new house. Levine was the production designer for the complete *Cycle*, collaborating with the three different directors and debuting as a director with *Das Rheingold* in the autumn of 2006. Levine designates this model as a significant 'player', a prescient presence woven into the four operas; its first appearance and its assembly onstage mightily refocuses spectatorial attention on a Valhalla that is *the* catalyst to the dramatic tensions, so that by the final opera its fragments exhibit the highly affecting fascination with 'ruins' of once monumental social perspectives. Finally, my last example will be from *Me on the Map* created by Adrienne Wong and Jan Derbyshire under the aegis of Neworld Theatre in Vancouver (2013–2015). This is a participatory urban planning event for young audiences during which the youthful participants are confronted with a professionally built architectural model that proposes unforeseen land use by a developer which would, on the one hand, solve the financial woes of their own plans for a happy city they have created for the site, but on the other, require compromises.

## Lepage's memory palace in *887*

The premise for *887* is Lepage's fascination with his difficulty to memorize Michèle Lalonde's landmark poem 'Speak White' for the fortieth anniversary of her recitation at *La Nuits de la poèsie*. Lalonde's text, written in 1968, invokes the rhetoric of racial oppression as analogous to the treatment of the Québécois under federal policies of bilingualism that effectively reinforced the currency of the English language and its cultural landmarks.[1] Lepage co-opts the architectural model as *his* rallying monument of the colloquial and his paean to his father as a marker of bilinguality. He uses his cell phone to locate 887 Murray Avenue on Google Maps and to provide a diagram of the human brain cortices where memory resides, and later uses its camera to capture brief sequences analogous to the fluidity of memory, which allow flow between temporal zones.

The model presents 887 Murray Avenue as a large structure on stage right; it becomes a flexible modular unit similar to those used in other shows by Lepage – the shoe boxes and booth in *The Dragon's Trilogy* (1987) and the mid-stage structure in *Seven Streams of the River Ota* (1994–1996) – and like a Piscatorian *praktikabel*;[2] it is used as a screen for selected projected images and is opened up in sections to reveal otherwise-scaled environments. Lepage

**Figure 10.1**  *887* (Ex Machina, Toronto, 2015, dir. Robert Lepage). Photo courtesy of Érick Labbé/Ex Machina.

introduces it to the spectators as a curbside view to show video scenarios of each of the eight apartments; metonymically the cultural and linguistic reality of Quebec City. By contrast, the poignant sequences follow a rotation of the model to arrive at his observation post of his father at the backdoor to the parking lot and the adjacent alley. In this quasi-private space, he disturbs a purely static view of the past captured in the model by the intervention of the traces and gestures of his father. A miniature black sedan car becomes the mode to remember specific traits of his father – the taxi is 'driven' (drawn) across the stage en route to a call, and a small red light in its interior signals his father's cigarette in its dark interior as he sits listening to French cover tunes, and the original English music on the car radio – either waiting for a call or as a refuge from the noise of the family home. From this vantage point, Lepage narrates a lived and sonic Québécois experience that he uses to fuel Lalonde's rhetoric, as private not publicly generalized experience.

For his own reality, Lepage rotates and opens up one end of the model, extending its sides to remake a portable set representing partial spaces in his chic condominium (hallway, kitchen and den). But what at first appears to allow for a spatial closure and thus a temporal one by the model as the remembered context (see Stewart 1993: 48) is contested by his narration that keeps both spaces in play visually. In a sequence ostensibly taking place in his condo library, he describes the reassignment of rooms in the apartment at 887 to accommodate his grandmother by 'replacing' a shelf of books in sections to become a latitudinal – cross-sectional – passage through the rooms of the apartment ranged across the span of a bookshelf. Similarly, elsewhere in the production, Lepage embodies the memory of his father's small acts of resistance reinforcing local initiatives against oppressive federalist policies. Wearing his father's driver's cap, he silently 'animates' the life-size fragment of an abandoned 1960s diner most crucially by unceremoniously rearranging the letters of the vocabulary of separatism into simple diner signage for fast food.

The scale of the model and the cell phone's camera coalesce in Lepage's staging of a seminal moment in Québécois nationalism. Lepage stages this sequence in the scale of the architectural model but brings the video animating it into the purview of his cell phone, unlike the initial introduction of the apartment building. A large table spans the stage to stand in for the Grande Allée along which French president Charles De Gaulle's motorcade passed in 1967, with scaled figurines representing the crowd lining the route skirting the historically significant Plains of Abraham.[3] The audience witnesses the view as *from* the motorcade *seeing* the crowds, as Lepage affixes his cell phone to the presidential limousine to see the crowds. Lepage uses the scale of the model to interpellate the crowds, and not the visiting president, as the focus so that he makes active the 'commemorative markers – the names of parks, streets, stelae and monuments – and the historical heritage around us that we no longer notice' ('*887*' 2015).

These vocabularies of modelling solve, in a material manner, the complexity of merging the social heteroglossia of the period with the double-voicedness of Lepage's memory (Bakhtin 1981: 326). While the model serves as a mnemonic device for Lepage, for the spectators it assists in a gestural ventriloquism; the scale of the model animates the expression of the coexistence of an authorial 'I' as an integral player in a Bakhtinian heteroglossia. The model establishes a grammar of possibilities from which 'the voice of the author, the voice of the performer, and the voice of the characters are simultaneously diversified and intertwined' (Meerzon 2015: 291).

## Doubling Valhalla for Levine's *Das Rheingold*

Michael Levine's production design and mise-en-scène employs a model to reassemble social processes within Richard Wagner's tetralogy as it becomes the nexus for performance energy that addresses ideological shifts. The model designed by Michael Levine for *Das Rheingold* becomes the material manifestation of a *leitmotiv* of Valhalla that is first ceremoniously assembled in the interlude between the first and second scene of the first of the four operas. This architectural model of the home for the gods, as envisioned by Levine (as designer)/Wotan (as character), is an assemblage consisting of almost two dozen units. Temples, colonnaded wings and other elements are brought on stage and ceremoniously assembled during the few minutes of the introduction and development of the Valhalla theme. A silent chorus of male attendants, dressed as late-nineteenth-century black-suited workers, roll into position nine black rectangular tables on which they place the components of the gleaming white, superbly detailed scale model. Levine's design thrusts Wotan's project for Valhalla into the immediate thematic foreground of the staging, distinct from many other designers who maintain the nuances of Wagner's didascalia that introduces a castle bathed in the glowing rays of the dawn, seen across the valley of the Rhine.[4]

The assembly of the model engenders a material dramaturgical architectonics. Stylistically, the model is a complex composite of neoclassical features. Not surprisingly, the details for the model point to historical instances of neoclassical epic redesign of cities coincident with social revolution. The monumentality of the model evokes the designs for magnificent civic monuments by Etienne-Louis Boullée (1728–1799) for revolutionary Paris, as well as Vienna's Imperial Forum (1873) of imposing Roman proportions by Gottfried Semper (1803–1879), Wagner's artistic collaborator and fellow revolutionary from his days in Dresden in the 1840s. Levine's choice of a maquette (as opposed to drawings which might have suggested these earlier examples) resonates with the white architectural model of a re-envisioned Berlin created by Albert Speer for Hitler in the 1930s, a project recorded in notorious photos showing Hitler poring over the scale model in an architectural atelier. An imperious theatricality epitomizes the overall grandeur of Levine's Valhalla conceptualization, including the arrival of the final element, a ponderous ceremony in which the imposing central section with a large dome is lowered from the flies on four chains to the waiting attendants. Now the completed model for Valhalla evokes the architectural marvel of Speer's model for the Nazi Kuppelhalle, or Great Hall. Such careful attention to monumentality links Wotan's project for domestic architecture to a much more far-reaching invasive social programme.

Significantly, even the miniaturized monumentality of the completed model consumes the stage with its placement and its striking symmetry: it could hardly

**Figure 10.2** *Das Rheingold* (Canadian Opera Company, Toronto, 2006, dir. Michael Levine). Photo courtesy of Gary Beechey.

be any wider and still fit within the given stage space, which is thus defined, for the scenic occasion, as an architectural atelier. This is the site at which the promised Valhalla is envisioned in its totality by Wotan, giants, gods and spectators also, while another structure shielded from direct view by scaffolding and construction curtains remains unacknowledged upstage. Levine completes this sequence by focusing on Wotan, seen in profile, in a similar shaft of light to that striking the descending cupola, but behind a scrim as he traverses the scaffolding on the façade of the almost completed Valhalla, upstage of the model. A crossfade between the two areas of the stage presages the 'trade' involved in the creation of Valhalla. It is not surprising that Fricka discovers Wotan asleep in an area midway between these two events. This near oneiric staging presents Wotan as suspended between the model and the building site with an 'illusion of mastery, of time into space and heterogeneity into order' (Stewart 1993: 171). This sequence of assembly and view of the reconfigured stage triggers witnessing of additional ideological shifts.

This visible transformation by Levine of the stage space into Wotan's atelier is a liminal moment when the innocence and fluid environment of the Rhinemaidens is replaced by Wotan's clearly defined ambitious construction; while the model is emblematic of transcendent aspirations, even in its miniature scale it reorients the energy of the stage space. Levine highlights the concomitant social reverberations simultaneously with the assembly of the model mid-stage, as he presents the recostuming of the Rhinemaidens along the downstage edge of the stage. This act of transformation is all the more significant since the Rhinemaidens are not normally on stage in this scene – at least there are no voice parts or stage directions to signal their inclusion. Their new costumes not only obliterate the Rhinemaidens' white silk shifts of the previous scene, they transform them into the sociocultural Victorian likenesses of the dressers. The now historicized Rhinemaidens thus become aligned with the onstage women (including Fricka and Freia) who are all now absorbed into the current of power being exerted to realize the Valhalla project; they assume a custodial role in Wotan's atelier as they retreat to their stations around the model to ensure its safety.

The assembled model also animates the contractual negotiation between Wotan and the giants. The model remains 'geometrically' intact until Freia disturbs it, as she runs in to ask for her sister's help, and it is finally pushed out of shape as the giants Fasolt and Fafner make their violent entry to confront Wotan. They assert their indifference, even contempt, for the carefully ordered arrangement that they have wrought. They destroy the symmetry designed to fulfil the desires of their client: Levine forces the clash of these two orders spatially and symbolically. Here, the relation between the model, its creators who remain indifferent to all but the price, and their client, whose yearning it will realize, is scenographically figured in such a way as to bring out the historical, political and social resonances of the mythical action. Wagner's own promotion of social revolution that would enable theatre to proceed beyond the 'tempting exhibition of the heterogeneous wares of art manufacture' (Wagner 1964: 38) is powerfully figured in the model – in its style, its size and placement, its assemblage and violent disassembly.

Levine's conceptualization of the giants at their entrance initiates an important interplay of persons and objects, without resorting to visual perspective. The giants are assemblages no less than the model: each giant is composed of seven men, the singer held aloft within a composite of dancers and extras. As the giants confront Wotan, their choreography deposits them on the tables that have been used for the model, as if onto platform stages. Standing next to parts of the model, they clearly demonstrate an alternative to Wotan's relationship to Valhalla; the model becomes an active arbiter of scale and proportion. This animating effect is immediate and demands a reconsideration of any oversimplified view of the giants as misshapen grotesque beings merely incidental to Wotan's larger plan. Levine's scenography offers a searing dynamic imagery of Wotan's ambitions and its implications as the connections between the two Valhalla structures are made as a harsher and more historical ironical vision than that of Wagner's rainbow bridge.

For the spectators, Levine presents an instance of morphogenesis of the 'emergence and evolution of form' (Kwinter 2001: 4). The prominence of the scale model creates an event-space into which Levine brings an essential 'objective element of form' (Malevich [1928] 1971: 11) around which activity coalesces to reveal otherwise 'invisible dynamic processes' (Kolarevic 2005: 199). In Levine's direction, the model takes on a role as a system of relay, without an imperative for a sustainable relationship in the way it figures social ties 'with completely different shape and figures' (Latour 2005: 80). By the final scene of the tetralogy when the fragments of the model are brought onto the stage, it is into a very different landscape; their presence is poignantly atemporal, their 'ruin value' (see Speer 1970: 56) is too deeply ironized, not least by their status as mere model fragments, to remain monumental. By this treatment of the model, Levine provides a figure for the spectator to organize and narrativize Wotan's ambitions in the much-expanded political and cultural fields of the twentieth and twenty-first centuries.

## Practising inclusivity in Wong and Derbyshire's *Me on the Map*

*Me on the Map* concentrates the acts of making a model as at once representational and virtual as it mediates morphogenetically between the concept and its realization. This production initiates a dynamic material dialogue, a form of research in urban design, so that the audience/spectators actively contribute preliminary architectural models that become the 'stuff' of the production. Adrienne Wong and Jan Derbyshire distilled the energy of the outpouring of civic pride and sense of citizenship in the city of Vancouver following the Stanley Cup riots in 2011 in this show to empower children in larger civic processes.[5] Their dramaturgy co-opts for its performance modes the city's commitment to implement the UN definition for inclusive design for accessibility in its public spaces for use by the greatest number of people, regardless of age, height, skill or physical ability.[6] The architectural models created by the participants concentrate the efforts of the audience thematically, exchanging a focal perspective with a haptic inquiry into the texture of the city. This event plays out a network of deontic relationships as an architectural practice.

Wong and Derbyshire developed the show through a series of brainstorming sessions and workshops where participants' three-dimensional models built up an urban environment on a grid that was spread out on the floor. Such development resulted in a kit that is sent out to schools and introduces five main categories of land usage that could be negotiated: attractions (playground, waterpark, zoo and amusement park), green space (forest, wetlands, fruit orchard and community gardens), community spaces (outdoor stage, community centre, interfaith chapel and library), sports spaces (sports field, skate park, tennis court and swimming pool) and services (day care, co-op housing, fire station and hospital). Students in their classes prepare plans for their parcel of land based on these categories as an equitable embodiment of their values as potential residents; as such, the plans challenge not only the way in which the city might be built but also the way in which the participants think of a functional 'happy city' (Montgomery 2014: 455).

Development of the production has instituted processes of mapping and re-evaluating as a primary mode of performance in sessions with groups of children to produce possible models of happy use of this land (Wong 2015). In each component of the performance, there is an active development of models that show the choices of an individual and of the group, a sense of fair use of the lot and the values that such choices demonstrate. The kit guides the students

**Figure 10.3** Photo of a hands-on activity as part of *Me on the Map* at the Vancouver International Children's Festival, 2013. Photo courtesy of Jan Derbyshire/Neworld Theatre.

through two fifty-minute periods in the classroom to prepare a ground plan for their actual parcel of land. Each student designs a plan for this lot using a grid accommodated to the shape of the lot: the grid is comprised of 100 units so that four segments of ten units each are designated for public use, and six segments of ten units are to be designated by the student. Students draw their choices from the four categories outlined earlier onto individual ground plans which are accompanied by a separate sheet of a legend. This process was adapted for weekend performances at the Vancouver International Children's Festival so that this planning segment was prepared in an ante-tent where the participants could design their ground plans. Before a class comes to the Happy City Design Lab, the organizers run the plans through software that generates radar charts showing the most popular choices scored against Happiness Values – the space to be inclusive, happy, healthy, friendly and surprising. Participants bring their hand-drawn maps to the lab and in small groups assemble ground plans using this information and coloured shapes keyed to the legend of design elements. The facilitator leads a discussion about the popular features and how each one of them might be linked to Happiness Values so that the participants can collaborate to adjust their designs to reflect the group's values and achieve an equitable use of space in a potential Happiness Model. Up to this point the students have created three maps: the first shows how their individual selections define their design, the second is a map that demonstrates a sense of fairness derived from the software algorithm and a third is of the Values Map based on the groups' values.

At this juncture, the production introduces a real-life complication that informs participants that the redevelopment of the empty lot can be realized only by their agreement to a compromise of land usage: this possible solution is unveiled as a professionally made architectural model for a luxury high-rise scaled to take up thirty of the available 100 units of space. In small groups the students are asked to evaluate whether they accept this offer from the developer and propose which features from their second Happiness Model they would like to include. Derbyshire moderates the discussion to help the students shape what they are ultimately striving to achieve in the design of this parcel of land. The experience at the Design Lab triggers explorations that play out social responsibility and contribute to the final events of the exercise – a letter to the mayor explaining the choices and the group's own model of their negotiated design. Once completed this is uploaded to the production's website and is available for other design groups to see.

The Happy City Design Lab integrates both two- and three-dimensional modelling as integral to the event and to stimulate dramatic interpersonal dialogue. The architectural modelling operates in several scales of magnitude simultaneously as the participants map their desired and negotiated presences into an urban environment. The acts of assembling the models shifts the narrative into what Echenique identified as sorting out static and dynamic temporal relationships, and effectively explores different grammars of what might happen in this urban space. The collaborative performance also resituates the role of emotions in performance to modelling a happy city to configure and spatialize affective responses to urban living in the re-assembly of subjectivity. Happiness and contentment is made performative as a collective phenomenon in which the participants experience their agency.

## Concluding remarks

In each of these examples, one can see the tension engendered by the material object that has been made and by its integration into the performance; the perspective that ensues complicates the narrative architectonics of performance. The conceptualization of such circumstances returns the spectator to a public space in each production, a space in which the architectural model becomes a 'test' of an agonistic space that remakes the social fabric. The assembly of the architectural model asserts a resistance to one perspective, guiding the spectator instead to seeing the gestural performance: the handling of the architectural model, and the act of spectators observing it, affecting the bearing in reality of the actors on the stage. The presence of the distinct scale meets the challenge of 'grasping, remembering, and understanding vast entities of information – such as one's persona, with its entire historicity, or the continuum of time and places through one's life' (Pallasmaa 2011: 32). These instances of architectural models on the stage reinforce a complex vision in which the representational does not necessarily follow the actual, and the achievement of the architectural models, within the architecture of the theatres, precipitates acts of assembly that contribute to a remaking of the stage space as an unmarked space. Moreover, as the inclusion of these architectural models interrupts acts of cognition, sign systems are adjusted and idioms of architecture become present not only as forms but as the knowledge that emerges from event-spaces; that is to say, envisioning liminality, and proposing agonistic spaces that enable an articulation of dissensus. The crafting of the architectural models for performance emphasizes details that are played out in performance, but the effect is longer-lasting than the production, since by their presence the models probe 'what kind of change is wrought upon the world when the artist's work is complete' (Lamarque 2010: 33).

# Notes

1   As Lalonde later commented: '*La langue ici est l'équivalent de la couleur pour le noir américain. La langue français, c'est notre couleur noire!* (Here language is equivalent to colour in black America. The French language is our blackness!)' (Lalonde cited in Mezei 1998: 234).

2   Erwin Piscator used architectural structures in his mises-en-scène that enabled multiple locations to be present on stage, picked out by lighting and defined by film projections. Traugott Müller's design for *Hoppla wir Lebben* (1927) allowed the action to be presented vertically, rather than horizontally on the stage floor. A central three-storey staircase was flanked by cubicals on either side, and the gauze curtains over this structure were deployed as film screens.

3   The Plains of Abraham is a public park in Quebec City, which commemorates the decisive battle in 1759 between British and French colonial forces that wrested New France from French control. During President de Gaulle's visit to Canada, he publicly encouraged the sovereignty movement of which Lalonde was an exponent.

4   Richard Wagner introduces Valhalla co-incident with the orchestral theme in the stage directions as a magnificent castle seen across a mountain meadow and lit by the rising sun. Wagner's didascalia maintains Valhalla as a projected vision of Wotan's plan for a great hall for the warriors.

5   The Stanley Cup riots took place after the Vancouver Canucks ice hockey team lost the deciding game of the National Hockey League play-offs in 2011. The destruction in Vancouver's downtown appalled many residents, who responded by arriving early the next morning to clean up the city. This spontaneous mobilization became an animating marker for an imperative of stewardship of the city.

6   The City of Vancouver has adopted the definition of inclusive design from the Division for Social Policy and Development of the United Nations Department of Economic and Social Affairs: 'Universal design' and 'inclusive design' mean 'the design of products, environments, programmes and services to be usable by all people, to the greatest extent possible, without the need for adaptation or specialized design' (*Design for Inclusion Toolkit* 2008: 2).

11

# *In Orbit* of *Dead Man Friend*

Alex Schweder

Autobiography is not so much about revealing the facts of one's life as it is a construction of one's self through the telling of experiences. Architectural theorist Jane Rendell, drawing on the insights of Susan Rubin Suleiman, puts forward this understanding of autobiography in her *Site-Writing* (2010: 50). And in Rendell's writing I find permission to think about architecture, which is also an act of construction, as a mode of autobiography through its requirements for cleaning and decoration, through its hosting of life events, and through its structuring of human relationships. An amalgam of these actions, buildings stage the performance of our life stories, not only expressing the subjectivities of their occupants but also shaping them. Can the making of one's own home be conceptualized as autobiographical in this sense? The domestic drama of constructing and performing one's self?

Conceived of in this way, as an autobiographical cycle, architecture builds subjects who then author new buildings, which in the context of this chapter can be understood as dramaturgical acts. 'Performance architecture' (Gratza 2013: 141) is a term I coined a decade ago to encapsulate this idea and put forward an understanding of architecture as giving cues for how occupants are to behave and offering itself as a prop for inhabitants to form and perform their identities (see Butler 1990). This term emerged during my first collaboration with artist Ward Shelley called *Flatland* (2007), where we built a two-foot-wide, four-storey-tall building to occupy for three weeks with four other people (Schweder 2012: 105–106; 112–113). The gap between who we thought we would be upon entering *Flatland* and who we were upon leaving compelled Shelley and I to make new works to spatialize and share these new selves. Living in each work to discover who we become in the situation has become our methodology for discovering ideas that lead to new works. Our collaborations, now seven works old, have all repeated this process of designing a building to produce a relationship between us, living in it without leaving for a predetermined time, experiencing the ways we are changing, reflecting upon those changes and the work's meaning both among ourselves and in real-time conversations with those who visit us, and then conceiving of a new inhabitational performance that we think might communicate our discoveries to an audience. In a way, viewing our performances is like looking at stars; they offer glimpses into the past by communicating who we were at the end of our last performance.

Jealousy and dementia can both be characterized by their circularity, each producing endless loops – the former because one cannot forget and the latter because one cannot remember. Sitting in a living room loaned to me by friends who were out of town, I regrouped from my wife's decision to be with a younger man. Ward tried to direct my attention towards more productive things: a new work maybe? He'd been there for my first divorce as well, but it was easier the first time. After all, we were Rome Prize winners back then, and the American Academy in Rome's august architecture was somehow a fortress for my confidence. It was as though the walls were made of sponge that had soaked in a century's worth of pride from accomplished artists and architects, available to be drained and drunk by living within them. But the second time around, moving from place to place, week to week, no house was inhabited long enough to steep me with dignity.

I cannot remember who first thought of a circular house to function like a hamster wheel, Ward or myself, but that never really matters between us; we don't compete like that. The circle resonated that day. Some works happen slowly – over years – picked up every so often and turned around to be seen from a different angle. *In Orbit* happened like that: a flash in the pan of ideas we were collecting turned just right that day. A hunch became a project.

Both just sketches of what and who we would become, *In Orbit* and I both needed sites to call home and build ourselves. 'Hi Mom, it's Alex. Things didn't go according to plan.' And with that she welcomed me back to my childhood home to spin my jealousy in the safety of her care. While I thought I was there to rehearse having a home, I found that I was in fact there to rehearse loving. What better leading lady than a mother? When she kept repeating her lines, though, her dementia announced itself through this circling, asking the same questions again and again. After a few months of our doubled but opposite orbits, her revolving queries became rotating fictions that she was convinced were real. A

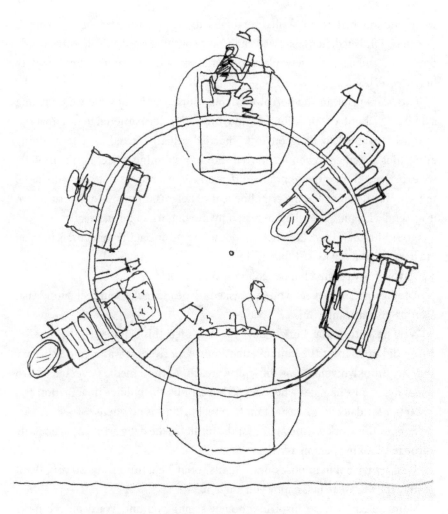

**Figure 11.1** Sketch of *In Orbit*. Image courtesy of Alex Schweder.

murderous cadre from the neighbourhood would come at eleven each night to 'take us out'. Through patience and endless hours addressing voices only she could hear, the importance of being loving as much as being loved gradually stilled my jealousy.

With our twinned fates, *In Orbit* and I found homes of our own two years later through Ward. He paid the deposit for a private flat and arranged for his gallery, Pierogi, to publicly present *In Orbit* in a decommissioned power plant that was used for commerce-free installations. The small disc-shaped medicine that would come to calm my mother's mind had not yet been prescribed and we brought her to work with us. She sat in Ward's chair before it was attached to the wheel and watched us, enthralled yet unable to imagine what we were making. It was finally finished, her borrowed chair now spinning right side up then upside down, and she needed a new place to sit, first on a train, and then in the safety of a friend's home.

Two years prior, in the borrowed living room, we thought we were making a building about cooperation. At the time, this idea offered me a toehold in a self I wanted to hang on to, a married self that acted as a team doing everything together. When we moved into our spinning wheel home, though, we experienced the situation quite differently. Ward moved onto the outside of the wheel in deference to my crippling fear of heights. In turn I took care of him by carefully keeping the wheel at rest, only moving when he was ready.

One visitor observed: 'You two are doing everything at the same time, but you are never together. Doesn't that get lonely?'

Maybe this was what happened to my marriage.

Another person – very young – asked: 'Does it make you feel funny that everyone is watching you?'

Were he a little older I might have replied: 'I feel this exposed all the time.'

We did not expect the kind of attention we received. It was a cold February and our Brooklyn venue was difficult to reach, but the media coverage of two artists living on a hamster wheel seemed to capture the public's imagination as a metaphor for daily life's constant motion that brings us nowhere.

'For me, this work is a metaphor for the futility of the daily grind', a particularly burdened-looking person asked.

'Well, we try not to impose our thoughts about what this means on you', Ward gently replied. 'We're just happy you are here.'

Mom called: 'It is so inspiring, honey, seeing you and Ward on the news walking for peace.'

I thought she meant world peace at the time, but as I write I like to think she meant a more personal kind. 'Thanks Mom, I love you.'

Like the hundreds of other audience members that we spoke with, Mom had her own interpretation of what we were up to. With them Ward and I would discuss the work, our experiences and what we thought it meant. Different answers were given depending on when the conversation occurred. You could say we were lying, but in fact we were recounting our thoughts in real time as we were reconciling our intentions with the lived emotions. *In Orbit*'s meaning was made collaboratively, with our visitors, in this way.

'Hey Alex', Ward called down to me in the quiet of the gallery's afterhours. 'You know I feel kind of guilty up here.'

**Figure 11.2** Ward Shelley, *In Orbit*. Photo by Double Cyclops and courtesy of Alex Schweder.

'What do you mean, Ward?'

'Every time I have to go to the bathroom, I need to interrupt what you are doing. It's like being the passenger with a small bladder on a long road trip, always asking the driver to pull over. It challenges my identity as someone who is self-reliant. I feel dependent on you.'

'Interrupt me as often as you want, I could never live on top and am just so thankful that you can.'

'You know I think this piece is more about care taking than cooperation. It feels similar to what taking care of my dad was like.'

'Yeah, or taking care of my mom.'

With this, the tacit experience of caretaking that was such a part of my life at the time felt like it could become sharable. It wasn't fully embodied in this piece, but we started to talk about making a new piece that might do this. A person walking into the exhibition space of this new work would immediately read a relationship of caretaking through the building and our occupation of it, just as *In Orbit* visualized cooperation.

Our ten days' living *In Orbit* ended publicly with cheers and a closing party, the two of us climbing off the wheel and out of our brightly coloured suits. As soon as I was back in street clothes, I had to rush and fetch my mom from the train our family friends had put her on. Over ten days my needs, actions and thoughts had been sensed and responded to by Ward through the rotating building. I was jarred by sadness at the indifference of the crowds to my rush. Without seeing me, shouldn't they have felt me coming through the subtle somatic cues of the sidewalk? I could feel them; why couldn't they feel me? I had not accounted for the mass of people that I needed to push through and was five minutes late. The loneliness that abated while performing *In Orbit* returned among this indifferent crowd. It all went wrong. Mom got confused and lost, and I had to enlist the police to find her in the station. Both in tears, we returned to our apartment – once again safe in mutual care.

Living in our work is how Ward and I make new work, to discover the difference between intention and experience. Our discoveries of performing *In Orbit* led us to thinking about a new building that requires caretaking between its occupants in order to live in it. At the time of writing, this work, provisionally titled *Dead Man Friend*, is still an idea. When the time comes, we will make a building where one artist is in bed for the duration of the performance. The other artist will occupy a full apartment and can come and go as he pleases. The freely moving artist will need to feed, bathe and toilet the bedridden one. Architecturally, the large living space will be designed such that when the artist gets out of bed, the rooms of the freely moving artist's apartment will come crashing down, suggesting that the one in bed is also taking care of the one who moves freely. *Dead Man Friend* points in this way to the doubled nature of care taking – the need to love and to be loved.

Our works set up a proposition for who we are to become. There is a relationship in mind that we want the building to shape us into. As Ward and I live in our works, however, that intended self is in contrast to the selves we bring to the project, shaped by other things that are happening in our lives, like learning to love again. It is in the ways that we don't fit the proscribed relationship that become most interesting; illuminating the misalignments of who we are and who we would like to be is an outcome of the architectural artworks we make. We would not necessarily see ourselves so clearly or tell our stores in the same way without this contrast of intention and experience, and it is here that I find architecture and autobiography to be in their most productive tension.

# Part Three

# Pedagogies

# 12

# Towards a Tectonics of Devised Performance: Experiments in Interdisciplinary Learning/Teaching

Juliet Rufford

*Productions at the limit of literature, at the limit of music, at the limit of any discipline, often inform us about the state of that discipline, its paradoxes and its contradictions. Questioning limits is a means of determining the nature of discipline.*

Tschumi 1983: 66

## Introduction

What might it mean to approach performance by way of architecture? How might such a move help question the limits of performance and of pedagogy? In this essay, I argue that exercises in spatial organization and articulation, formal manipulation and tectonics might prove useful in learning/teaching postdramatic devised performance (defined below). In exploring this idea, I am interested in how architecture might stimulate artistic daring and originality, and inform the relationship between the aesthetic and the political in performance practice. Indeed, for those of us committed to building a new politics of performance, the interdisciplinary challenge is always how to use unfamiliar source materials, methodologies and techniques not merely for their novelty value but as the critical means by which to unveil, disrupt or transform disciplinary orthodoxies and hegemonic structures in the world beyond (Kristeva 1997; Rendell 2006: 10–12, 2014: 103–112). This is risky business; it asks students and teachers to look closely at the foundations of their practice and, at times, to dismantle the systems of meaning that have supported both their work and their world-views for a long time. The central notion I am working with is that architecture, as the discipline *par excellence* of space, form and order, might aid performance's internal organization and, equally, might strengthen our sense of its position in relation to the structures and spaces that condition its production and dissemination.

In seeking to elaborate an architectural framework for devised performance pedagogy, to outline some of the particular directions that learning/teaching could take and to highlight some of the resources it could use in so doing, I draw on a range of different architectural ideas and influences, including the theory and practice of Bernard Tschumi, current redefinitions of the tectonic in architecture and contemporary methods in architecture education. While my approach to devised performance owes much to the work of Hans-Thies Lehmann and others who have examined and further developed his *Postdramatic Theatre* (Lehmann 2006, 2011; see also Harvie and Lavender 2010; Jürs-Munby 2013), my pedagogical practice is underpinned by the insights of constructivist and critical pedagogies (Bruner 1961, 1971; Freire 1970, 2000; Giroux 2011; Vygotsky 1978). Finally, in working across and between the disciplines of architecture and performance, I engage with theories and practices of interdisciplinarity that 'undermine the very foundations, framework, constitutive presuppositions, of the specialized disciplines' not in order to collapse or blur them but rather to disclose 'an *Other* of the discipline, an outside, a limit, the revelation of the *extrinsic*' by which, in Fredric Jameson's view, an area of thought and practice can test itself and renew its connections to the world in general (1988: 42–43). Folding into a discussion that builds upon these various intellectual and practical contexts, my own experiences of teaching group devising, I claim that the interdisciplinary pressure exerted on performance by architecture affects all aspects of devised performance practice; furthermore, that it might also lead to future transformations of performance and pedagogical processes. I begin by surveying some of the chief strengths and weaknesses of learning/teaching devised performance in the UK (where I live and work) and I introduce the style of interdisciplinary pedagogy I consider most useful in this context. Then, I examine the question of what might be gained from bringing architecture into performance pedagogy through three topics – space, form and construction – that have long been recognized as central to architecture but have not received as much attention as they deserve in theatre and performance studies. These three discrete themes are brought together, at the end, in an extended example of student practice.

## Existing frameworks, expanded possibilities

Over the past forty years, devised performance – as collaborative creation among group members working without a director or a single, pre-scripted text – has come to occupy an increasingly prominent position on degree programmes in theatre and performance (Harvie and Lavender 2010: 2–3; Heddon and Milling 2006: 218; Ledger 2009: 241–242; Mermikides and Smart 2010: 3–5). The evidence of current syllabi for courses in devised performance in the UK as well as recent appraisals of learning/teaching devising shows that pedagogy is broad-based and inclusive of both theory and practice. Typically, students are encouraged to make connections between their developing practice and the insights they gain from set readings on postdramatic theatre theory, site-specific performance and the history of devising practices as well as the critical cultural commentaries making up the 'expanded field' of performance studies. They are introduced to the work of significant practitioners, whose work may be seen live or on video, and are introduced to a variety of practical devising strategies. While learning/teaching devised performance makes use of many of the somatic and other training techniques used in learning/teaching acting for text-based theatrical performance, the movement away from dramatic theatre and towards postdramatic devised performance has brought about a concomitant shift in pedagogy from methods that are based on textual analysis, character and scene study, and mimetic representation to methods that are prompted by expanded conceptions of performance as a 'postmimetic' practice, and by the 'interdisciplinary stimuli and new media' that have transformed dramaturgical practice (Trencsényi and Cochrane 2014: xi–xii). Altogether, as Julia Wilson and Helen Manchester's 2012 PALATINE report on learning/teaching in higher education institutions across the UK notes, pedagogy is successfully aligning inspiration with analysis, and is imbuing a richly varied studio practice with the practices of reading, thinking and reflecting critically on our contemporary postdramatic context.

However, devised performance pedagogy is not without its problems. Wilson and Manchester note as a problem widely acknowledged by both teacher and student respondents difficulties in shaping, structuring and refining performance material into a coherent whole (Wilson and Manchester 2012: 13; for a similar assessment see Heddon and Milling 2006: 200). The Wilson and Manchester report also cites a shared concern among teachers that students may be relying too heavily on the creative models to which they are introduced with the result that learning can be more passive than active, and that student work can show signs of 'unconsidered and uncritical imitation' (2012: 18). To these pedagogical problems, directors, dramaturgs and educators have added a number of others, which they see reflected back and forth between the theatre industry, theatre and performance research, and dominant models of teaching theatre at pre- and post-16 levels. These include: little or no training in spatial awareness or exploration of spatial relationships in performance (Bogart and Landau 2014: 10; Halprin 1995: 31–33); little or no consideration of the role of architecture in constructing meaning in performance (McAuley 2000: 4–8; Rufford 2015: 1–6; Wiles 2003: 258); little or no understanding of architectural readings of 'site' (Taylor 2004: 17–18); and poor integration of theatre design or scenography into the practice and study of dramaturgy and performance (Knowles 2004: 28–30; McKinney and Butterworth 2009: 84–85). Given theatre's postdramatic, spatial and scenographic turns, I am keen to develop methods that will equip emerging performance makers with the tools they need to build original forms of theatre, and to better articulate the myriad connections between the performative, the political, the social and the spatial – in short, between theatre and world.

Architecture is helpful in learning/teaching performance in a number of ways. First, architecture is increasingly being seen as analogous to dramaturgy and as a valuable point of reference for playwriting as well as performance that breaks with traditional text-based theatre (see, for example, Frisch 2002: 277; Stegemann 2016: 48; Turner 2010, 2015). Second, an architectural understanding of spaces in and of performance can help us work more consciously and precisely with the 'relational aesthetics' and spatial politics set up by particular stage types and/ or spatial arrangements and dynamics within or beyond the theatre auditorium (Bourriaud 2002; see also Bishop 2012). Third, at the level of metaphor, architecture can denaturalize or deconstruct institutionalized knowledge and facilitate the kinds of meta-level thinking about epistemology that performance studies aims to promote (see, for example, Jackson 2004; Kirshenblatt-Gimblett 2004; Stucky and Wimmer 2002). In place of cross- or multidisciplinarity, both of which leave disciplinary boundaries in place, the radical interdisciplinarity that interests me redefines our understandings of what performance *is* and *does* even while questioning where, how, for whom, and under what conditions post-16 learning/teaching takes place. Looking at theatre architecturally is an important first step in recognizing theatrical structures and conventions (such as mimetic representation, character, performer–spectator relationships and spaces, etc.) as cultural *constructs*, and beginning to develop ways of working with or against them in devised performance. By shaking the edifice of performance in this way, architecture helps deconstruct its various constitutive presuppositions and its normative methods and values, redistributing its weight along less predictable lines.

Like many teachers intent on helping their students to take up a more reflexive approach to theatre and performance making, I am of the opinion that one essential prerequisite to learning to make devised performance is the opening up of a space in which all those involved can question received wisdom about theatre and performance in general, and about devising in particular. In this safe space, I ask my students to discuss as many of the assumptions, frameworks, methods, foci, key questions, tools and techniques as we can think of in relation to performances we have experienced, read about, or made ourselves. Invariably, we discover that performance contains within it a series of internal divisions and differences of approach, and that it seems, at times, to fold within it and, at other times, to more aggressively rub up against a variety of different artistic dimensions, media and practices. From these questions about what devised performance is and does (and how it does it), we ask questions about performance's underlying values, and about what we might want it to do and to mean in the future. We also meditate on what we think it is that contemporary performance does not do (or, does not do as well as it might) and dream up hypothetical solutions to the problems we perceive. For instance, we might agree with Nick Ridout (2015) that while performance 'does' transience very well indeed, it could use some help in addressing larger, longer-term structures. However, as a counterweight to the emphasis in drama and literary studies on language and text, we might look not to grammatical structures (as Ridout suggests) but to architecture for assistance with this problem, and we might draw, demonstrate, diagram or debate all the possible (and impossible) ways in which a performance, like an urban master plan, might engage and index issues on a monumental scale and/or might form a semi-permanent fixture in public life.

This kind of preparatory work serves a number of pedagogical functions. In keeping with constructivist and critical pedagogical practices, it defers to learners' lived experiences of performance and of life, and asks learners both to locate themselves within the concrete conditions of their culture and society and build on 'intimate' starting points to engage broader modes of knowledge and practice (Freire 2000: 36; see also Bruner 1961, 1971; Gruber and Vonèche 1995; Vygotsky 1978; Wood 1976). It also introduces metacognitive, self-reflective, 'co-intentional' and strongly dialogical elements into learning/ teaching so that our individual and collective engagement with performance ideas and processes can be seen to be 'related to the specificity of particular contexts, students, communities, and available resources' and can be left open to individual and group reconsideration (Giroux 2011: 4; see also Freire 1970: chapters 3 and 4). Additionally, while sensitizing learners to the productive tensions between disciplinary problems, interdisciplinary dynamics and a larger realm of transdisciplinary problematics, it arouses learners' curiosity for the practical problem-solving techniques they might develop through active experimentation between disciplines (Hayes cited in DeZure 1999). This last point is directly linked to the question of particular interdisciplinary approaches and to a certain tension or paradox that I try to keep alive in teaching and to manage in accordance to differing learner needs. On the one hand, since architecture can seem far removed from theatre and performance – and there is no reason that someone who wants to be a theatre maker should willingly sign up for methods, skills and techniques in another discipline – I try to avoid simply introducing the 'salient bits' of architecture education and then applying them 'to' performance. While there is much to be gained from such an approach, most learners are better able to internalize and make use of new interdisciplinary knowledge if it is presented through an 'integrative' approach – one in which architectural thinking is presented as implicit within performance (Klein 2005: 8–10). On the other hand, as my references to the arguments of Julia Kristeva, Fredric Jameson and Jane Rendell make plain, interdisciplinarity can be beneficial precisely because of the sometimes quite violent 'Otherness' it entails.

## Space

In contrast to the way it has been classified for much of its history, performance is as much a spatial as a time-based art and, as such, requires a spatially turned mode of learning/teaching. In establishing a performance studies degree at Aberystwyth University, Mike Pearson and colleagues were among the first educators in the UK to reassert this under-acknowledged facet of performance, and to develop an overtly architectural approach to site-specific performance. Using a model that combines dramaturgy and scenography, space and place, Pearson draws on the architectural ideas and practices of Clifford McLucas and Bernard Tschumi to nurture student work that examines 'the implications of social, cultural, political and historical contexts for the nature, form and function of performance' (Pearson 2005: 255–256; see also Pearson 2010). And, while Nick Kaye (2000) and Alan Read (2000) have enlivened the conversation between architecture theory, site-specific performance and urban intervention, Anne Bogart and Tina Landau have turned to architecture for help with performer training and performance composition. Bogart and Landau's system of Viewpoints offers devising and compositional techniques based in movement, time and space that can not only add to, or replace, the dominant psychologizing techniques of American (and other Stanislavskian traditions of) actor training but can be used in theatre as well as in spatially unconventional places of performance. *The Viewpoints Book*, which outlines nine different Viewpoints of space and time as part of an open methodology for devising and shaping performance, addresses head-on the thought that performance is a situated practice and is, more often than not, situated in architectural space (Bogart and Landau 2014: x). The book includes practical exercises that require performance makers to work at different scales and to be conscious of how architecture frames and articulates meaning in performance (see, in particular, 'Spatial Relationship', 45–47; 'Framing Devices', 158; and 'Architecture', 192–193). Together with the emphasis they place on learning to treat performance space as a dynamic cubic volume (see, in particular, the exercises outlined in 2014: 39–45), the directors' entreaty to emerging performance makers to consider space as both a dramaturgical element and as the medium through which real-world orders play out constitutes an invitation to the next generation of performance makers to challenge habitual spatial relationships and behaviours in theatre and everyday life (Bogart and Landau 2014: 10).

Early on in the Viewpoints process, Bogart and Landau introduce the performers to exercises that they need to perform on an imaginary rehearsal room-sized grid, the corners of which correspond to those of the (real) room. The purpose of this is to encourage students to move beyond the 2–5 metre arena in which most of our daily interactions take place and explore extremes of tempo, duration, spatial organization and spatial relationship for the meanings they might begin to suggest. As in architecture education, the grid is a strategic tool – one that brings together space, organization, rhythm, hierarchy and action (see Simitch and Warke 2014: 180–187 for an approach to gridwork in architecture education that can be adapted for use in learning/teaching performance). In the drama studio or at site, different kinds of grid (whether regular, irregular or distorted) might be used as performance scores. While each kind of grid will impose its own peculiar order on material that may seem disordered, gridwork opens fledgling performance makers to a more fully three-dimensional realm through a rare-for-theatre emphasis on the vertical axis. Paradoxically, then, it comes to feel more liberating than regulatory. At the same time, as Bogart and Landau make clear, the insights that gridwork yields about the body's orientation in space and about spatial hierarchies remind us that historical shifts to the actor's primary axis – from playing to the gods, to royalty, to the audience, to other actors, and, with Beckett, to nothingness – are culturally contingent and politically loaded (2014: 92–93). Thus, in addition to enhancing practitioners' spatial awareness and paving the way for spatial dramaturgies, Bogart and Landau's major focus on space in devised performance folds over into questions about ideologies of space.

Why I think this matters is because we live in a world in which space is increasingly contested. From housing crisis to environmental crisis, urbanization to globalization, and geopolitics to biopolitics, our everyday realities are haunted by issues of inclusion/exclusion, displacement, incarceration, detention and more. If performance is to remain relevant and meaningful today, it must find ways of demonstrating, deconstructing and intervening in the spatial logic through which these issues are played out (see, for example, Harvey 2001 on spaces of capital; Foucault [1982] 1998 on architecture and the practice of liberty; Agamben 1998, 2000 and 2005 on the spatial logic of the state of exception). It must, in other words, seek out a spatial language through which to communicate issues that are manifesting spatially. To be sure, architecture is not the only spatial language that performers might harness to this task, and performance pedagogy has already made productive use of critical readings which view contemporary theatre and/or performance through the lenses of geography, cartography, topology and urban studies in order to support student work that connects performance and space and/or place to social and political life (see, for instance, Birch and Tompkins 2012; Fischer-Lichte and Wihstutz 2013; Fuchs and Chaudhuri 2002; Harvie 2009, 2013: 108–147; Hopkins and Solga 2013; Whybrow 2014). However, architecture's characteristic concerns not only with mapping or sensing space but more specifically with spatial design and control make it especially useful in linking questions of space to the performative assertion of socio-political orders. What socially engaged performance makers gain from architecture, then, is the means to recognize and reclaim spaces of power and control.

Such a moment of recognition and of spatial counter-agency is supported by the ideas and teaching of Bernard Tschumi. Tschumi's theoretical work since the early 1970s has been directed against the 3,000-year-old ideology that holds that 'architecture is about stability, solidity, foundation' (Tschumi 1996: 19). Noting that 'there is no cause-and-effect relationship between the concept of space and the experience of space, or between buildings and their uses', Tschumi argues that while architecture has been used to stabilize and institutionalize social life it is not innately repressive (1996: 16). For, if architecture is designed to channel us along passageways and contain us within its walls, it cannot finally dictate our actions or determine our experiences. Tschumi's braided observations that idealized, abstract conceptions of architecture rarely coincide with architecture as it is actually lived, and that there is thus a radical disjunction between buildings and their prescribed uses – or functions – allows for architecture–user relations to be renegotiated in bottom-up and other unexpected ways. What he claims his approach offers students of his discipline is 'a reading of architecture in which space, movement and events are ultimately independent, yet stand in a new relation to one another, so that the conventional components of architecture are broken down and rebuilt along different axes' (Tschumi 1983: 67). There is also, I think, a real sense in his writings of how this claim might be re-written as a pronouncement about the deconstructive influence of architecture on performance since both disciplines – and not architecture alone – are continually interwoven in his thought. In short, Tschumi's focus on actions, movements and unscripted uses of space destabilizes normative practices in architecture and performance alike.

Throughout the provocations and project documents collected together in his *Manhattan Transcripts* (1983) and in the *Event Cities* series of illustrated textbooks (1994, 2000, 2004, 2010), Tschumi provides methods for unbuilding and critically re-building architecture that glance between spaces and events – what he sees as the architecture-performance complex event-space. These methods, which rely on tactics of cross-, dis- and transprogramming different spaces and activities (clashing the activity of bowling with the architecture of a church, say, or combining the activities and spatial configurations of a planetarium and a roller coaster), borrow heavily from drag performance, film and theatre in order to shatter notions of causality, fixity, natural order and synthesis and to expose architectural, cultural and social norms as performatively constructed (Tschumi 1994; for definitions of terms see pages 155, 221 and 327). Transposing these ideas back into performance pedagogy, whether by adapting exercises from the *Transcripts* oneself or by using Pearson's Tschumi-inspired instructions for making site-specific performance (e.g. Pearson 2010: 38–40, 86–87, 136–139, 179–180, 186–187), promotes a new aesthetics and politics of spaces and events. For example, Tschumi's distinction between 'function' (as the institutionally-sanctioned activities that *should* take place in a given space) and 'programme' (as the multiple, unpredictable events that *could* conceivably occur there) highlights just how limited are our customary arrangements of performing and spectating areas – whether at site or in a theatre building – and opens up possibilities for troubling questions of sociality, spatiality, spectatorship and participation to which conservative ideologies have blinded us (Tschumi 1983: 71; compare with Pearson 1998: 35–36). At the limits of architecture and performance practice, where students are encouraged to confront their assumptions about architectural and performative cues and sociospatial codes, we see the transgression of disciplines and the performance of subversive spatial strategies.

# Form

Approaching the formal aspects of devised performance through architecture raises as many problems as it offers possibilities. For one thing, form in the time-based medium of performance is not quite the same thing as form in the three-dimensional context of architectural composition. For another, the centrality of form to architecture education has been called into question in recent decades – partly as a positive effect of Tschumi's emphasis on architectural programmes and lived experiences of space and partly because of concerns about shallow formalism and the commodification of eye-catching architectural forms. Michael Stanton, in a critique of traditional architecture education, argues that exercises taught to students at the initial stages of learning architectural design (including geometry, transformation of the cube and nine-square manipulations) privilege architecture's aesthetic impact in ways that threaten to seal off aesthetics from social issues and cultural acts (2001: 28–33; see also Robinson 2001: 73). The consequence of architectural education that treats the formal 'product' as separable from architecture's lived effects is that architecture appears as a self-sufficient object rather than a force for cultivating positive relationships between people and the built environments they occupy. Highlighting a further problem, Colin Davies writes:

> Form and matter – the shape of a thing and the material that it's made of – are inseparable companions. Everything that physically exists has both form and matter. Even a 'formless' mass has some kind of form, like a cloud or a heap, and form devoid of matter is a mere ghost or apparition. So why do we, in language and thought persistently treat form and matter as if it were possible to separate them? (2011: 42)

The problems that these educators perceive with learning/teaching form in architecture are highly relevant to debates about postdramatic aesthetics and the politics of performance and, as such, are a useful point of departure for student–

teacher dialogue about making devised performance. For if, as Lehmann (drawing on the critical theory of Georg Lukács, Walter Benjamin and others) has pointed out, the search for new forms and strategies of theatre reveals the potential for a 'truly political dimension' of performance, the pedagogical challenge in performance, as in architecture, is one of how best to enable processes of form-making, form-breaking, formal manipulation and production that are attuned to 'the situation, the relation, the social moment which theatre as such is able to constitute' (Lehmann 2011: 35).

To this end, one of the things the 'expanded' or 'new' dramaturgies aim to promote is greater sensitivity to the issue of how and with what consequences content, form and matter, or material, relate (see, for example, Gritzner 2009; Romanska 2015; Trencsényi and Cochrane 2014; Turner and Behrndt 2008, 2010; Van Kerkhoven 1994a). In so doing, these new dramaturgies highlight the shift from dramatic composition to an 'architectonics of performance' (Turner 2009) and from constructional support to comprehensive framework for 'connect[ing] theatre to social and political life' (Eckersall 2014: 19). For if performance is, to a significant extent, the 'form' that gives shape to social and cultural 'matters' for contemplation by members of an audience, form–content and form–matter relations cannot be dismissed as 'merely' abstract, part of an 'extreme' understanding of theatre (see Lehmann 2006: 36 for a defence of Michael Kirby's formalist theatre). Addressing form–content relations through dramaturgical analysis of an intentionally varied selection of play-texts, Cathy Turner and Synne Behrndt demonstrate how patterns of congruence, collision and subversion 'tend towards a particular view of the world' (2008: 26). Addressing form and matter, I have previously examined how the devising process by which composer Heiner Goebbels and scenographer Klaus Grünberg developed their 2008/2012 sound-performance installation *Stifters Dinge* allowed for interplay between the conceptual, formal, material and structural aspects of the piece, and tied these various elements of performance to questions of global power relations and environmental politics (Rufford 2015: 67–85). There is, then, a resonance between content, form and matter that connects aesthetics to politics within and between architecture and performance.

Finding literature that is geared towards learning/teaching of form–content and/or form–matter relationships in devising is not easy as the overwhelming emphasis has been on the key issue of helping learners to generate material (see, for example, Margolin 1997 on learning/teaching performance composition). Where teachable literature exists, it shows how students are encouraged to consider how one combination or order of events will give a different inflection

– perhaps, quite a different meaning – from another in performance. Adam Ledger shares a helpful exercise on how to play about with the eventual form of devised material by re-ordering index card descriptions of component sections of the developing piece (2009: 259). And, while Heddon and Milling recommend an open-ended 'trying out of combinations in order to consider how different components work together [...] and what their combinations might variously signify' (2006: 200), Jessica Swale uses exploratory storytelling, word games, experiments with genre and convention, and visualizations of narrative arcs to help 'hone' and 'edit' an unwieldy piece (2012: 81–98). These approaches reflect the emphasis in contemporary experimental theatre on automatic writing techniques and spontaneous collective authorship. They also honour the role that accident and chance can play in performance composition. Yet, as the members of the Australian workshop-research unit 'The Dramaturgies Project' argue, there is a need for focused learning that addresses the dramaturgical aspects of devised performance in ways that balance such creative openness with attention to structural, ideological, compositional and contextual 'lines of force' (Eckersall 2014: 29–33). While the growing awareness of this need has led some dramaturgs and educators to borrow from disciplines such as mathematics, music and science in order to introduce learners to forms, formats and structures that might aid them in performance composition (see Odendahl-James 2015; Roesner 2010; Romanska 2015), I see architecture as a means not only to question the limits of aesthetic form, and formal and spatial organization but also to test these aspects of composition against the physical forms – i.e. buildings – that shape our ways of life.

My own teaching practice has been inspired by architecture education's widespread use of *charrettes* or *esquisses*: short, sharp exercises in intuitive form-making, which can foster the same attitude of discovery and play in relation to the object as improvisation does in relation to the making of a performance and which, in performance (unlike in the 'abstract', 'out-of-body' world of orthodox architecture education), tend not to push aside, or get separated from, embodied, sociocultural, thematic or technical aspects of the devising process (Robinson 2001: 73). In performance pedagogy, the use of readily-available materials such as card, corrugated cardboard, foamboard and textiles has the beneficial effect of making things tangible while the speed at which *charrettes* are executed keeps alive the quality of provisionality that is needed if work is to grow and improve through critically informed change. A favourite exercise of mine draws on first year architecture exercises designed by Raimund Abraham, and described in John Hejduk's *Education of an Architect* (1988: 14–17, 24–31; see also Habraken,

Mignucci and Teicher 2014; Hanlon 2009 for architectural *charrettes* that can be readily adapted for use in learning/teaching devised performance). It steers learners through a process of taking to pieces the component parts of a three-dimensional form (a demountable architectural model or a bicycle will do nicely) and either rebuilding the whole or, as a more advanced alternative, recombining its components into a new form that is as imaginative and/or nonsensical as the students want it to be so long as it is also robust. The pedagogical aim of such an exercise is to demonstrate how the analysis of precedents provides knowledge about historical forms and principles of composition, a basic strategy for formal composition, and the research methods by which such a strategy is revealed. It also enables students to see that existing forms are neither 'natural' nor 'unchangeable' but are conditioned by – and, in turn, condition – the society that produced them. Varying these architectural exercises in formal analysis, deconstruction and manipulation by introducing combinations of two- and/or three-dimensional and time-based elements, which might be adapted as 'found' elements or created by students, produces complex hybrid forms while sharpening awareness of the relationships between part and whole. In placing the onus on students to actively intervene in and manipulate the form they are given to work on, exercises like these diminish the risk of passive learning and/or over-reliance on creative models, increase students' confidence in themselves as *makers* and inform the choices students make about form as powerfully communicative of meaning in performance.

## Construction

In contrast to dramatic theatre, where a play-text provides content, form and structure, contemporary devised performance is often the result of a simultaneous and quite chaotic process of generating content while also shaping and structuring the developing material. Noting as a paradox of group devising the fact that a 'seemingly free and open-ended process might require an even stronger sense of structural organization and overview than a production of a conventional play would demand', Turner and Behrndt highlight the need for 'tangible practical strategies' to help guide and shape the beginning of the devising process and 'construct' or 'wright' the more fully developed performance material (2008: 173, 171). I first read their words as a (terrified) new teacher of drama, theatre and performance. I was struck both by the way that Turner and Behrndt seemed to be issuing a call to teachers to *act* on their

knowledge of the difficulties faced by devising companies and by the fact that
the authors' vocabulary echoed that of building and craft. Allowing research I
was undertaking on the intersections between theatre and architecture to feed
into my teaching practice, I began to see how an approach to devising based on
tectonics – the branch of architecture that deals with the poetics of construction
– might prove useful to students grappling with composition. Over several years
of adopting this approach with (mainly) UK drama undergraduates, I believe the
tectonic can, indeed, offer guiding principles for making postdramatic theatre
because of the very precise yet practical way in which it asks us to attend to the
intersections between place (*topos*), format, model or type (*typos*), and artful
construction (*tectonic*), and to mediate between the driving concept for a work,
that work's multiple contexts, and the structural force that guarantees its viability
(Rufford 2015: 71–74).

The tectonic entered architectural discourse and practice in nineteenth-
century Germany (Frampton 1995: 4), and was reintroduced into debates about
building design culture in 1990 by the architectural historian Kenneth Frampton
(1990). Its chief value, now as at earlier moments in architecture's history, is in
treating construction as a conscious artistic act – one that connects creative
ideas, design and structure into a coherent and expressive whole without
blurring, hiding or merging aspects of the whole (as in a *Gesamtkunstwerk*) but
rather by exploring meaningful juxtaposition and the conjoining of components.
But, whereas Frampton follows Karl Bötticher, Gottfried Semper and other late
nineteenth-century advocates of a tectonic approach to architecture in focusing
on the rigorous and locally responsive connection of structure, materials and
form, other commentators on the twenty-first-century tectonic have expanded
its core logic to attend to the connections between architecture's physical form, its
conditions of possibility and the environmental and sociocultural contexts with
which it is (inevitably) in relationship (Bech-Danielsen et al. 2012; Hartoonian
1994; Lecuyer 2001; Schwarzer 1996). As an analogue for dramaturgical practice,
the tectonic offers a route into performance composition that privileges the
concrete act of *making* through collaborative, corporeal, formal, material and
technical processes that are always project specific and that, therefore, cannot
be standardized and imposed on performance as a set of pre-determined
compositional rules. Work undertaken by some second year undergraduates
I taught in the 2013–14 academic year provides just one example of what a
tectonics of devised performance might look like in practice.

By week five of twelve, the students taking my practical module in making
group devised performance had built upon their embodied knowledges of

improvisation and other tried-and-tested devising techniques, and had spent time doing – as devising practice in adaptation, object theatre, scenography and spatial dramaturgy – many of the architectural exercises noted above. They were more than commonly spatially aware and were alert to the fact that different kinds of material tend to take different forms. They were also aware that spaces, forms and events can be consciously combined in ways that worked against the grain of received artistic practice but that their cross-, dis- or transprogramming must always be as thoughtful provocation and not as 'trendy' eclecticism. It was now time for them to set out in smaller groups of three to five people to create the twenty-minute pieces of postdramatic devised performance on which they were to be assessed. Drawing directly on the language of the tectonic, I asked each of the small groups within the bigger class to think about how they were crafting their pieces: what was holding them together, enabling their ideas to stand up? What significance might an audience for each of the groups' performances attribute to the interweaving or juxtaposing of different elements, ideas and/ or materials in their work? How would they connect the different moments within their performance, and facilitate an audience's transition between them? I encouraged the students to consider how their chosen form might rise above its role as mere carrier of content to act as a communicative force in its own right, and I urged them to remain alert to the possibility of articulating between the content of their emerging works and the physical, social, ideological and other contexts for that work.

The simple act of re-situating performance composition in these terms helped break down the dramaturgical process into a more manageable series of tightly-focused concerns and allowed each of the student groups to find its own project-specific answers to my questions through active, experiential learning. This learning included playing with objects and materials and assembling and disassembling impromptu constructions at 1:1 scale as well as drawing ground plans for the projected performance and analysing human circulation patterns around a number of different public, private and performance spaces. While basic techniques in selecting and joining materials held out obvious advantages to the students who were interested in scenography, these and other approaches to *constructing* performance (e.g. awareness of how particular materials behave or what a certain fabric or form might 'say' to an audience about a piece's underlying ideology) added an important new dimension to learning/teaching performance composition. As the weeks passed, and I watched four very different yet equally well-crafted pieces take shape, I began to see the pedagogical value of a tectonics of performance composition as:

- Liberating learners from disciplinary exemplars and creative models by supplying them with tools for unbuilding, questioning and reconfiguring performance
- Enabling approaches that integrate dramaturgy and scenography
- Supporting learners in fully distinguishing and harnessing structure, form and content, and in exploring the slippage between the symbolic and the structural aspects of their work
- Providing a framework for analysing and making theatre that refuses to privilege any one format, genre or style of performance over another
- Extending issues of how form and content relate to promote similar attention to the connections between process and product, analogue and digital technologies, space and time, performance and spectatorship

The tectonic, then, spans questions of space, form and the poetics of construction. It focuses attention on questions of how and why materials are joined in the ways they are and on the need to forge meaningful connections between performance, context and conditions of production.

While all four devising groups produced work that was unswerving in its dedication to its chosen aesthetic, work by one group of four students, which drew together the students' layered experiences of devising with space and form, provides a vivid example of what can be gained by treating architecture as foundational to performance and by taking up a tectonic approach to performance composition. The group was made up of three young women and one man who all shared interests in feminism and gender and queer theory, and who had all expressed a desire to make a spatially inventive piece that might show off group members' existing strengths in solo cabaret performance and physical theatre while enabling them to discover their own visuospatial dramaturgy. Three group members had done some important groundwork on theatre architecture and performer-spectator relationships with me during their first year; additionally, they had taken core first year modules in technical theatre and site-specific performance. The fourth student – an associate on a semester-long visit from the United States – had a dance background and was familiar with both Lawrence and Anna Halprin's RSVP Cycles and the Viewpoints system (L. Halprin 1970; A. Halprin 1995). In my second-half-of-semester role as devising 'mentor' rather than 'tutor', I suggested that they begin every session with warm-up exercises that would attune them spatially to the white L-shaped rehearsal room that was also the allocated presentation space for second year students on the module, and set themselves improvisation tasks that would necessitate interaction between their bodies and the images, objects, spaces and textures they were interested in using. As a result of diagramming, modelling and improvising in the space, the students decided to build a number of discrete though thematically inter-related environments within which to examine different aspects of their broad topic: female identity construction and representations of women. Their choice of a clustered organization of spaces saved them the logistical nightmare of having to install and strike in its totality the scenographic components of their developing piece while enabling them to express themes (e.g. fragmentation of the self) and realize artistic goals (e.g. disavowal of dramatic narrative, mixing performance with sculpture) through stucture and construction (for performance-friendly work on clusters, see Ching 2007: 222).

The resulting work, in its use of Lewis Carroll's *Alice in Wonderland* to provide a structural through-line, recalled our learning/teaching both of formal manipulation and the braiding together of symbolism and structure in tectonics. The piece, entitled *Who Are You?*, after the caterpillar's question to Alice, took audiences on a journey of compression (entry into what is normally a spacious room was along a tunnel or 'rabbit hole') and release into a large central space, which hosted a sizeable and meticulously detailed 'tea party' installation. This part-Wonderland, part-Dadaist Merz installation visually linked 'Alice' imagery to a larger set of ideas about female rites of passage and mythologies of womanhood while directing visitors along the different paths they might take next. In the surrounding cluster of differently sized spaces, group members each took up an issue that the Carroll text had triggered for them personally and examined it in ways that departed sharply from the aesthetic and tone of children's literature. For instance, in the largest of the discrete performance spaces, scaled-up scenographic objects (a vast bed and a super-sized chair formed from 'at hand' objects) accentuated the petite frame of one solo performer while also acting expressionistically as a comment on her perception of her 'lesser' stature as a young, mixed-race woman in a world where most 'heroines' (from the Alices, Hermiones and Wendys of children's literature to the Hollywood actresses and celebrities, CEOs and cabinet ministers of our everyday lives) are white. In another space – the floor of which was almost entirely covered with small glass vases – a female performer knelt pouring water from one receptacle to another over and over again – her parodic actions, in this 'pool of tears', evoking and challenging the stereotype of the 'emotional' (perhaps 'mad') woman. In yet another space, a 'court-room' with gossamer thin walls, a hypnotically slow performance of dressing and undressing, first in 'female' and then in 'male' attire, became the vehicle by which the male performer, struggling to maintain his balance as he raised one leg with infinite precision, exposed the structures of heteronormativity as similarly precarious: a mere 'house of cards'. In all, the students had constructed a piece in which conceptual, contextual, material, performative and visuospatial elements were impressively well put together according to the laws of the project's own universe, and where every question of aesthetic form – from the piece's fragmented, hybrid nature and the connotative power of its scenographic materials to its preference for manifestation over straightforward signification, its non-linear organization and its invitation to visitors to act as authors of their own spatial dramaturgies – was also, implicitly, a question of the politics of postdramatic performance (see Lehmann's 'note in passing'; Lehmann et al. 2008: 16).

In its own small way, *Who Are You?* might be described in Professor of Design Mohsen Mostafavi's words as an act of 'constructed imagination' designed to challenge an existing institutional set-up (2014: 194). By re-configuring beyond all recognition the unpopular, 'dumb' rehearsal room which they had been assigned, and introducing into a building that is not equipped for learning/teaching (or even storing) scenography and sets an unapologetically architectural logic, the students had intervened in an environment which they perceived as unsupportive of their ambitions and built a new space in which it was possible for them to learn and make performance without restriction. The confidence with which my students determined anew what performance might be is reason enough for me to want to continue bringing an architectural inflection to my teaching of theatre and performance. Yet there is a bigger point to be made here about the architecture of disciplinary and/or institutional structures and the mental spaces we might free up through interdisciplinary transformation. It is this larger constellation of questions around the politics of teaching performance that I wish to turn to by way of conclusion.

# Conclusion

More interesting than accounts that acknowledge individual disciplines and practices as always already the meeting places of many different knowledges, peoples and skills are those attempts to address the social implications of training and education that remain (largely) divided by more-or-less well-respected categories of subject. As Tim Culvahouse argues of the way professional practice in architecture and the construction industry is split into separate specialisms, one of the main benefits of newly expanded definitions of the tectonic might be in ensuring productive working relations between the different players whose combined contributions are needed to produce the end result (1996: 11). In architecture education, this has already led to a re-thinking of the ways that architects, clients, construction workers, local interest groups, planners, project managers and structural engineers interact with one another. In performance pedagogy, it might lead to greater awareness of the nature of the various social and artistic inter-dependencies that exist between performers, scenographers, spectators, technicians and others involved in making contemporary performance. In this respect, the decision by new media company and makers of postdramatic devised performance The Builders Association to include architects, set builders and other technical workers within its network of regular collaborators and to place acts of construction – and, on occasion, construction workers – centre-stage draws attention to a schism in contemporary experimental theatre and performance that many of us find uncomfortable: that is, the hierarchical structure that posits theory above practice, artists above designers, university-educated directors and writers above conservatoire-trained actors, and members of a creative collective above the technicians and builders whose efforts make their artistic productions possible. If we are to break apart the system that perpetuates such inequalities and clear the way for constructing new forms of education and imagination, this change, I would suggest, needs to be brought about in the places where children and young adults first learn to categorize, differently value and, eventually, 'distrust and disdain' people and practices that are Other to their own (Dolan 2001: 1).

While university drama departments cannot always provide the space and equipment that students would like, and do not always have enough flexibility in their timetables to schedule mixed classes with other departments, there is a growing desire among learners and teachers – both within and outside higher education institutions and other official educational contexts – to forge closer working relations between scenographers and builders, architects, dancers and performance makers to venture outside their comfort zones in order to combine, exchange and question established knowledge and skills. Examples include Beatriz Colomina's ongoing 'Radical Pedagogies' project; Ephemera Collective's workshops in architecture and performance intervention (see Ephemera Collective 2015); Station House Opera's builder-led training for participants of *Dominoes* and other breezeblock performances; the 'Shared Pedagogies' programme of learning/teaching between architecture and performance that Andrew Filmer and I organized for PQ15 (the Prague Quadrennial of Performance Design and Space 2015); and recent workshops and writings by

Kyveli Anastasiadi, Aliki Kylika and Alex Schweder of the Viral Institute of Performance Architecture (see Kylika and Anastasiadi 2016). Other possibilities might involve setting up exchanges between conservatoires or university drama departments and schools of architecture or, more broadly, between those learning theatre or performance and those learning woodwork, metalwork and other construction skills in nearby schools, colleges or community education facilities. Exchanges between such different types of learner have implications that are at once pedagogical, personal and socially turned. They suggest not only a bridging of artistic, intellectual and manual labour across subject fields and categories of educational institution but also (potentially) a bringing together of learners across age groups, ethnicities, gender identities and social classes. Ultimately, such exchanges could begin to dismantle entrenched practices and prejudices in education and to posit new ways in which to build and share knowledge in ways that are more genuinely democratic.

Architecture and performance share overlaps of material, concern and practice that range from a focus on time and space to interests in the production, articulation and programming of space, in the structuring of action and event, in the construction and contestation of social relations and in the meeting between human bodies and the built forms they occupy. Yet, they are stubbornly, wonderfully Other. Whether as organizing principle, material presence or compositional practice, architecture can transform how we learn to make theatre. As I have argued, an architectural approach to learning/teaching performance stresses the fact that both disciplines are centrally concerned with world building and with notions of sociality and shared space. At the same time (and as this chapter's epigraph implies), architecture troubles the very nature of performance – pushing at its boundaries and exposing its paradoxes and its contradictions. For those of us seeking to promote interdisciplinarity within and beyond the academy, the issue of how we might best enable the theorists and makers of tomorrow not only to recognize and, if necessary, overturn disciplinary conventions but also to think outside the norms of education and established creative practices is essential for the formation of active citizens. It is because tectonic thinking is helpful at the levels of performance composition, design and space and in terms of a far larger 'architecture' of institutionalized structures that a tectonics of devised performance might help forward radical practices in postdramatic theatre and performance pedagogy alike.

# 13

# Bringing Performance into Architectural Pedagogy

Beth Weinstein

Architects frequently refer to Michel de Certeau's assertion that 'space is practiced place' (de Certeau 1984: 117), a statement suggesting repeated being and doing in physical space. Yet the practices that are central to architectural ideation of space – drawing and modelling – are, necessarily, removed in time, location and scale from site and future architectural work. Diagrams may help anticipate human movement, or other performances, in space, yet tools to directly explore human performances in, of and with space are largely absent in architectural pedagogy. These mediating tools form an incomplete set where students' developing embodied knowledge of live, iterative practices of space is concerned. Despite the ubiquity today of the term *performance* in architecture, I would argue for a more nuanced understanding of performance, drawing from performance studies. With the help of case studies, this chapter demonstrates instances for bringing questions and practices from performance into architectural education – through the projective designing, processual making and inhabiting of space – as complementary and critical tools.

In architecture, the term performance most commonly refers to how a building, space, envelope or constructive component responds to changing environmental conditions or human activity. Digital modelling and simulation software are essential to exploring such environmental, material and formal performances. Recent publications such as *Performance-Oriented Architecture* (Hensel 2013), *Performative Architecture: Beyond Instrumentality* (Kolarevic and Malkawi 2005) and *Performalism: Form and Performance in Digital Architecture* (Grobman and Neuman 2012) explore this form–performance nexus. We can interpret this as architecture's technological performance, similar to performance studies scholar Jon McKenzie's idea of *techno-performance* explored in *Perform or Else*. In theorizing performance, McKenzie identifies three types, the second being *organizational performances* – those 'evaluated in terms of [the] [...] efficiency' of business structures that are 'service-based, globally oriented and electronically wired' (McKenzie 2001: 5–6). Architectural education is currently consumed by techno- and organizational performance anxieties. While recent volumes reflect upon enduring principles, practices and milestones in architectural education (Nicol and Pilling 2000; Ockman and Williamson 2012; Simitch and Warke 2014), others focus on shifts responding to global economic and climate changes, and the 'great tsunami of technology that has affected how we work, what we work on, what it is made of and when we work on it' (Spiller and Clear 2014: 11). Changes to teaching in this economy parallel McKenzie's organizational paradigm. The 'perform or else' mandate incessantly monitors faculty and student 'training' – to meet accrediting bureau standards with industry-approved tools – and convolutes objectives through funded studios that often tie corporate interests to the academy's economic health (Miessen 2010). Meanwhile, critics of the ivory tower challenge students and faculty to redefine the roles they perform, as architects in communities, with clients and collaborators. So, to complement globally-oriented, digitally-networked investigations, schools of architecture increasingly are valorizing local engagement and hands-on learning through Design-Build or Live-Project studios.[1] While these projects are platforms for developing embodied understanding of materials and construction, what McKenzie defines as the third performance largely remains unexplored.

McKenzie's *cultural performance* refers to both the tricks of showbiz and the 'living, embodied expression of cultural traditions and transformations' with the efficacy of 'foregrounding and resisting dominant norms' (McKenzie 2001: 9). The study of cultural performances feeds back between ritual and theatre, critical theory and performance art; through iterative practices and theories *performances challenge* (McKenzie 2001: 44) – challenge what is and has been and rehearse possible futures. Challenging traditions through performance echoes architect Bernard Tschumi's proclamation that 'architecture('s) social relevance and formal invention [...] cannot be dissociated from the events that *happen* in it' (1996: 139). Architectural historian David Leatherbarrow, in affirming 'a shift of orientation in architectural theory and practice from what the building *is* to what it *does*' (2005: 7), places cultural performances among techno- and organizational performances. Leatherbarrow argues:

> [O]perations can indeed be managed, functions can likewise be scripted, but the *events* that we take as important cannot – or what is planned is not what makes them important. [...] If the *event* is only what was anticipated it will have been both uneventful and unmemorable. (2005: 11)

Central to architecture's performances are the living, embodied occasions, events and actions, the intended as well as unscripted practices and improvisations of space. Space is 'practiced place', as de Certeau suggests, and, following McKenzie, performances of space challenge. Cultural performances of architecture afford critical questioning of ways of being in and with space; they are not predetermined but rather constructed, akin to philosopher Judith Butler's claim that gender is constructed through its repeated performance (1988: 583). Thus, while architecture's scripts may appear to be written (drawn or built) in bricks and mortar, critical practices in architecture must repeatedly be performed.

Pre-existing places, I would argue, are not the only sites and occasions in architecture's design–build–inhabit cycle in which performance can be leveraged as a critical tool to interrogate and otherwise inform architecture. Performance, I would argue, may be a critical tool during three phases in the architectural life cycle. First, performances in and of space may be a potent conceptual springboard at a project's outset. For example, during the pre-design phase architects normally analyse *programme* – space-use requirements or projected performances – in relation to precedents. Through programme analysis architects challenge received ideas about rooms and functions and research and speculate about human activity in relation to past (precedent) and future built-form. Analysis of performance spaces and events, in particular, helps students understand space from the perspective of temporal events, and more critically question how time and event inform their design work. In the case studies *SHiFT* and *ICON* (discussed below), students' designs were developed through research, analysis and ultimately the design of event-spaces and temporal structures.

Second, performance may inform the leap from designing to building – the performance of constructing – space. Dominant design processes work through scalar media – drawings and models – that privilege visual aspects and spatial, geometric ordering. The design process may also include full-scale mock-ups of building components, particularly in design-build studios – a rehearsal of sorts. Given that construction is generally carried out by people other than those who create the drawings, these drawn instructions tend to prescribe every detail – a very tight score or script to be followed. However, when designers perform the act of building, the role or necessity of mediating instructions is called into question. A robust feedback loop between scalar work and full-scale prototyping may in fact lead to other kinds of design solutions – ones open to live improvisation in the performance of building informed by the physically present, multi-sensory designing-building being and body. Philosophers Maxine Sheets-Johnstone (1981) as well as Erin Manning and Brian Massumi (2014) theorize 'thinking in movement' and 'thought in the act' as underacknowledged, valuable ways of knowing and creating space. While design-build projects are increasingly popular pedagogical vehicles, these opportunities rarely consider students' bodies as sites for learning or embrace improvisation as a positive, desirable practice. The 'Dance Lab' and 'Design in Movement' studios (discussed later) explore liveness within the designing and building processes.

As already suggested, opportunities to explore inhabitation as a performance or a practice of space are infrequent in architectural curricula. *Architectes/Actions* and 'Performative Renovations' critically rethought and designed alternative inhabitations. While design-build studios offer students opportunities to grapple with materiality and full scale, they do not foreground the third phase – practising space. Embodied, live performances offer architecture students opportunities to learn through exploring tensions between what built spaces suggest and other ways of being *in* and *with* space.

The six examples, taken from my teaching and those of colleagues within architectural schools internationally, in no way comprise the definitive and exhaustive survey of instances of architecture instructors bringing performance into architectural pedagogy. Many exciting examples have been left out and many more remain unknown to me. The examples presented each pulled architecture students out of their comfort zone (the studio) and de-emphasized or eliminated use of the dominant learning/teaching tools, i.e. analogue and digital scalar drawings and modelling. They introduced performance space and event case studies, concepts and practices as ways of rethinking, making and inhabiting space. They challenged students to work directly with materials, live, full-scaled, in embodied explorations. The projects and pedagogies put students on the spot, challenged them to perform, with distinct and complementary tools from those typical of architectural education and practice.

## About performing

The objective of my semester-long undergraduate elective that resulted in *SHiFT* (University of Arizona, 2010) was for students to learn *about* and *through*

**Figure 13.1** *SHiFT*: a performed reinterpretation of visionary theatre (University of Arizona, Tucson, 2010), Beth Weinstein (architect-instructor) with Cruz Crawford, Tyler Jorgenson, Corey Kingston, Lara Lafontain, Heiman Luk, Kevin Moore, Andy Rodrigue and Nicole Sweeney (architecture student team). Above: performance photo. Below: score showing plan, elevation and theatre architecture research. Photo courtesy of Tabitha Rodrigue. Score courtesy of Tyler Jorgensen and team.

performance space design and the performance of space (Weinstein 2011). This course broke from standard formats by combining seminar and workshop modes of learning. Similar to the projects that follow, it rejected typical outcome formats – papers, drawings, models or even installations. My students interpreted their research through performance.

At the outset, each student researched one pre-twentieth-century architectural space associated with a historical form of theatre or performance, followed by research about one experimental twentieth-century performance space. This built a common vocabulary and contrasted traditional and avant-garde examples. The students then abstracted and re-presented their twentieth-century case study in a two-step exercise. They first created digital models revealing the primary spatial elements and performer–audience relationships. I then challenged them to further abstract these through small *performative models* – models performing one quality. The elements and relations that emerged through this process included steps to ascend towers and projections to surround an audience. We collectively discussed how to share their understanding of performance space through an experience, deciding to create a performance of space about performance space. In the next leap, they developed a set of elements that could, in one configuration and then another, convey the experience of each theatre. Informed by their precedents, they adopted a Bauhaus/Constructivist vocabulary of lines, planes and simple volumes. A collective exploration through scale models, during one intense *charrette* session, resulted in the final design – a set of long rectangular volumes (columns/steps) and fabric panels to suspend. The performance would be a *stage-hand ballet* of moving these elements into and out of different configurations, one after another, on the basis of the salient features of each theatre.

The next phase of research was through full-scale, real-time explorations with their bodies. Constraints of material availability, weight, elasticity, attachment and budget were similar to those of design-build projects. Once built, this kit of parts afforded students opportunities to explore with their bodies the still evolving configurations. This *spatial sketching* – iterative, live exploration with full-scale components – offered vital feedback, revising the choreography of constructing and deconstructing the theatre-analogues. In addition to designing the configurations and movement of the physical elements between these, the students looked to the performer–audience relationships in their case studies to score their being and movement in each theatre-analogue. Designing within the space-in-the-process-of-becoming – not virtually, but live – privileged simultaneous working with mind and body. The process placed value on 'the body as a medium for learning' and demanded deliberate attention to and development of a kinaesthetic sensibility (Pineau 2002) in direct relation to the space of investigation. While it is common for architects to place value on phenomenological and kinaesthetic experience (Pallasmaa 1996) or to reflect upon the image or proportions of the body inscribed within built architectures (Dodds, Tavernor and Rykwert 2002), this learning context challenged dominant pedagogies that repress or forget bodies (hooks 1993; Pineau 2002). *SHiFT* and the projects that follow subverted dominant practice by valuing embodied learning as integral to the design process. The learning environment foregrounded the tension between intellectual and embodied modes of working, and challenged students to mine past performances to design future events, spaces and inhabitations.

*Iconography* (or *ICON*), at the University of Waterloo, similarly challenged students to reformulate and reinterpret the past through performance. The programme's founder, Larry Cummings, initiated the *ICON* performance project, and Tracey Winton led this endeavour between 2006 and 2016. While the teaching of Renaissance history was the official objective, Winton approached history as dynamically constructed from a particular viewpoint, and challenged the students to not only 'think like an architect' but also leverage their diverse abilities to construct – through space, prop, movement and narrative – and perform their layered interpretation of cultural history.

*ICON* is the final course in the cultural history series, occurring during the summer after students' second year. Winton began each semester by presenting two kinds of prompts. The first was a thematic or topic, such as the construction of memory, with several texts, images and even pieces of music or art works for students to research and weave together. During the semester that focused on memory, Winton paired Homer's recounting of the Trojan War with *Blade Runner* replicants' 'memories'. The second prompt or informing constraint was place, one capable of holding a complexity of cultural references, experiences and information; sometimes the location was given, other times scouted by the students. The performance content developed through the '[r]euse and interpretation of historical materials, images, [...] textual materials [...] deploying [them] and bodies in space, more like performance art, or installation art' (Winton 2014: 6) than a narrative-based play.

This annual performance was a massive undertaking involving approximately eighty undergraduates. The students self-organized into teams, with elected spokespeople, to take on the diverse responsibilities: researching and developing the performance structure, writing scripts, designing objects, costumes and environments, choreographing performers and audience members, developing lighting and soundtracks, and performing. The students made use of social media to communicate their ideas, inspirations, reference materials and the work-in-progress, as well as for fundraising and publicity. While all participants were students of architecture, they drew upon their diverse life skills – as organizers, managers, musicians and dancers – to realize the work.

Student feedback remarked on the talent and trust developed in their peers, new collaboration skills and respect for budgets and deadlines. They were surprised that, in spite of having drawn everything beforehand, they 'had to change everything based on what [they] experience[d] and learned while [they] were building it in real life' (Winton 2014: 8). The 'rehearsing' or testing of design ideas through mock-ups or prototypes, and the tweaking and remaking of these prototypes, gave new perspective on the uses and limitations of drawing versus full-scale construction. Another student commented on the movement between writing or drawing and making or sensing:

> Reading a play in words on a script is like understanding a building in lines
> on a drawing. It's entirely different from the actual presence of material and
> experience. I believe there is a middle ground of understanding … between the
> plan and carrying it out that can only come from experience. (Winton 2014: 8)

Similar to *SHiFT*, the *ICON* projects moved historical research out of the library
and creative exploration away from the drawing board; it moved students
into wood shops and buildings around their city. The compressed schedule
and ephemerality of the performance afforded more playful approaches. As a
'construction of history', students felt authorized to explore ambiguity, affect
and atmosphere – qualities that are not always embraced in architectural
studio courses (Weinstein 2016b). Learning took place through the movement
of artefacts from the past into a sensible, spatial, eventful present. This in
turn afforded embodied knowledge development, a modality of learning too
frequently absent from architectural pedagogy.

While both *SHiFT* and *ICON* admittedly involved multiple types and occasions
for learning – historical research and analysis as well as research through
designing, fabrication and embodied action – these projects are examples of
leveraging research *about* past performances, spaces, bodies, atmospheres and
temporal structures to inform new performances of space.

## Performing making

'Dance Lab' and 'Design in Movement' both exemplify performances of making
that afforded emergent or improvised architectures. In dialogue with University
of Illinois Urbana-Champaign dance faculty and students, architects Julie
Larsen and Roger Hubeli engaged upper-level architecture students in designing
and fitting out a new graduate student 'Dance Lab' (University of Illinois
Urbana-Champaign, 2010). They structured this design-build project semester
in two parts – research to inform the design process and the performance of
constructing the design. One significant constraint was the donation of a
basketball court's worth of wood flooring.

In the first exercise, teams comprising one dance and two to three architecture
students explored dance videos to question the relationship between dance and
space and to develop a shared vocabulary. One video in particular, by Montreal-
based La La La Human Steps, featured a dance within a small wooden vessel
in which the floor seamlessly curved up to become the walls. This image of a
containing space informed the design they developed – that of a vessel of space

defining the dance lab, with its sprung floor, inside the volume of the existing building. A second set of somatic exercises led by dance faculty member Jennifer Monson involved the students listening to the building's sonic performance, attuning to near and far, and sensing the distance and space between (Weinstein 2016a). These exercises led the students to develop ideas for interruptions in the surface of the inner vessel – allowing views to the exterior, light into the interior, revealing the interstitial space, accessing storage or framing previously overlooked elements in the space. A third exercise asked students to question how the repurposed floorboards might perform differently than usually conceived, drawing both from the dance video and the embodied space exercises. Using the physical material, students explored aggregations, flexibility and adaptation, leading to several design strategies. From these they chose a proposal with a flexible meshwork made from the scrap end bits of the reclaimed wood, strung together with piano wire.

**Figure 13.2** 'Dance Lab 1' (UIUC, Urbana-Champaign, 2010), APTUM: Roger Hubeli and Julie Larsen (architects-instructors) with UIUC architecture and dance students. Above: photo of dancer between existing building and new woven wood wall. Below: diagram of the process of making the woven wall assembly – from old basketball court to chopped elements to new draped wall. Photo courtesy of Wallo Villacorta. Diagram courtesy of APTUM.

What emerged through this was a material assembly strategy – a process in lieu of a fixed plan – allowing for improvisation during the construction. It involved two material systems. First, the team laid a new sprung floor using the repurposed boards from point A, in one corner, towards point B, in the opposite corner, until the available 'good' material was exhausted; the limit of the dance floor was unforeseeable, emerging through performing the construction. Second, the team created the enclosing vessel from the mesh, woven into modular panels and suspended from the ceiling, in such a way as to allow for change. Once suspended, the panels were pulled into shapes responding to performance criteria – accommodating changes in ceiling height and pitch, allowing passage from the dance floor into the interstitial space, accessing storage and draping to mimic the silhouette of bodies. While architectural drawing and modelling was used to *approximate* a layout of 'good' floorboards for the sprung floor, the inner vessel and its subdivision into modules, the materials and construction process demanded ongoing improvisation, proving the drawings to be mere approximations. Both the architects and student participants remarked on how the open-ended, bottom-up, improvisational nature of the construction contrasted sharply with experiences in other design-build studios, which tended to favour definitive outcomes (Weinstein 2012, 2017a, b). In one way, the donated material, with its unknowns, pre-conditioned this improvisation; the geometry of the inner vessel and the residual space between it and the outer wall and ceiling were contingent upon the surface area of the new sprung floor. Additionally, the dancer-clients modelled improvisation repeatedly, with micro-performances throughout the semester. Ironically, since the dancers' project goal was having a 'clean' workspace, they had dismissed the interstitial space as 'lost' space. Once constructed, its unique spatial constraints and qualities prompted the dancers to explore it and create site-specific dances.

While typical architectural learning and practice aim to predetermine the final form of a design, this learning environment privileged the emergence of form and space through the performance of a construction strategy. Larsen and Hubeli, as well as the student-assistant on the project, remarked that since this experience they continue to work with open-ended, material and fabrication-driven processes as a critical form of practice. The shift of priority from form to performance, from the thing to the doing, created opportunities to work discursively with material, site and client-user, and develop methods open to variables beyond control. Learning agility of mind through improvisation with

matter equips designers to consider processes, not just products, in their practice
– valuable from a human, environmental and economic perspective.

Whereas improvisation was an unforeseen outcome of the 'Dance Lab'
project, it was a fundamental starting point of architect Frances Bronet and
philosopher John Schumacher's pedagogy. Their 'Design in Movement' studio
(Rensselaer Polytechnic Institute, 1996–1997) explored 'dance as the basis for
explaining [the] contrast [of] space – or movement *in* space – with movement'
(1999: 97). Contact improvisation – a dance form developed by Steve Paxton –
was key to introducing the ideas and practices of *space-in-the-making* to the
beginning design students. Citing dance scholar Eleanor Luger, Bronet and
Schumacher pointed out that '[c]ontacters come to regard the geography of
the body differently than other types of dancers or pedestrians. Rather than
distinguishing the body by its parts (as the eye would tend to do), they think
more of body surfaces, as planes of support' (1999: 97).

At the semester outset, dancers demonstrated contact improv, and
students engaged in embodied exercises, such as multi-body shape-making
and transformations. Through these exercises, and the main project to create
environments for dance, Bronet and Schumacher challenged students to
prioritize space's coming into being, live, through embodied exploration, over
the shaping of space to be seen at a distance. They suggest:

> [F]or the hypothesis of body as opposed to eye, we should speak of bodily
> actions as making space (space-making actions, not spatializing actions), what
> we think of as *space-in-the-making*. [...] In our design pedagogy we are trying to
> push to the limit of the tensive play of eye and body. Can we achieve a primacy
> of body in architectural design? (Bronet and Schumacher 1999: 97, 100–101)

Six student teams developed proposals for environments to support both *space-
in-the-making* and *dance-in-the-making* – environments in which 'movement
determines space'. As with the previous projects, testing ideas at full-scale was
an integral part of the process. Here, too, the use of conventional practices,
such as scale models, was a starting point; students' direct explorations with the
behaviours of materials, such as fabric and rolled paper, quickly revealed what
would not work and yielded unforeseen opportunities. Working at full-scale,
students asked how materials and components would occupy space, respond to
dancers' movements and enable emergent and transforming spaces. In keeping
with the principle of *space-in-the-making*, both the elements and their layout in
the site were conceptualized not as 'ready-made', pre-existing, but as designs-in-

development. In this spirit, students continued adjusting and tuning elements during the installation process. The 'Entropy' project, for example,

> developed into an array of malleable, transparent, and rotating elements that could be dense when the dancers were not there, but could readily be cleared when they were present – a kind of space-in-the-making. The turnstiles were also transparent, so that the coming together of the performers was not completely accidental. [...] The advantage was the tension between the eye being drawn through the hangings to the walls beyond and the body being called upon to move where there was space, a 'moving' condition of hangings and human bodies. (Bronet and Schumacher 1999: 104–105)

The student designs aspired to create spaces that did not reveal themselves as images to be visually enjoyed from afar but rather as spaces that had to be explored through movement. As I have argued above, the normative tools of architectural practice (scalar drawings and models) privilege the eye and visual aspects of designs. These develop thought processes that distance the designer – spatially, through scale and time – from the imagined space in formation. This is a necessity for the design of most buildings. However, normative practice and teaching tend to forget the body as a locus of and tool through which to develop spatial thinking, knowledge and proposals. Bronet and Schumacher challenged students to develop skills that extend beyond these norms, to work with their mind and body in real time and improvisationally, and to take into consideration multi-sensory moving bodies' temporally unfolding experiences of space. 'Design in Movement', as with 'Dance Lab', drew students' attention to present-tense unfolding of the design through construction or movement. They set aside practices of predetermination for performances of improvisation – open-ended processes shaping and manipulating materials, and fostering the emergence of movement and space together.

## Performing inhabitations

*Architectes/Actions* and 'Performative Renovations' shifted attention away from research *about* past performance or *through* performance of building, to the design of new embodied performances within existing spaces. The undergraduate architecture elective course in 'art and movement', collaboratively taught by artist-architect Emmanuelle Bouyer and choreographer Catherine Baÿ, sought to draw attention to normative versus unexpected actions, inhabitations and body–architecture relationships latent within a familiar space – their school of architecture. The semester-length exploration culminated in an informal performance, *Architectes/Actions* (ENSA Paris-Val de Seine, 2012).

In their recently constructed school, students identified the diversity of spatial relationships the building suggested, in detail and at large scale, and that could be questioned. Bouyer and Baÿ asked the students to develop a catalogue of typical architecture student gestures – related to drawing, model making, presenting and discussing works – as well as movements and actions commonly performed by people their age – movements taken from sports and other leisure activities. The students were then challenged to defamiliarize relationships between action and space through techniques such as displacement, juxtaposition, simultaneity and so on. The most common means for architecture students to learn to speculate about and communicate proportional relationships between human bodies and spaces is through section drawings in which they integrate *entourage* – images of people doing everyday things – to scale. This technique is also used to communicate activities occurring in a space. Instructors sometimes complement this drawing-based method with embodied methods, such as

**Figure 13.3** *Architectes/Actions* (ENSA Paris-Val de Seine, Paris, 2012), instructors Catherine Baÿ (artist-choreographer) and Emmanuelle Bouyer (artist-architect) with architecture students. Photos courtesy of the author.

students measuring a space with a part of their body. *Architectes/Actions* asked students to work with their own bodies as primary tools of investigation to explore the specific slopes of floors, depths of ledges, capacities of handrails to bear weight, visual and sonic connections from one part of a space to another, as well as questioning the activities one anticipated finding there.

For the final project the students chose three spaces to perform through inhabitation. The event began in a wide hallway, unique because of the slight split into two levels with a bench marking the edge. This split complicated inhabitation of the space, leading the students to juxtapose two distinct activities in the space. The event continued several floors below in a vestibule with one wall interrupted by several floor-to-ceiling glass panels. The students intervened in the space by installing modular tables on both sides of the glass partition, creating the appearance of a long table and its occupants' activities split/ mirrored by this glass. The third and final scene explored the two-level entrance hall. The students occupied the reception desk as if it were their design studio where they were working on a collaborative project. Meanwhile other student activities moved between the upper-level mezzanine, connecting ramp, ground level and various remote corners of the volume. The students' bright orange and green jerseys signalled to passers-by that something unusual was happening; actions carried out simultaneously by jerseyed students in different parts of the space prompted the accidental audience to look around the space with curiosity to ask 'what's going on here?' The students were encouraged to bring a playful inquisitiveness to every detail and spatial relation in their investigation, and through this develop keener embodied knowledge of proportions, ergonomics and scale, as well as tools for critically questioning assumed relations between programme and space. *Architectes/Actions* affirmed that space is practised place and the identity of the space and its occupants is constructed through performance.

Similar ideas informed Alex Schweder's undergraduate architecture studio, 'Performative Renovations' (Pratt Institute, 2013). This studio asked students to approach performance as 'an aesthetic way of looking at program', use, action and event (Schweder 2014: 22). This enquiry built upon his own practice through which he was asking subjects to 'use a familiar environment in an unexpected way' in order to develop new perceptions of that space, and of themselves in relation to it; Schweder was questioning the definition of *architectural renovation* (Schweder 2015: 98). Normally, when architects are asked to design a space for a given purpose, they ask what is involved in the activities that the space will accommodate. Furthermore, when adapting a space for a new activity, the assumption is that the 'renovation' will involve some material construction and/or demolition, not mere shifts in the inhabitants' behaviour or perception. However, renovations without material alteration can be seen as a radically sustainable and economic approach to solving the problem, in line with the position that building is not necessarily the solution to an architectural problem.

For the initial exercises Schweder drew on *The Décor Project* (2001–2006) by artists Hadley + Maxwell and Erwin Wurm's *One Minute Sculptures* (various locations, ongoing since 1996). In the latter, untrained subjects create ephemeral relations between their bodies, found objects and spaces. Schweder's first short assignment, 'One-Minute Building', challenged students to design similar kinds of relations, quickly, with a sense of humour. In working with their bodies and found elements, students were also challenged to think and work in ways that did not draw from their familiar skill set, and to develop confidence performing in front of each other. One student outcome of this exercise was the *Purposeful[ly] Ambiguous Object #2*, a wooden element attached to two metal tubes. Depending on how one held it and its relation to other people, the object could perform, when held frontally, as a serving tray or a classroom writing tablet, or, when overhead, a sign. A performance's duration would depend on the performer's fatigue holding the object in position, in relation to physical weight placed on it. To explicitly link performance and architectural practices, students wrote and drew instructions and documented the performance. Whereas architectural 'orthographic' drawings – plans and sections – are instructions for the performance of construction, these instructions were made to inform the performance of use, based upon rehearsals.

For 'Performative Renovations', each student was to renovate the dwelling space of another student. Their first task was to uncover the needs of their client and ultimately design other actions to redefine the way the space performed. Students interviewed their clients, modelled after Hadley + Maxwell's practice, to uncover their client's less-evident desires and frustrations in relation to their dwelling space. This was an iterative process, both to develop interview skills and to reveal the compelling problem to be approached from a spatial *and* performance perspective. One student-client sought greater privacy within the context of his shared university dormitory room to do what he felt uncomfortable doing when his extrovert room-mate was present – playing music, spending time with his girlfriend or cleaning. The normative architectural approach would be to design a physical element creating separation and visual/acoustical privacy between the room-mates. The performative approach taken addressed time – time alone in the apartment. To the student-designer, Schweder suggested two means to control the extrovert room-mate's non-use of the space – *bait* or *poison*. To construct times for privacy, the student-designer proposed finding the extrovert room-mate a girlfriend. An internet dating page and time-tracking system were the 'things' designed. Through this design, the student-client gained agency over time – time 'home' for himself in correspondence to designed time 'out' for the extrovert room-mate.

While the students initially struggled with this unfamiliar mode of thinking, they came to understand programme and performance as interrelated, and that our daily use of space is performed. Both assignments asked students to take a critical stance vis-à-vis the architect's purpose and practice, and the relation of these to construction versus performance of space. Through this pedagogy, students challenged normative design practices, problematized 'performance criteria' and questioned how space performs; in doing so, they developed intelligent, economic and ecological alternatives to *common* practice.

## Conclusion

These pairings of pedagogical case studies, framed through three instances in the design process or architectural life cycle, demonstrate occasions when performance can fruitfully expand how we think about and explore space, and make and inhabit space. Focusing on predesign and design-phase research and speculation *about* performance, the first pair foregrounded the eventfulness of space. Students examined past performances within avant-garde environmental scenographies, scripts, films and histories to inform the design of temporal structures and spatial events. They used expanded skills to bring history into the present. The second pair illustrated opportunities within the space-making process, the *performing of designing*, as a liminal space-time that opens up to unknowns. This challenged students to develop 'game plans' rather than plans, ones open to interpretation and improvisation. In designing processes to be carried out, the end result remained to be seen, literally. The process, rather than the space or object, was the object of design. Students in Bronet and Schumacher's studio explored the body as tool for researching, for perceiving, and for feedback about designs intended for bodies in movement, rather than for eyes at a distance. The third instances challenged students to perform space with their bodies as a way of critiquing space-programme expectations, gaining embodied knowledge of the fit between body and space, and to expand the architect's palette to include time and performance in addition to matter.

While many of these case studies engaged students of architecture in the making of some form of performance event, the goal was not to make dancers or actors of them. Rather the objectives were to empower designers to consider performance as a lens through which to understand and imagine the eventfulness within and of space. As humanist pedagogies, the courses drew upon the diversity of students' skills, interests and abilities as whole people. The projects offered multimodal forms of learning – learning *about* performance and its relation to architecture and learning *through* performing. As promoted through '21st century pedagogies' and current university 'engagement policies', as well as decades of research in performance studies, embodied learning 'deepens experiential and participatory engagement with materials both for the researcher and her audience' (Conquergood 2002: 152). These case studies leveraged the performance challenge for students to step out from behind the computer screen into the picture or space-in-the-making and perform space as a practice. Through these course projects, they developed complementary and empowering skills to challenge architectural practices through embodied performances.

# Note

1  Design-Build (USA) or Live (UK) Projects mimic forms of practice in which the designer is also the builder. These studios generally provide design services to underserved communities and non-profit organizations and they engage students in the pre-design phase of developing the project brief with the client, the various design and approval processes, and the execution of the construction.

# 14

# The Watermill Center: An Interview with Robert Wilson

Andrew Filmer

*Robert Wilson's prolific career as artist, director, designer and performer has profoundly influenced the look and sound of contemporary theatre. Through seminal works including* Deafman Glance *(1970), the seven-day epic* KA MOUNTAIN AND GUARDenia TERRACE *(1972), the silent opera* The Life and Times of Joseph Stalin *(1973) and* Einstein on the Beach *(1976), Wilson has established a signature style of structured images, movement and deconstructed language. The sheer range of Wilson's work has crossed traditional artistic boundaries, encompassing drama, dance, opera, visual art, sculpture and installation.*

*Wilson has a long-standing fascination and engagement with architecture. As a student at the Pratt Institute in New York in the early 1960s, Wilson was taught by the architectural historian Sybil Moholy-Nagy: 'What I learnt from her', he recalled, 'was to apply order and disorder in a way that was meaningful. I think that's my fascination with architecture. An architect can design a structure, but within that structure, you can let your imagination run free' (Otto-Bernstein 2006: 38). Wilson has frequently used the term 'architecture' to describe the compositional dimensions of his theatre work, in particular the way he uses the geometry of vertical, horizontal and diagonal arrangements to create space. Such arrangements hold in tension different elements – shape, colour, movement – allowing a play of relationships to evolve within an overall structure. 'I do not have a message', stated Wilson in an interview, 'What I do is an architectural arrangement' (Lesschaeve in Shevtsova 2007: 52).*

*In 1990 Wilson founded The Watermill Center on Long Island, New York, a centre for artistic exploration and experimentation that he has described variously as his home, as a laboratory and as a place for asking questions. Watermill functions not only as a place of meeting, collaboration, art making and experimentation, but also as a work of art in itself. Watermill's design and its positioning in a carefully maintained landscape reflects Wilson's own aesthetic, offering striking experiences of symmetry, geometry and the precise juxtaposition of forms and objects. Gideon Lester observes that Wilson's aesthetic choices operate as the frame to any creative work that is done there and that the artistic freedom afforded at Watermill 'is contingent on strict rules: beds must be made and plates washed on a particular way; each room must be left pristine' (2011: 289). Through this, Watermill functions as a place that heightens perception and awareness. It also embodies Wilson's world view: a place where life, art and learning are intermingled.*

*This interview with Wilson, which serves as the final chapter to this book, provides an insight into how architecture can mediate a pedagogic vision through co-producing spaces for learning and development. It serves as a coda to this section on interdisciplinary pedagogies, first by reinforcing Beth Weinstein's discussion of the importance of the body as a site of learning and the value of inhabitation and the practising of space in the development of architecture students as 'whole people'. It also returns to Juliet Rufford's argument that an engagement with architecture can transform how emerging performance makers learn to make theatre and come to occupy a position of active, engaged citizenship. The materiality of Watermill's buildings and landscape encourages an ethics of care and attentiveness, deepening awareness of one's relationship with others, with the environment, and with the past. Watermill stands as an implicit critique of institutionalized spaces of formal education which fail to offer such a holistic ethical vision. It provides an inspiring example of how architecture might stage and embody pedagogy. The interview was conducted via email in March 2017.*

**Andrew Filmer: Could you start by telling us a little bit about why you established Watermill?**

**Robert Wilson:** My first works were developed in a loft space in Soho in the mid-1960s at 147 Spring Street. It was where I lived and worked. At the time I was an educational consultant at various institutions around New York City: public schools, private schools, community centres, hospitals. It occurred to me that these very diverse people in their own communities never came together, so

I began to invite them to my loft, and out of this grew my first theatrical works. I brought together housewives, schoolteachers, factory workers, artists, homeless people, children and elderly people. All, for the most part, non-professional performers or actors.

In 1976 I had no money after having produced *Einstein on the Beach* myself. I had to give up my loft on Spring Street and worked mostly in major European theatres. Towards the end of the 1980s, I wanted to go back to my roots, to work with people with no formal education and others with high degrees of formal education; to bring together people from a variety of communities and backgrounds. I found an abandoned laboratory building in Water Mill, a hamlet of Southampton, Long Island. It reminded me very much of the loft I formerly had in Soho. I acquired it and began to remodel it. It was built by Western Union in the 1920s and had been vacant since 1959.

By this time I had met people from all over the world, from Latin America to North America to Europe and the Far East. In 1990 I officially established The Watermill Center, a laboratory for creative thinking. It was a place to bring together people from different backgrounds for an open exchange, where art and culture are the core.

**AF: Could you tell us a bit about it as place? Are there any features that you are especially fond of?**

**RW:** The Watermill Center is situated on ten acres of land. To the west we are protected by the Peconic Land Trust, an environmental preserve. It is in a farming community, a place where some of the first colonists landed. I like that it is in a natural environment.

On the grounds are a circle of stones from Flores, Indonesia. They are like Stonehenge, over 4,000 years old; markers of an ancient burial site. In the west courtyard there is a wooden funeral post from Borneo. To the north of the main building is a flower garden inspired by the paintings of Clementine Hunter, an African-American self-taught painter who has been very influential on my work. We also built a small house modeled after the place she lived and covered in murals. She called it 'Africa House'.

The building has a north–south and an east–west axis. The roof has gardens on both the north and south wings, and underground, in the core of the building is a library and an archive room, which houses works in the art collection. They comprise a kind of visual history of humanity.

**AF: Teaching is an integral part of your work and life as an artist. Could you tell us about your approach to teaching?**

RW: The basic premise is that you learn by doing, with a firm belief that the mind is a muscle. You learn to walk by walking, or falling down.

**AF: How does Watermill embody this understanding?**

RW: I think of The Watermill Center as a kind of Library of Inspiration where one lives with an awareness of artefacts from the past as one creates new work. We work alongside people from different parts of the world who speak different languages, integrated with people from the local community. When he was Minister of Culture in France, André Malraux said: 'We must maintain a balance of interest in protecting the art of the past with a balance of interest in protecting the art of our time; creation, and a balance of interest in the art

**Figure 14.1** The Rehearsal Hall, South Wing, Watermill Center. Photo courtesy of Lovis Ostenrik/The Watermill Center.

of our Nation, our homeland, with a balance of interest in the ART OF ALL NATIONS!'

At Watermill, one lives with an awareness of light; the special light of Long Island. The central building which connects the north and south wings has a floating roof, so rain and snow and light can fall in around the perimeter of the space. It is open to the elements. Inside the building there are big open spaces, and narrow spaces with high skylights. The South side of the building has wooden floors and it is more for workshops, exhibition space, and collaborative study. The north side has concrete floors and is used for the preparation and sharing of meals, sleeping, private study. It is like two hands of a body. The central building has no door, but an opening with a formal entrance following the east–west axis of the building. One can walk all the way from the street through the building to the circle of stones from 3500 BC in a single line.

**AF: Watermill embodies a strong collaborative artistic and ethical vision and this is modelled in the rules and protocols that govern its use. Can you tell us about these?**

**RW:** The design for the renovation of the building was done by a German architectural student from Berlin. Watermill was her thesis. The tables that we eat on, we have made ourselves. During the summer program, which I run, we all share in 'chores', which means cleaning, gardening, preparation of food. You have a different feeling for something you make than for something you buy. An artist works differently in an environment that they help to maintain and care for.

I like to think of a Noh mask, which is as beautifully finished on the interior as on the exterior. One is seen and one is hidden, but they are a part of the same work.

**AF: How have the responses and contributions of artists at Watermill changed your own view of the place?**

**RW:** It is constantly evolving. I do not want to have one school of thought. I do not want to have a Robert Wilson School of doing things. My own life and work always change because of the diversity of people who I meet and with whom I work.

**AF: Could you tell us about Watermill as a place of memory and history? It is striking that Watermill houses your personal archive and collection of objects and that its architecture embodies the memory of your theatre work.**

RW: It is living with an awareness of culture throughout the history of humanity. Culture is rapidly changing, and works of art are often the little that remains of a certain time. We learn about the nature of society through the nature of the individual, and we learn about the nature of the individual from the work of art. If we lose a culture, we lose our memory.

**AF: Currently there isn't a theatre at Watermill, but I understand there are plans to build one as part of a proposed underground extension. What was behind your original decision not to include a theatre at Watermill, and why are you interested in building one there now?**

RW: Actually, there are no plans to build a 'theatre' per se, but a space that is multipurpose. So a space that can on one hand be a theatre, but could also be a space for exhibition or performance or a conference of scientists. The spaces are not clearly defined. There are some spaces that are quieter and more for contemplation, and other spaces that are more interactive. It is important to have both.

**AF: What can theatre artists learn from architecture?**

RW: Theatre started out as being architectural in its setting and staging. For me, theatre should not be a place for decoration. The light, the stage set, the props, the gesture, the word, the sound/music are all structural and integral to the whole. They are the components of a complete book.

**AF: What are your hopes for the future of The Watermill Center?**

RW: That people of the next generations will take the space and make it their own.

# References

*28 Days Later* (2002), [Film] Dir. Danny Boyle, London: DNA Films.

'*887*' (2015), *Ex Machina*. Available online: http://lacaserne.net/index2.php/theatre/ eight_eight_seven/ (accessed 4 February 2016).

Adams, D. (1996a), *Stage Welsh, Changing Wales*, Llandysul, Ceredigion: Gomer Press.

Adams, D. (1996b), Review of *Prydain*, details unknown, Brith Gof Archive, PK8, National Library of Wales.

Agamben, G. (1998), *Homo Sacer: Sovereign Power and Bare Life*, trans. D. Heller-Roazen, Stanford, CT: Stanford University Press.

Agamben, G. (2000), *Means Without End: Notes on Politics*, trans. V. Binetti and C. Casarino, Minneapolis, MN: University of Minnesota Press.

Agamben, G. (2005), *State of Exception*, trans. K. Attell, Chicago, IL: University of Chicago Press.

Anelli, R. L. S. (2010), 'Ponderações sobre os relatos da trajetória de Lina Bo Badi na Itália', *Pós. Revista do Programa de Pós-Graduação em Arquitetura e Urbanismo da FAUUSP*, 17: 86–101.

Appleton, I. (1996), *Buildings for the Performing Arts: A Design and Development Guide*, Oxford: Butterworth.

Aristotle (1987), *The Poetics of Aristotle*, trans. S. Halliwell, Chapel Hill, NC: University of North Carolina Press.

Aronson, A. (2005), 'New Homes for a New Theater', in *Looking into the Abyss: Essays on Scenography*, 38–43, Ann Arbor, MI: The University of Michigan Press.

Artaud, A. (1958), *The Theater and Its Double*, trans. M. C. Richardson, New York: Grove Press.

Austin, J. L. (1962), *How to Do Things with Words: The William James Lectures Delivered at Harvard University in 1955*, Oxford: Oxford University Press.

Awan, N., T. Schneider and J. Till (2011), *Spatial Agency: Other Ways of Doing Architecture*, Abingdon: Routledge.

Badiou, A. (2007), *The Century*, Cambridge, MA: Polity.

Bakhtin, M. (1981), 'Discourse in the Novel', in M. Holquist (ed.), *The Dialogic Imagination*, trans. C. Emerson and M. Holquist, Austin, TX: University of Texas.

Bal, M. (1999), 'Narrative Inside Out: Louise Bourgeois' Spider as Theoretical Object', *Oxford Art Journal*, 22 (2): 103–126.

Barbieri, D. (2007), 'Proposing an Interdisciplinary, Movement-Based Approach to Teaching and Learning as Applied to Design for Performance Related Areas', working paper, London: Prague Quadrennial. Available online: http:// ualresearchonline.arts.ac.uk/1755/ (accessed 10 March 2017).

Barnett, J. (1986), *The Elusive City*, New York: Harper & Row.

Baudrillard, J. and J. Nouvel (2002), *The Singular Objects of Architecture*, trans.
R. Bononno, Minneapolis, MN: University of Minnesota Press.

Baugh, C. (2005), *Theatre, Performance and Technology: The Development of Scenography
in the Twentieth Century*, Basingstoke: Palgrave Macmillan.

Bech-Danielsen, C., A. Beim, C. Bundgaard, K. Christiansen, T. B. Jensen, U. S. Madsen
and O. E. Pedersen (2012), 'Tectonic Thinking in Architecture'. Available online:
https://issuu.com/cinark/docs/tectonic_thinking_in_architecture (accessed 22 June
2017).

Bell, C. and K. Beswick (2014), 'Authenticity and Representation: Council Estate Plays
at the Royal Court', *New Theatre Quarterly*, 30 (2): 120–135.

Benjamin, W. (1977a), 'Der Ursprung des Deutschen Trauerspiels', in R. Tiedemann and
H. Schweppenhäuser (eds), *Gesammelte Schriften*, vol. I.1, 203–430, Frankfurt am
Main: Suhrkamp.

Benjamin, W. (1977b), 'Was ist das Epische Theater? Eine Studie zu Brecht', in R.
Tiedemann and H. Schweppenhäuser (eds), *Gesammelte Schriften*, vol. II.2, 519–531,
Frankfurt am Main: Suhrkamp.

Bennett, S. (1990), *Theatre Audiences: A Theory of Production and Reception*, London
and New York: Routledge.

Birch, A. and J. Tompkins, eds (2012), *Performing Site-Specific Theatre: Politics, Place,
Practice*, Basingstoke: Palgrave Macmillan.

Bishop, C. (2012), *Artificial Hells: Participatory Art and the Politics of Spectatorship*,
London: Verso.

Blake, W. (2008), *The Complete Poetry and Prose of William Blake*, 2nd edn, Berkeley,
CA and London: University of California Press.

Bleeker, M. (2008), *Visuality in the Theatre: The Locus of Looking*, Basingstoke: Palgrave
Macmillan.

Blesser, B. and L. Salter (2007), *Spaces Speak, Are You Listening? Experiencing Aural
Architecture*, Cambridge, MA: The MIT Press.

*Blitz* (2011), [Film] Dir. Elliott Lester, London: Lionsgate.

Bo Bardi, L. (1958), 'Crônicas de arte, de história, de cultura da vida. Arquitetura,
Pintura, Escultura, Música, Artes Visuais', *Diário de Notícias*, 8 (26 October): n.p.

Bo Bardi, L. (1960), 'Técnica e arte', *Artes e letras. Terceiro caderno do Diário de Noticias*
(Salvador), 23–24 (October): 1–2.

Bo Bardi, L. (1967), 'Cinco Anos entre os Brancos', *Mirante das Artes* (São Paulo),
November/December: 1.

Bo Bardi, L. (1992), 'Uma Aula de Arquitetura', *Projeto*, 149 (January/February): 59–64.

Bo Bardi, L. ([1986] 1993), 'Sesc da Pompeia', in M. Ferraz (ed.), *Lina Bo Bardi*,
220–240, São Paulo: Instituto Lina Bo bardi e P.M. Bardi.

Bo Bardi, L. ([1958] 2001), 'The Theory and Philosophy of Architecture', in O. de
Oliveira (ed.), *2G: Revista Internacional de Arquitectura*, 23–24, 210–214, Barcelona:
Editorial Gustavo Gili.

Bo Bardi, L. and M. Gonçalves (1959), *Catálogo da Exposição Bahia no Ibirapuera*, São Paulo: Exhibition leaflet.

Bo Bardi, L., E. Elito and J. C. M. Corrêa (1999), *Teatro Oficina*, Lisbon: Editorial Blau, Instituto Lina Bo e P. M. Bardi.

Boal, A. ([1974] 2000), *Theatre of the Oppressed*, trans. C.A. McBride, M.-O. Leal Mcbride and E. Fryer, New York: Theatre Communications Group.

Boal, A. (1992), *Games for Actors and Non-Actors*, trans. A. Jackson, London and New York: Routledge.

Boenisch, P. M. (2014), 'Acts of Spectating: The Dramaturgy of the Audience's Experience in Contemporary Theatre', in K. Trencsényi and B. Cochrane (eds), *New Dramaturgy: International Perspectives on Theory and Practice*, 225–241, London: Bloomsbury.

Bogart, A. and T. Landau (2014), *The Viewpoints Book: A Practical Guide to Viewpoints and Composition*, London: Nick Hern Books.

Borden, I. (2001), *Skateboarding, Space and the City: Architecture and the Body*, Oxford: Berg.

Bourriaud, N. (2002), *Relational Aesthetics*, trans. S. Pleasance and F. Woods with M. Copeland, Dijon: Les Presses du Réel.

Boyer, C. (1996), *The City of Collective Memory: Its Historical Imagery and Architectural Entertainments*, Cambridge, MA: The MIT Press.

Brandi, C. (1963), *Teoria e Historia del Restauro*, Rome: Edizioni di Storia e Letteratura.

Brejzek, T. (2012), 'Scenography or: Making Space', in A. Aronson (ed.), *The Disappearing Stage: Reflections on the 2011 Prague Quadrennial*, 15–23, Prague: Arts and Theatre Institute/Prague Quadrennial.

Breton, G. (1991), *Théâtres*, New York: Princeton Architectural Press.

Brett, R., ed. (2004a), *Theatre Engineering and Architecture, Vol. 1: Engineering and Technology*, London: Theatrical Events Ltd.

Brett, R., ed. (2004b), *Theatre Engineering and Architecture, Vol. 2: Architecture and Planning*, London: Theatrical Events Ltd.

Brett, R., ed. (2004c), *Theatre Engineering and Architecture, Vol. 3: Operations, Safety, Cost and Risk*, London: Theatrical Events Ltd.

Bronet, F. and J. Schumacher (1999), 'Design in Movement: The Prospects of Interdisciplinary Design', *Journal of Architectural Education*, 53 (2): 97–109.

Brookes, M. (2014), 'On a Clear Day You Can See For Ever: Mediation as Form and Dramaturgy in Located Performance', PhD thesis, Aberystwyth University.

Brookes, M. and M. Pearson (2015), 'Commentary: Making *Iliad*', in *Iliad*, Theatre Programme.

Bruner, J. S. (1961), 'The Act of Discovery', *Harvard Educational Review*, 31: 21–32.

Bruner, J. S. (1971), *The Relevance of Education*, New York: W. W. Norton and Co.

Buergel, R. M. (2011), 'This Exhibition Is an Accusation: The Grammar of Display According to Lina Bo Bardi', *Afterall*, 26 (Spring). Available online: http://www.afterall.org/journal/issue.26/this-exhibition-is-an-accusation-the-grammar-of-display-according-to-lina-bo-bardi1 (accessed 12 January 2016).

Burte, H. (2007), 'Performers as Placemakers', in R. Brett (ed.), *Theatre Engineering and Architecture*, vol. 5, PA4 2-7, London: Theatre Engineering and Architecture.

Burte, H. (2008), *Space for Engagement: The Indian Artplace and a Habitational Approach to Architecture*, Kolkata: Seagull Books.

Busch, A. (1991), *The Art of the Architectural Model*, Hong Kong: Design Press.

Butler, J. (1988), 'Performative Acts and Gender Constitution: An Essay in Phenomenology and Feminist Theory', *Theatre Journal*, 40 (4): 519–531.

Butler, J. (1990), *Gender Trouble: Feminism and the Subversion of Identity*, New York: Routledge.

Cameron, N. (2004), 'Understanding Ernö', *The Architects' Journal*, 220 (2): 44.

Carlson, M. (1989), *Places of Performance: The Semiotics of Theatre Architecture*, Ithaca, NY: Cornell University Press.

Carlson, M. (2003), *The Haunted Stage: The Theatre as a Memory Machine*, Ann Arbor, MI: University of Michigan Press.

Chaudhuri, U. (1995), *Staging Place: The Geography of Modern Drama*, Ann Arbor, MI: University of Michigan Press.

Cherry, B., C. O'Brien and N. Pevsner (2005), *The Buildings of England, London 5: East*, London: Yale University Press.

Ching, F. (2007), *Architecture: Form, Space, and Order*, 3rd edn, Hoboken, NJ: John Wiley and Sons.

Coates, N. (2012), *Narrative Architecture: Architectural Design Primers Series*, London: John Wiley & Sons.

Cohn, R. (2001), 'Sarah Kane, An Architect of Drama', *Cycnos*, 18 (1): 39–49.

Conquergood, D. (2002), 'Performance Studies: Interventions and Radical Research', *TDR: The Drama Review*, 46 (2): 145–156.

Cousin, G. (1992), 'An Interview with Mike Pearson of Brith Gof', *Contemporary Theatre Review*, 2 (2): 37–47.

Coutinho, C. N. (2006), *Intervenções: O Marxismo na Batalha das Ideias*, São Paulo: Cortez.

Croce, B. (1921), *History: Its Theory and Practice*, trans. D. Ainslie, New York: Harcourt Brace, and Company.

Culvahouse, T. (1996), 'Book Review: Kenneth Frampton, *Studies in Tectonic Culture*', in M. Schwarzer (ed.), 'Tectonics Unbound', special issue of *ANY*, 14: 11–12.

Curtis, W. (1996), *Modern Architecture Since 1900*, 3rd edn, New York: Phaidon.

Darton, E. (1999), *Divided We Stand. A Biography of New York's World Trade Centre*, New York: Basic Books.

Davies, C. (2011), *Thinking about Architecture: An Introduction to Architectural Theory*, London: Laurence King.

de Certeau, M. (1984), *The Practice of Everyday Life*, trans. S. Rendall, Berkeley, CA: University of California Press.

de Oliveira, O. (2002), 'Interview with Lina Bo Bardi', in O. de Oliveira (ed.), *2G: Revista Internacional de Arquitectura*, 23–24, 230–255, Barcelona: Editorial Gustavo Gili.

Deleuze, G. (2006), *Nietzsche and Philosophy*, trans. H. Tomlinson, New York: Columbia University Press.

Derrida, J. (1997a), 'Point de Folie – Maintenant l'Architecture', in N. Leach (ed.), *Rethinking Architecture: A Reader in Cultural Theory*, 324–336, London: Routledge.

Derrida, J. (1997b), 'Why Peter Eisenman Writes Such Good Books', in N. Leach (ed.), *Rethinking Architecture: A Reader in Cultural Theory*, 336–347, London: Routledge.

*Design for Inclusion Toolkit* (2008), Research Report, Vancouver: Canada Mortgage and Housing Corporation and City of Vancouver. Available online: ftp://ftp.cmhc-schl. gc.ca/chic-ccdh/Research_Reports-Rapports_de_recherche/eng_unilingual/Design_ for_%20Inclusion_Toolkit.%20pdf.pdf (accessed 15 February 2016).

DeZure, D. (1999), 'Interdisciplinary Teaching and Learning', *Essays on Teaching Excellence: Toward the Best in the Academy*, 10 (4). Available online: http:// podnetwork.org/content/uploads/V10-N4-DeZure.pdf (accessed 20 July 2017).

Dickson, A. (2015), 'Iliad review - Homer's epic is the theatrical event of the year', *Guardian*, 28 September. Available online: https://www.theguardian.com/ stage/2015/sep/28/iliad-review-homer-ffwrnes-national-theatre-wales (accessed 5 October 2015).

Dillon, D. (1985), *Dallas Architecture 1936–1986*, Austin, TX: Texas Monthly Press.

Dodds, G., R. Tavernor and J. Rykwert, eds (2002), *Body and Building: Essays on the Changing Relation of Body and Architecture*, Cambridge, MA: The MIT Press.

Dolan, J. (2001), *Geographies of Learning: Theory and Practice, Activism and Performance*, Middletown, CT: Wesleyan University Press.

'Duisburg-Nord – The Railway Park' (n.d.), *Latzundpartner.de*. Available online: http:// www.latzundpartner.de/en/projekte/postindustrielle-landschaften/duisburg-nord- bahnpark/ (accessed 7 January 2016).

Dunnett, J. (1983), 'Ernö Goldfinger: The Architect as Constructor', *Architectural Review*, 173: 42–48.

Dunnett, J. (2014), 'Brownfield Estate: Grade 2* Listing Nomination Reasons Text', in D. Roberts (ed.), *Balfron Tower: A Building Archive*. Available online: http://www. balfrontower.org (accessed 2 October 2017).

'East End's Tallest Block of Flats Make "Ideal Homes"' (1968), *East London Advertiser*, 1 March.

Echenique, M. (1970), 'Models: A Discussion', *Architectural Research and Teaching*, 1 (1): 25–30.

Eckersall, P., P. Monaghan and M. Beddie (2014), 'Dramaturgy as Ecology: A Report from The Dramaturgies Project', in K. Trencsényi and B. Cochrane (eds), *New Dramaturgy: International Perspectives on Theory and Practice*, 18–35, London: Bloomsbury.

Ephemera Collective (2015), 'Layers of Space', *Ephemera Collective*. Available online: https://www.ephemeracollective.org/layers-of-space (accessed 18 May 2017).

Feuerstein, M. and G. Read (2013), *Architecture as a Performing Art*, Burlington, VT: Ashgate.

Filmer, A. (2006), 'Backstage Space: The Place of the Performer', PhD thesis, University of Sydney.

Filmer, A. (2015), Mike Brookes, unpublished interview.

Filmer, A. (2016), '*Coriolan/us* and the Limits of "Immersive"', in J. Frieze (ed.), *Reframing Immersive Theatre: The Politics and Pragmatics of Participatory Performance*, 289–302, Basingstoke: Palgrave Macmillan.

Fischer-Dieskau, D. (1976), *Wagner and Nietzsche*, New York: Seabury Press.

Fischer-Lichte, E. and B. Wihstutz, eds (2013), *Performance and the Politics of Space: Theatre and Topology*, London: Routledge.

Forty, A. (1995), 'Being or Nothingness: Private Experience and Public Architecture in Post-War Britain', *Architectural History*, 38: 25–35.

Foucault, M. (1970), *The Order of Things: An Archaeology of the Human Sciences*, New York: Vintage Books.

Foucault, M. (1980), *Power/Knowledge: Selected Interviews and Other Writings, 1972–1977*, ed. C. Gordon, New York: Pantheon Books.

Foucault, M. ([1982] 1998), 'Space, Knowledge, and Power', in K. M. Hays (ed.), *Architecture Theory Since 1968*, 428–439, Cambridge, MA: The MIT Press.

Foucault, M. (1986), 'Of Other Spaces', trans. J. Miskowiec, *Diacritics*, 16 (Spring): 22–27.

Frampton, K. (1990), 'Rappel à l'Ordre: The Case for the Tectonic', *Architectural Design*, 60 (3–4): 20–32.

Frampton, K. (1995), *Studies in Tectonic Culture: Poetics of Construction in Nineteenth and Twentieth Century Architecture*, Cambridge, MA: The MIT Press.

Frampton, K. and S. Kolbowski, eds (1981), *Idea as Model*, New York: Rizzoli.

Freee (2010), 'Interview with Freee', in J. B. Slater and A. Iles (eds), *No Room to Move: Radical Art and the Regenerate City*, 80–90, London: Mute Books.

Freire, P. ([1968] 1970), *Pedagogy of the Oppressed*, trans. M. B. Ramos, London: Continuum.

Freire, P. (2000), *Pedagogy of Freedom: Ethics, Democracy and Civil Courage*, trans. P. Clarke, Lanham, MD: Rowman and Littlefield.

Frisch, N. (2002), 'Norman Frisch Interviewed', in J. Rudakoff and L. M. Thomson (eds), *Between the Lines: The Process of Dramaturgy*, 273–299, Toronto: Playwrights Canada Press.

Fuchs, E. and U. Chaudhuri, eds (2002), *Land/Scape/Theatre*, Ann Arbor, MI: University of Michigan Press.

Geiger, J. (2015), *Entr'acte: Performing Publics, Pervasive Media, and Architecture*, New York: Palgrave Macmillan.

Giroto, I. R. (2010), 'Poesia da democracia. Cultura e transformação social na obra de Fábio Penteado', *Arquitextos*, 123 (3). Available online: http://www.vitruvius.com.br/revistas/read/arquitextos/11.123/3520 (accessed 18 May 2016).

Giroux, H. A. (2011), *On Critical Pedagogy*, London: Continuum.

Gokhale, S., ed. (2016), *The Scenes We Made: An Oral History of Experimental Theatre in Mumbai*, New Delhi: Speaking Tiger.

Goldberger, P. (1988), 'Winter Garden at Battery Park City', *New York Times*, 12 October. Available online: http://www.nytimes.com/1988/10/12/arts/review-architecture-winter-garden-at-battery-park-city.html (accessed 18 January 2016).

Golds, P. (2013), 'Towers of London', *Conservativehome.com*, 1 November. Available online: http://www.conservativehome.com/localgovernment/2013/11/towers-of-london.html (accessed 5 January 2016).

Goodstein, E. (2017), *Georg Simmel and the Disciplinary Imaginary*, Stanford, CT: Stanford University Press.

Gramsci, A. (1975), *L'alternativa pedagogica*, Florence: La Nuova Italia.

Gramsci, A. (1999), *Selections from the Prison Notebooks,* trans. Q. Hoare and G. Nowell Smith, New York: International Publishers.

Gratza, A. (2013), 'Open House', *Frieze*, 157 (September): 140–144.

Greenwood, E. (2009), 'Sounding Out Homer: Christopher Logue's Acoustic Homer', *Oral Tradition*, 24 (2): 503–518.

Grinover, M. M. (2010), 'Uma Ideia de Arquitetura. Escritos de Lina Bo Bardi', MA diss., University of São Paulo.

Gritzner, K., P. Primavesi and H. Roms, eds (2009), 'On Dramaturgy', special issue of *Performance Research*, 14 (3).

Grobman, Y. and E. Neuman, eds (2012), *Performalism: Form and Performance in Digital Architecture*, London and New York: Routledge.

Gruber, H. and J. J. Vonèche, eds (1995), *The Essential Piaget: An Interpretive Reference and Guide*, Lanham, MD: Jason Aronson Inc.

Habraken, N. J., A. Mignucci and J. Teicher (2014), *Conversations With Form: A Workbook for Students of Architecture*, London: Routledge.

Hall, S. (1987), 'Gramsci and Us', *Marxism Today*, June: 16–21.

Halprin, L. (1970), *The RSVP Cycles: Creative Processes in the Human Environment*, New York: George Braziller.

Halprin, A. (1995), *Moving Toward Life: Five Decades of Transformational Dance*, ed. R. Kaplan, Middletown, CT: Wesleyan University Press.

Hanlon, D. (2009), *Compositions in Architecture*, Hoboken, NJ: John Wiley and Sons.

Hannah, D. (2008), 'State of Crisis: Theatre Architecture Performing Badly', in A. Aronson (ed.), *Exhibition on the Stage: Reflections on the 2007 Prague Quadrennial*, 41–49, Prague: Arts Institute–Theatre Institute.

Hannah, D. (2011), 'Editorial/Sceno-Architecture', *ERA21*, 3: 5.

Hannah, D. (2018), *Event Space: Theatre Architecture and the Historical Avant-Garde*, London and New York: Routledge.

Hannah, D. and O. Khan (2008), 'Performance/Architecture: An Interview with Bernard Tschumi', *Journal of Architectural Education*, 61 (4): 52–58.

Harling, R. (2015), 'Turning Balfron Tower Inside Out', Balfron Social Club. Available online: https://50percentbalfron.tumblr.com/post/124053438534/turning-balfron-tower-inside-out (accessed 17 January 2016).

Hartford, R., ed. (1980), *Bayreuth, the Early Years: An Account of the Early Decades of the Wagner Festival as Seen by the Celebrated Visitors & Participants*, Cambridge: Cambridge University Press.

Hartoonian, G. (1994), *Ontology of Construction*, Cambridge: Cambridge University Press.

Harvey, D. (2001), *Spaces of Capital: Towards a Critical Geography*, London: Routledge.

Harvie, J. (2009), *Theatre and the City*, Basingstoke and New York: Palgrave Macmillan.

Harvie, J. (2013), *Fair Play: Art, Performance and Neoliberalism*, Basingstoke and New York: Palgrave Macmillan.

Harvie, J. and A. Lavender (2010), *Making Contemporary Theatre: International Rehearsal Processes*, Manchester: Manchester University Press.

Hatherley, O. (2013), 'Balfron Tower', in *Lesser Known Architecture*, Design Museum.

Hays, K. M., ed. (2000), *Architecture Theory Since 1968*, Cambridge, MA: The MIT Press.

Heddon, D. and J. Milling (2006), *Devising Performance: A Critical History*, Basingstoke: Palgrave Macmillan.

Hejduk, J. (1988), *Education of an Architect*, New York: Rizzoli.

Hemmings, S. and M. Kagel (2010), 'Memory Gardens: Landschaftspark Duisburg-Nord', *German Studies Review*, 33 (2): 246–248.

Henderson, M. (1973), *The City and the Theatre: New York Playhouses from Bowling Green to Times Square*, Clifton, NJ: White.

Hensel, M. (2013), *Performance-oriented Architecture: Rethinking Architectural Design and the Built Environment*, Chichester: John Wiley & Sons.

Hill, J., ed. (1998), *Occupying Architecture: Between the Architect and the User*, London and New York: Routledge.

Historic England (2015), *Balfron Tower: List Entry Summary*. Available online: https://historicengland.org.uk/listing/the-list/list-entry/1334931 (accessed 20 May 2016).

Hodgson, W. (1795), *The Commonwealth of Reason*, London: Printed for and sold by the author.

Hollier, D. (1989), *Against Architecture: The Writings of Georges Bataille*, Cambridge, MA: The MIT Press.

hooks, b. (1993), 'Eros, Eroticism and the Pedagogical Process', *Cultural Studies*, 7 (1): 58–63.

Hopkins, D. J. and K. Solga, eds (2013), *Performance and the Global City*, Basingstoke: Palgrave Macmillan.

Houston, A. (1998), 'Postmodern Dramaturgy in Contemporary British Theatre: Three Companies', PhD thesis, University of Kent, Canterbury.

Howard, P. (2002), *What is Scenography?* London: Routledge.

Jackson, S. (2004), *Professing Performance: Theatre in the Academy from Philology to Performativity*, Cambridge: Cambridge University Press.

Jacobs, J. (1958), 'The Miniature Boom', *Architectural Forum*, 108 (5): 106–111.

Jameson, F. (1988), 'Architecture and the Critique of Ideology', in *The Ideologies of Theory Essays, 1971-86: Syntax of History*, 35–60, Minneapolis, MN: Minnesota University Press.

Jürs-Munby, K., J. Carroll and S. Giles, eds (2013), *Postdramatic Theatre and the Political: International Perspectives on Contemporary Performance*, London: Bloomsbury.

Kaye, N. (2000), *Site-Specific Art: Performance, Place, and Documentation*, London and New York: Routledge.

Kershaw, B. (1999), *The Radical in Performance: Between Brecht and Baudrillard*, London and New York: Routledge.

Kirshenblatt-Gimblett, B. (2004), 'Performance Studies', in H. Bial (ed.), *The Performance Studies Reader*, 43–55, London: Routledge.

Klein, J. T. (2005), 'Integrative Learning and Interdisciplinary Studies', *Peer Review*, 7 (4): 8–10.

Knowles, R. (2004), *Reading the Material Theatre*, Cambridge: Cambridge University Press.

Kolarevic, B. (2005), 'Computing the Performative', in B. Kolarevic and A. M. Malkawi (eds), *Performative Architecture: Beyond Instrumentality*, 193–202, New York: Spon Press.

Kolarevic, B. and A. Malkawi, eds (2005), *Performative Architecture: Beyond Instrumentality*, New York: Spon Press.

Koolhaas, R. ([1978] 2004), *Delirious New York*, New York: Monacelli Press.

Kostka, A. and I. Wohlfarth, eds (1999), *Nietzsche and An Architecture of Our Minds*, Los Angeles: Getty Research Institute for the History of Art and the Humanities.

Krauss, R. (1979), 'Sculpture in the Expanded Field', *October*, 8: 30–44.

Kristeva, J. (1997), 'Institutional Interdisciplinarity in Theory and Practice: An Interview', in A. Coles and A. Defert (eds), *The Anxiety of Interdiscipinarity, De-, Dis-, Ex-*, vol. 2, 3–21, London: Black Dog Publishing.

Kwinter, S. (2001), *Architectures of Time: Toward a Theory of the Event in Modernist Culture*, Cambridge, MA: The MIT Press.

Kylika, A. and K. Anastasiadi (2016), 'Viral Institute of Performance Architecture', *Performance Research*, 21 (6): 87–93.

Lahiji, N., ed. (2014), *The Missed Encounter of Radical Philosophy With Architecture*, London: Bloomsbury.

Lamarque, P. (2010), *Work and Object*, Oxford: Oxford University Press.

Lang, J. (2005), *Urban Design: A Typology of Procedures and Products*, Oxford: Architectural Press.

Latour, B. (2005), *Reassembling the Social: An Introduction to Actor-network Theory*, Oxford: Oxford University Press.

Lavender, A. (2016), *Performance in the Twenty-First Century: Theatres of Engagement*, London: Routledge.

London Borough of Tower Hamlets (2006), *Formal consultation on the proposed regeneration and transfer of the East India Area to Poplar*, HARCA.

London Borough of Tower Hamlets (2010), 'Poplar HARCA Report'. Available online: http://www.towerhamletsfoi.org.uk/documents/2625/Poplar%20HARCA%20 Report.pdf (accessed 30 September 2017).

Leacroft, R. (1973), *The Development of the English Playhouse: An Illustrated Survey of Theatre Building in England from Medieval to Modern Times*, London: Eyre Methuen.

Leacroft, R. (2011), *Civic Theatre Design*, London: Tansill Press.

Leacroft, R. and H. Leacroft (1984), *Theatre and Playhouse: An Illustrated Survey of Theatre Buildings from Ancient Greece to the Present Day*, London: Methuen.

Leatherbarrow, D. (2005), 'Architecture's Unscripted Performance', in B. Kolarevic and A. Malkawi (eds), *Performative Architecture: Beyond Instrumentality*, 6–19, New York: Spon Press.

Lecuyer, A. (2001), *Radical Tectonics*, London: Thames and Hudson.

Ledger, A. (2009), 'Finding a Way: Considering the Pedagogies of Devising in the University Context', in A. Fliotsos and G. Medford (eds), *Teaching Theatre Today*, 241–266, Basingstoke: Palgrave Macmillan.

Lefebvre, H. (1991), *The Production of Space*, trans. D. Nicholson-Smith, Oxford: Blackwell.

Lefebvre, H. (2002), *Critique of Everyday Life, Volume II*, trans. J. Moore, London and New York: Verso.

Lehmann, H.-T. (2006), *Postdramatic Theatre*, trans. K. Jürs-Munby, London: Routledge.

Lehmann, H.-T. (2011), '"Postdramatic Theatre", A Decade Later', in I. Medenica (ed.), *Dramatic and Postdramatic Theatre Ten Years After: Conference Proceedings*, 31–46, Belgrade: Faculty of Dramatic Arts.

Lehmann, H.-T., K. Jürs-Munby and E. Fuchs (2008), 'Lost in Translation?' *TDR: The Drama Review*, 52 (4): 13–20.

Lester, G. (2011), 'Paradoxical Playground: The Watermill Center as a Laboratory for Collaboration', in J. E. Macián, S. Jane Stoker and J. Weisbrodt (eds), *The Watermill Center: A Laboratory for Performance*, 288–289, Stuttgart: Daco Verlag.

Lima, E. F. W. (2008), 'O espaço cênico de Lina Bo Bardi: uma poética antropológica e surrealista', *ArtCultura*, 9: 31–42. Available online: http://www.artcultura.inhis.ufu.br/PDF15/H&T_Lima.pdf (accessed 12 December 2015).

Lima, E. F. W. (2009), 'Estudo das relações simbólicas entre os espaços teatrais e os contextos urbanos e sociais com base em documentos gráficos de Lina Bo Bardi', *Arquitextos*, 107. Available online: http://www.vitruvius.com.br/revistas/read/arquitextos/09.107/58 (accessed 12 December 2015).

Lima, Z. R. M. de A. (2009), 'Lina Bo Bardi, Entre margens e centros', *Arquitextos*, 14: 110–144.

Lima, Z. R. M. de A. (2013), *Lina Bo Bardi*, New Haven, NY: Yale University Press.

Lima, E. F. W. and C. Monteiro (2012), *Entre Arquiteturas e Cenografias. A arquiteta Lina Bo Bardi e o teatro*, Rio de Janeiro: Contracapa/FAPERJ.

Logue, C. (2001), *War Music: An Account of Books 1–4 and 16–19 of Homer's Iliad*, London: Faber and Faber.

Lubow, A. (2004), 'The Anti Olmsted', *New York Times Magazine*, 16 May: 1.

Mackintosh, I. (1993), *Architecture, Actor and Audience*, London: Routledge.

Malevich, K. ([1928] 1971), 'Painting and the Problem of Architecture', in T. Andersen (ed.), *Kazimir Malevich, Essays on Art, 1915–1933*, trans. X. Glowacki-Prus and A. McMillin, New York: George Wittenborn.

Manning, E. and B. Massumi (2014), *Thought in the Act: Passages in the Ecology of Experience*, Minneapolis, MN: University of Minnesota Press.

Margolin, D. (1997), 'A Perfect Theatre for One: Teaching Performance Composition', *TDR: The Drama Review*, 41 (2) 68–81.

McAuley, G. (2000), *Space in Performance: Making Meaning in the Theatre*, Ann Arbor, MI: University of Michigan Press.

McGrath, J. (2009), 'Rapid Response', *New Welsh Review*, 85: 9–14.

McKenzie, J. (2001), *Perform or Else: From Discipline to Performance*, London and New York: Routledge.

McKinney, J. and P. Butterworth (2009), *The Cambridge Introduction to Scenography*, Cambridge: Cambridge University Press.

McKinnie, M. (2007), *City Stages. Theatre and Urban Space in a Global City*, Toronto: University of Toronto Press.

McKinnie, M. (2013), 'Performing Like a City: London's South Bank and the Cultural Politics of Urban Governance', in E. Fischer-Lichte and B. Wihstutz (eds), *Performance and the Politics of Space: Theatre and Topology*, 66–80, London: Routledge.

McLucas, C. (c. 1993–1994), 'The Host and the Ghost: Brith Gof's Large-Scale Site-Specific Theatre, Wales, Some notes for an illustrated lecture', CA12, Box 54, Cliff McLucas Archive, National Library of Wales, Aberystwyth.

McLucas, C. (c. 1995–1996), 'Devising Notebook', PK1, Brith Gof Archive, National Library of Wales, Aberystwyth.

McLucas, C. (1996), 'Scenography', PK2, Brith Gof Archive, National Library of Wales, Aberystwyth.

McLucas, C. (c. 1998), mock-up pages for a book, *The Host and the Ghost*, GA/13, 2, Cliff McLucas Archive, National Library of Wales, Aberystwyth.

McMillan, J. (1996), 'National Diffusion', *Scotland on Sunday*, 5 May: 10.

Meerzon, Y. (2015), 'Between Je et Moi: Staging the Heteroglossia of Immigrant Autobiography', *Theatre Research in Canada*, 36 (2): 291–312.

Mermikides, A. and J. Smart, eds (2010), *Devising in Process*, Basingstoke: Palgrave Macmillan.

Merrick, J. (2010), 'Shock of the Nouvel', *Independent*, 23 May. Available online: http://www.independent.co.uk/arts-entertainment/architecture/shock-of-the-nouvel-1981016.html (accessed 19 January 2016).

Merrifield, A. (1993), 'Place and Space: A Lefebvrian Reconciliation', *Transactions of the Institute of British Geographers*, 18 (4): 516–531.

Mezei, K. (1998), 'Bilingualism and Translation in/of Michèle Lalonde's *Speak White*', *The Translator*, 4 (2): 229–247.

Miessen, M. (2010), *The Nightmare of Participation: Crossbench Praxis as a Mode of Criticality*, New York: Sternberg Press.

Monk, J. (1998), 'Ceremonies and Models', in R. Gullstrom-Hughes and J. Monk (eds), *The Book of Models: Ceremonies, Metaphor, and Performance*, 33–46, Milton Keynes: Open University.

Monk, J. (2012), 'Creating Reality', in C. Bissell and C. Dillon (eds), *Ways of Thinking: Ways of Seeing*, 1–28, Berlin: Springer-Verlag.

Montgomery, C. (2014), *Happy City: Transforming Our Lives Through Urban Design*, London: Farrar, Straus and Giroux.

Moore, R. (2015), 'The 10 Best Theatres', *Guardian*, 11 December. Available online: http://www.theguardian.com/artanddesign/2015/dec/11/the-10-best-theatres-architecture-epidaurus-radio-city-music-hall (accessed 20 December 2015).

Morgan, R., C. McLucas, M. Pearson and L. Hughes Jones (1995), *Brith Gof: Y Llyfr Glas: 1988–1995*, Aberystwyth: Brith Gof.

Morris, M. (2006), *Models: Architecture and the Miniature*, Chichester: Wiley-Academy.

Mostafavi, M. (2014), 'Instigations: Reimagining Better Futures', in N. Spiller and N. Clear (eds), *Educating Architects: How Tomorrow's Practitioners Will Learn Today*, 190–199, London: Thames & Hudson.

Nicol, D. and S. Pilling, eds (2000), *Changing Architectural Education: Towards a New Professionalism*, London and New York: Spon Press.

Nietzsche, F. (1954), 'Twilight of the Idols', in *The Portable Nietzsche*, trans. W. Kaufmann, 463–563, New York: Penguin Books.

Nietzsche, F. (1966), 'On Great Events', in *Thus Spoke Zarathustra: A Book for All and None*, trans. W. Kaufmann, 129–133, New York: Penguin Books.

Nietzsche, F. (1969), *Thus Spoke Zarathustra*, trans. R. J. Hollingdale, London: Penguin Books.

Nietzsche, F. (1974), *The Gay Science*, trans. W. Kaufmann, New York: Vintage.

Nietzsche, F. (1997a), *Daybreak: Thoughts on the Prejudices of Morality*, trans R. J. Hollingdale, New York: Cambridge University Press.

Nietzsche, F. (1997b), 'Richard Wagner at Bayreuth', in *Untimely Meditations*, trans. R. J. Hollingdale, 195–254, Cambridge: Cambridge University Press.

Nietzsche, F. (2000), *Basic Writings of Nietzsche*, ed. W. Kaufman, New York and Toronto: Random House.

Ockman, J. and R. Williamson, eds (2012), *Architecture School: Three Centuries of Educating Architects in North America*, Cambridge, MA: The MIT Press.

Odendahl-James, J. (2015), 'The Science of Dramaturgy and the Dramaturgy of Science', in M. Romanska (ed.), *The Routledge Companion to Dramaturgy*, 381–387, London: Routledge.

O'Sullivan, F. (2014), 'The Pernicious Realities of "Artwashing"', CityLab. Available online: https://www.citylab.com/equity/2014/06/the-pernicious-realities-of-artwashing/373289/ (accessed 17 January 2016).

Otto-Bernstein, K. (2006), *Absolute Wilson: The Biography*, Munich and London: Prestel.

Ouroussoff, N. (2006), 'On the Mississippi, A Vision Steeped in an Industrial Past', *New York Times*, 4 July. Available online: http://www.nytimes.com/2006/07/04/arts/design/04nouv.html (accessed 19 January 2016).

Pallasmaa, J. (1996), *The Eyes of the Skin: Architecture and the Senses*, Chichester: John Wiley and Sons.

Pallasmaa, J. (2011), *The Embodied Image*, Chichester: John Wiley and Sons.

Panofsky, E. (1991), *Perspective as Symbolic Form*, trans. C. S. Wood, New York: Zone.

Pearson, M. (1994), 'Anecdotes and Analects', unpublished paper, presented at '"We are searching"... A Forced Entertainment Symposium', 16–17 October, University of Lancaster, Lancaster.

Pearson, M. (1998), 'My Balls/Your Chin', *Performance Research*, 3 (2): 25–41.

Pearson, M. (2004), '"Prydain", an Evocation...', unpublished paper presented to TRAWS, coach journey to former site, March, Cardiff.

Pearson, M. (2005), 'Way Out West!', *Studies in Theatre and Performance*, 25 (3): 253–262.

Pearson, M. (2010), *Site-Specific Performance*, Basingstoke and New York: Palgrave Macmillan.

Pearson, M. and M. Shanks (2001), *Theatre/Archaeology*, London: Routledge.

Pelli, C., M. Gandelsonas and J. Pastier (1990), *Cesar Pelli. Buildings and Projects 1965-1990*, New York: Rizzoli.

Pérez-Gómez, A. (2013), 'Architecture as a Performing Art: Two Analogical Reflections', in M. Feuerstein and G. Read (eds), *Architecture as a Performing Art*, 15–26, Burlington, VT: Ashgate.

Petralia, P. S. (2010), 'Headspace: Architectural Space in the Brain', *Contemporary Theatre Review*, 20 (1): 96–108.

Pineau, E. L. (2002), 'Critical Performative Pedagogy: Fleshing Out the Politics', in N. Stucky and C. Wimmer (eds), *Teaching Performance Studies*, 41–54, Carbondale and Edwardsville, IL: Southern Illinois University Press.

Plato (1997), 'The Allegory of the Cave', in *The Republic*, ed. D. Lee, New York: Penguin Classics.

Poláček, V. and V. Pokorný, eds (2015), *Recyklované divadlo/Recycled Theatre*, Prague: Národní Muzeum.

Poole, A. (2005), *Tragedy: A Very Short Introduction*, Oxford: Oxford University Press.

Rancière, J. (2009), *The Emancipated Spectator*, trans. G. Elliott, London: Verso.

Rao, U. (2009), 'Theatre Infrastructure Baseline Study', unpublished study for the India Foundation for the Arts (IFA), Bangalore.

Read, A., ed. (2000), *Architecturally Speaking: Practices of Art, Architecture and the Everyday*, London: Routledge.

Rendell, J. (2006), *Art and Architecture: A Place Between*, London: I. B. Tauris.

Rendell, J. (2008), 'You Tell Me: A Topography', in A. Harutyunyan, K. Hörschelmann and M. Miles (eds), *Public Spheres after Socialism*, 73–89, Bristol: Intellect.

Rendell, J. (2010), *Site-Writing: The Architecture of Art Criticism*, London: I. B. Tauris.

Rendell, J. (2011), 'May Mo(u)rn: A Site Writing', in N. Lahiji (ed.), *The Political Unconscious of Architecture: Re-opening Jameson's Narrative*, 109–142, London: Ashgate.

Rendell, J. (2014), 'The Transitional Space of Interdisciplinarity', in J. Calow, D. Hinchcliffe and L. Mansfield (eds), *Speculative Strategies in Interdisciplinary Arts Practice*, 103–112, Bristol: Underwing Press.

Rendell, J. (2015), 'Witness Statement', *Aylesbury Estate Public Enquiry*. Available online: http://crappistmartin.github.io/images/SummaryProfRendell.pdf (accessed 11 November 2016).

Rendell, J. (2017), *The Architecture of Psychoanalysis: Spaces of Transition*, London: I. B. Tauris.

Ridout, N. (2015), 'The Grammar of Politics and Performance', unpublished panel talk for *The Grammar of Politics and Performance*, The Shard, London.

Roberts, D. (2014), *Residents' Experiences of Balfron Tower*. Available online: http://www.balfrontower.org/document/88/listing-nomination-residents-experiences-supporting-document (accessed 11 November 2016).

Roberts, D. (2017), 'Make Public: Performing Public Housing in Ernő Goldfinger's Balfron Tower', *The Journal of Architecture*, 22 (1): 123–150.

Robinson, J. W. (2001), 'The Form and Structure of Architectural Knowledge: From Practice to Discipline', in A. Piotrowski and J. W. Robinson (eds), *The Discipline of Architecture*, 61–82, Minneapolis, MN: University of Minnesota Press.

Roesner, D. (2010), 'Musicality as a Paradigm for the Theatre: A Kind of Manifesto', *Studies in Musical Theatre*, 4 (3): 293–306.

Rohde, M. and R. Schomann, eds (2003), *Historische Gärten Heute*, Leipzig: Edition Leipzig.

Romanska, M., ed. (2015), *The Routledge Companion to Dramaturgy*, London: Routledge.

Roms, H. (2001), 'Identifying (with) Performance: Representations and Constructions of Cultural Identity in Contemporary Theatre Practice – Three Case Studies', PhD Thesis, Aberystwyth University.

Roms, H. (2013), 'Archiving Legacies: Who Cares for Performance Remains', in G. Borggreen and R. Gade (eds), *Performing Archives/Archives of Performance*, 35–52, Copenhagen: Museum Tusculanum Press.

Roms, H. (2014), *What's Welsh for Performance? Beth yw 'performance' yn Gymraeg?* Cardiff: Trace Samizdat Press.

Roms, H. and R. Edwards (2011), 'Oral History as Site-specific Practice: Locating the History of Performance Art in Wales', in S. Trower (ed.), *Place, Writing, and Voice in Oral History*, 171–192, Basingstoke and New York: Palgrave Macmillan.

Roulet, S. (2015) 'Jean Nouvel: Images in Colour', in E. Mattie (ed.), *The Colours of… Frank O. Gehry, Jean Nouvel, Wang Shu and other Architects*, 84–151, Basel: Birkhuauser.

Rufford, J. (2007), 'The Theatre Projects of Haworth Tompkins: Architecture and Performance in Theory and in Practice', PhD Thesis, King's College, London.

Rufford, J. (2015), *Theatre & Architecture*, Basingstoke and New York: Palgrave Macmillan.

Sabbag, H. (1986), 'A Metafora Continua (Entrevista a Lina Bo Bardi)', *AU: Arquitectura y Urbanismo*, 6 (August): 50–54.

Salter, C. (2010), *Entangled: Technology and the Transformation of Performance*, Cambridge, MA: The MIT Press.

Sasaki Associates (2014), 'Dallas Art District', *sasaki.com*. Available online: http://www.sasaki.com/project/176/dallas-arts-district/ (accessed 28 August 2016).

Sassen, S. (2005), 'The Global City: Introducing a Concept', *Brown Journal of World Affairs*, 11 (2): 29–32.

Schechner, R. (1968), '6 Axioms for Environmental Theatre', *The Drama Review: TDR*, 12 (3): 41–64.

Schechner, R. (1988), *Performance Theory*, New York: Routledge.

Schmidt, T. (2010), 'Unsettling Representation: Monuments, Theatre, and Relational Space', *Contemporary Theatre Review*, 20 (3): 283–295.

Schneider, R. (2011), *Performing Remains: Art and War in Times of Theatrical Reenactment*, London: Routledge.

Schwarzer, M., ed. (1996), 'Tectonics Unbound', special issue of *ANY*, 14.

Schweder, A. (2012), 'Performance Architecture', *Le Journal Special Z*, 4: 103–129.

Schweder, A. (2014), 'Pedagogy', unpublished notes.

Schweder, A. (2015), 'Performance Architecture: Spatialized Subjectivity & Enacted Renovations', PhD Thesis, Queens' College, University of Cambridge.

Serlio, S. ([1611] 1982), 'Book II', in *The Five Books of Architecture*, Toronto: Dover.

Shapiro, G. (2002), 'Review of *Nietzsche and an Architecture of Our Minds*', *Journal of Aesthetics and Art Criticism*, 60: 101–103.

Sheets-Johnstone, M. (1981), 'Thinking in Movement', *The Journal of Aesthetics and Art Criticism*, 39 (4): 399–407.

Shevtsova, M. (2007), *Robert Wilson*, London and New York: Routledge.

Simitch, A. and V. Warke (2014), *The Language of Architecture: 26 Principles Every Architect Should Know*, Beverley, MA: Rockport Publishers.

Soja, E. (2016), 'Regional Urbanization and the End of the Metropolis Era', in O. Nel-Lo and R. Mele (eds), *Cities in the 21st Century*, 41–56, London and New York: Routledge.

Speer, A. (1970), *Inside the Third Reich*, trans. R. and C. Winston, Toronto: Macmillan.

Spencer, D. (2016), *The Architecture of Neoliberalism*, London: Bloomsbury.

Spiller, N. and N. Clear, eds (2014), *Educating Architects: How Tomorrow's Practitioners will Learn Today*, London: Thames & Hudson.

Stanton, M. (2001), 'Disciplining Knowledge: Architecture between Cube and Frame', in A. Piotrowski and J. W. Robinson (eds), *The Discipline of Architecture*, 10–39, Minneapolis, MN: University of Minnesota Press.

Starkey, B. (2005), 'Architectural Models: Material, Intellectual, Spiritual', *Arq: Architectural Research Quarterly*, 9 (3/4): 265–272.

Stegemann, B. (2016), 'On German Dramaturgy', in M. Romanska (ed.), *The Routledge Companion to Dramaturgy*, 45–49, London: Routledge.

Stewart, S. (1993), *On Longing: Narratives of the Miniature, the Gigantic, the Souvenir, the Collection*, Durham, NC and London: Duke University Press.

Strong, J., ed. (2010), *Theatre Buildings: A Design Guide*, London: Routledge.

Stucky, N. and C. Wimmer, eds (2002), *Teaching Performance Studies*, Carbondale, IL: Southern Illinois University Press.

Studio Egret West (2015), *Balfron Tower: Design and Access Statement*. Available online: https://development.towerhamlets.gov.uk/online-applications/files/1EA796324438 8AC3EB83A639C5CFBCA5/pdf/PA_15_02554_NC-SECTION_00-02-1093631.pdf (accessed 17 April 2016).

Stungo, N. (1991), 'Goldfinger Becomes a Hero', *The Independent*, 18 September: 17.

Swale, J. (2012) *Drama Games for Devising*, London: Nick Hern Books.

TAAT (2016), *HALL05*, Exhibition Guide, 10–18 September, Deutsches Architektur Zentrum, Berlin, Germany.

Taussig, M., R. Schechner and A. Boal (1990), 'Boal in Brazil, France, the USA: An Interview with Augusto Boal', *The Drama Review*, 34 (3): 50–65.

Taylor, H. (2004), 'Deep Dramaturgy: Excavating the Architecture of the Site-Specific Performance', *Canadian Theatre Review*, 119: 16–19.

Thorne, S. (1996), 'Review of "Prydain", Brith Gof, Cardiff', *Live Art Mag*, 9: 30–31.

Tompkins, J. (2014), *Theatre's Heterotopias: Performance and the Cultural Politics of Space*, Basingstoke and New York: Palgrave Macmillan.

Tompkins, J. and A. Birch, eds (2012), *Performing Site-Specific Theatre Politics, Place, Practice*, Basingstoke and New York: Palgrave Macmillan.

Topalovic, M. (2011), 'Models and Other Spaces', *OASE*, 84: 37–52.

Trencsňyi, K. and B. Cochrane, eds (2014), *New Dramaturgy: International Perspectives on Theory and Practice*, London: Bloomsbury.

Tschumi, B. (1983), 'Illustrated Index: Themes from the Manhattan Transcripts', *AA Files*, 4: 65–74.

Tschumi, B. (1987), *Cinégramme Folie, Le Parc De La Villette: Paris, Nineteenth Arrondissement*, Seyssel: Champ Vallon.

Tschumi, B. (1990), 'Spaces and Events', in *Questions of Space: Lectures on Architecture*, 87–96, London: Architectural Association.

Tschumi, B. (1994), *Event Cities 1*, Cambridge, MA: The MIT Press.

Tschumi, B. (1996), *Architecture and Disjunction*, Cambridge, MA: The MIT Press.

Tschumi, B. (2000), *Event Cities 2*, Cambridge, MA: The MIT Press.

Tschumi, B. (2004), *Event Cities 3: Concept Vs. Context Vs. Content*, Cambridge, MA: The MIT Press.

Tschumi, B. (2005), 'The Manhattan Transcripts', *Bernard Tschumi Architects*. Available online: http://www.tschumi.com/projects/18/ (accessed 10 December 2016).

Tschumi, B. (2010), *Event Cities 4: Concept-Form*, Cambridge, MA: The MIT Press.

Tschumi, B. (2014), *Notations: Diagrams and Sequences*, London: Artifice.

Tschumi, B. and E. Walker (2004), 'Bernard Tschumi in Conversation with Enrique Walker', *Grey Room*, 17 (Fall): 118–126.

Turner, J. F. C. (1976), *Housing by the People: Towards Autonomy in Building Environments*, New York: Pantheon Books.

Turner, C. (2009), 'Architectonics of Performance Seminars', *Expanded Dramaturgies: Site, Walking, Dramaturgy*. Available online: http://expandeddramaturgies.com/ architectonics-of-performance-seminars/ (accessed 30 September 2017).

Turner, C. (2010), 'Mis-Guidance and Spatial Planning: Dramaturgies of Public Space', *Contemporary Theatre Review*, 20 (2): 149–161.

Turner, C. (2015), *Dramaturgy and Architecture: Theatre, Utopia, and the Built Environment*, Basingstoke: Palgrave Macmillan.

Turner, C. and S. Behrndt (2008), *Dramaturgy and Performance*, Basingstoke: Palgrave Macmillan.

Turner, C. and S. Behrndt, eds (2010), 'New Dramaturgies', special issue of *Contemporary Theatre Review*, 20 (2).

Van Gennep, A. ([1908] 1960), *The Rites of Passage*, Chicago: The University of Chicago Press.

Van Kerkhoven, M. (1994a), 'Introduction to "On Dramaturgy"', *Theaterscrift*, 5–6: 8–34.

Van Kerkhoven, M. (1994b), 'The Theatre is in the City and the City is in the World and Its Walls Are of Skin', trans. G. Ball, *Etcetera*, 46 (October). Available online: http:// www.kaaitheater.be/marianne/bulletin.jsp (accessed 3 March 2016).

Vidler, A. (2001), *Warped Space*, Cambridge, MA: The MIT Press.

Virilio, P. (2009), *Bunker Archeology*, New York: Princeton Architectural Press.

Vitruvius (1999), *Ten Books of Architecture*, trans. I. D. Rowland, Cambridge: Cambridge University Press.

Vygotsky, L. S. (1978), *Mind in Society: The Development of Higher Psychological Processes*, trans. M. Cole, Cambridge, MA: Harvard University Press.

Wagner, R. (1896a), 'A Retrospect of the Stage-Festivals of 1876', in *Richard Wagner's Prose Works*, vol. 6, trans. W. A. Ellis, 95–109, New York: Broude Brothers.

Wagner, R. (1896b), 'Bayreuth (The Playhouse)', in *Richard Wagner's Prose Works*, vol. 5, trans. W. A. Ellis, 320–340, New York: Broude Brothers.

Wagner, R. (1964), 'Mercury, God of Merchants, Reigns over Modern Culture', in A. Goldman and E. Sprinchorn (eds), *Wagner on Music and Drama*, trans. W. A. Ellis, 37–40, New York: DaCapo Press.

Wainwright, O. (2015), 'Revealed: How Developers Exploit Flawed Planning System to Minimize Affordable Housing', *Guardian*, 25 June. Available online: https:// www.theguardian.com/cities/2015/jun/25/london-developers-viability-planning-affordable-social-housing-regeneration-oliver-wainwright (accessed 5 January 2016).

Warburton, N. (2005), *Ernö Goldfinger: The Life of an Architect*, London: Routledge.

Weinstein, B. (2011), 'SHiFT: A Performed Reinterpretation of Visionary Theater', *Journal of Architectural Education*, 64 (2): 87–98.

Weinstein, B. (2012), Julie Larsen and Roger Hubeli, unpublished interview.

Weinstein, B. (2016a), Jennifer Monson, unpublished interview.

Weinstein, B. (2016b), Tracey Winton, unpublished interview.

Weinstein, B. (2017a), Diego Morell-Perea, unpublished interview.

Weinstein, B. (2017b), Julie Larsen and Roger Hubeli, unpublished interview.

Weiss, A. S. (1989), 'Possession Trance and Dramatic Perversity', in *The Aesthetics of Excess*, 3–11, Albany: State University of New York Press.

Weiss, A. S. (1995), *Mirrors of Infinity: The French Formal Garden and 17th-Century Metaphysics*, New York: Princeton Architectural Press.

Weiss, A. S. (2002), 'Drunken Space', in *Feast and Folly: Cuisine, Intoxication, and the Poetics of the Sublime*, 17–37, Albany, NY: State University of New York Press.

Wellacher, U. (2008), *Syntax of Landscape: The Landscape Architecture of Peter Latz and Partners*, Basel: Birkhäuser.

Whybrow, N., ed. (2014), *Performing Cities*, Basingstoke: Palgrave Macmillan.

Wigley, M. (1995), *The Architecture of Deconstruction: Derrida's Haunt*, Cambridge, MA: The MIT Press.

Wiles, D. (2003), *A Short History of Western Performance Space*, Cambridge: Cambridge University Press.

Williams, G. A. (1985), *When was Wales?: A History of the Welsh*, London: Pelican.

Wilson, J. and H. Manchester (2012), *Teaching Postdramatic Devised Performance in Higher Education*, London: The Higher Education Academy/PALATINE.

Winton, T. (2014), 'Think Like an Architect! Theater and Invention in the Architecture Program', ACSA. Available online: https://www.acsa-arch.org/docs/default-source/13-14-award-winners/ca-thinklikeanarchitect-winners-opt.pdf?sfvrsn=2 (accessed 11 June 2015).

Wong, A. (2015), 'Adrienne Wong: *Me on the Map*: Involving Children in Urban Planning', unpublished presentation, 18 November, Queen's University, Kingston.

Wood, D., J. Bruner and G. Ross (1976), 'The Role of Tutoring in Problem Solving', *Journal of Child Psychology and Psychiatry*, 17: 89–100.

Zancan, R. (2012), 'The Street is a Theatre', *Domus*, 21 May. Available online: http://www.domusweb.it/en/architecture/2012/05/21/the-street-is-a-theatre.html (accessed 20 November 2015).

Zaointz, K. (2012), 'Ambulatory Audiences and Animate Sites: Staging the Spectator in Site-Specific Performance', in A. Birch and J. Tompkins (eds), *Performing Site-Specific Theatre: Politics, Place, Practice*, 167–181, Basingstoke: Palgrave Macmillan.

Zevi, B. ([1948] 1996), *Saber ver a arquitetura*, São Paulo: Martins Fontes.

# Index

Note: The letter 'n' in a locator denotes an endnote and the letter 'f' following locators refers to figures.

CPSIA information can be obtained
at www.ICGtesting.com
Printed in the USA
LVHW03*2057110818
586684LV00010B/245/P

9 781474 247986